Safe at Last in the Middle Years

Safe at Last
in the Middle Years

The Invention of the Midlife Progress Novel:
Saul Bellow, Margaret Drabble,
Anne Tyler, and John Updike

Margaret Morganroth Gullette

UNIVERSITY OF CALIFORNIA PRESS

Berkeley / Los Angeles / London

University of California Press
Berkeley and Los Angeles, California

University of California Press, Ltd.
London, England

© 1988 by
The Regents of the University of California

Library of Congress Cataloging-in-Publication Data

Gullette, Margaret Morganroth.
    Safe at last in the middle years.
    1. Middle age in literature.   2. American fiction
—20th century—History and criticism.   3. English
fiction—20th century—History and criticism.
4. Progress in literature.   I. Title.
PS374.M49G85   1988   813'.5'093520564   87-34286
ISBN 0-520-06282-5 (alk. paper)

Printed in the United States of America

1 2 3 4 5 6 7 8 9

For David

Contents

Acknowledgments

Four colleagues have been especially supportive from the very earliest period, when I was writing essays on individual writers without yet having a sense that enough midlife progress novels were being written to warrant speaking of a new paradigm in fiction. For their initial encouragement and continuing interest, I would here like to thank Warner Berthoff, Mary Anne Ferguson, Patricia Meyer Spacks, and Mark Spilka.

William McClung's interest in the book at an early stage gave me the courage to drop what else I was doing at the time and produce it. The American Council of Learned Societies and the Bunting Institute provided me with a period of time and a congenial space in which to bring the book to completion. Many pages bear witness to conversations I have had with Bunting Fellows and members of the Feminist Theory colloquium at Harvard's Center for Literary and Cultural Studies. Three chapters in particular have benefited from the careful readings of Lisa Ruddick, Elizabeth Spelman, and Gish Jen. Philip Fisher, Robert Gooding-Williams, Celeste Schenck, and Andreas Teuber also helped me think better about some of the issues addressed in the final chapter. Barbara Haber gave me good advice about bibliography. Judith Borit, Maida Greenberg, David Schretlen, and Caroline Cross Chinlund have helped me understand what is going on in the therapeutic world. Over the years, associates at the Northeast Modern Language Association's session of "Literary Images of Aging" have constituted an invaluable network of people who were interested in the midlife and the ideology of aging in literature before anyone else thought them valid intellectual topics.

This book owes a special debt to the Radcliffe Seminars and its director, Nancy Downey, and to the students in my midlife courses there from 1978 on. Without their enthusiastic involvement, it might never have been begun; and without these opportunities to test my ideas, it might never have been finished.

Chapter Four originally appeared in a somewhat different version in *Modern Language Quarterly:* the text was improved by Edith B. Baras's meticulous attentions. Chapter Five originally appeared in a somewhat different version in the *New England Review and Bread Loaf Quarterly*. Sydney Lea offered exactly the right advice about an early version of the essay. At the Press, Jeanne Sugiyama and Mary Lamprech have paid kind, scrupulous attention to every detail of publication.

Many friends helped me survive and grow up. Just watching their life courses has been an education in midlife diversity, and their active involvement has steadied and confirmed me in my own erratic course. Among my counselors and models, I am lucky to have Caroline Cross Chinlund, Penelope Sales Cordish, Cornelia Wilson Higginson, Coppélia Kahn, and Suzie Scarff Webster. Sean Gullette's two decades in my life have also been an education and a delight. David Gullette has been my mainstay.

Both of my parents, in their different ways, and at different ages, came to tell safe-at-last stories about their own lives. My mother, in particular, made these explicit. From my childhood on, her conversation habitually made the future a reassuring place to be. As a first-grade teacher who had absorbed the ideology of childhood development and who treated every one of her "children" with concern for their promise, she simply ignored the idea that promise was supposed to run out after a certain age. She has never set a statute of limitations on hopefulness. Both of my parents taught me lessons in stoicism and recovery.

If any reader closes this book having applied some of its ideas personally, these (as well as the novelists) are the people to thank.

Introduction:
"The Years Teach Much . . ."

All our days are so unprofitable while they pass, that 't is wonderful where or when we ever got anything of this which we call wisdom, poetry, virtue. We never got it on any dated calendar day. Some heavenly days must have been intercalated somewhere, like those that Hermes won with dice of the moon, that Osiris might be born. . . . The years teach much which the days never know.

—Emerson, "Experience"

I. A New Ideology of Aging

This book is about change and invention. Specifically, it celebrates a new kind of novel, the progress narrative of the middle years. Although some literary historians think it next to impossible to distinguish the cultural phenomena of one's own time, part of what compelled me to write *Safe at Last in the Middle Years* was what Warner Berthoff has called "the pull of major invention whose overruling authority must somehow be accommodated."[1] To explain the fictional invention, the book needed a coinvention of its own, with psychosocial and narrative features: the hypothesis that people can grow over the course of their lifespan in ways that make it possible for them to come

1. Warner Berthoff, "The Way We Think Now: Protocols for Deprivation," *New Literary History* 7, no. 3 (Spring 1976):600.

to "write" what I call a happier genre. The adult lifespan may be full of sorrow and acquainted with grief, but when growth of this kind shows up, it argues for the existence of heavenly days.

Who can change, and who can write/tell this humanly privileged genre? My short answer has to be, "Potentially, everyone."

Especially in the past decade and a half, a number of fiction writers have been offering Anglo-American culture new heroines and heroes in their middle years; new plots of recovery and development in those years; and favorable views of midlife looks and midlife outlooks, midlife parenting and childing, midlife subjectivity. It's a revisionist genre, which means it's full of surprises.

Among those performing such acts of cultural prestidigitation, I have selected four, for the variety and the intrinsic interest of their changing attitudes toward aging: Saul Bellow and Margaret Drabble, Anne Tyler and John Updike. Such popular writers presumably reach readers across a wider than usual spectrum of class, gender, race, and national origin—they have a greater potential influence on other writers and nonwriters alike.[2] Moreover, although these writers have specific characteristics in common (in being white and heterosexual, and in having become over time older, well-off, married, and parents), the "conditions of possibility" for midlife progress narrative—to borrow Fredric Jameson's term[3]—exist in the culture at large and can be employed by others who do not match these exact specifications. Other writers have composed midlife progress narratives with protagonists who are poor, rural, and black or poor, urban, and white. We do not need to rely on the idea of direct influence to explain the (up-to-now modest) proliferation of the genre. Some will to revision is in the air.

About 1975, it was observable that the culture was giving its writers

2. "A proper work of popular fiction appeals ideally to a whole populace, rather than to a coterie or an elite. It cuts across lines of class, occupation and education. It is formed by the fears and desires that keep a populace together, rather than by those that keep special interest groups apart. . . . The formulas, or conventions, of our popular genres are shaped by the same forces that shape our national character" (George Stade, "The Big Chiller," *The Nation,* February 28, 1987, p. 259). Although I doubt that any single work of popular fiction appeals to "a whole populace," a group of works—like the midlife progress narrative—may approach that ideal through its overlapping audiences.

3. Fredric Jameson, "Magical Narratives: Romance as Genre," *New Literary History* 7, no. 1 (Autumn 1975): 158: "The historical moment blocks off a certain number of formal possibilities . . . all the while opening up certain determinate new ones which may or may not then come into being. To put it another way, the *combinatoire* aims at revealing, not the causes behind a given form, but rather the *conditions of possibility* of its existence" (italics in original).

permission to overthrow the traditional decline view that the middle years are a time of devolution, on a spectrum from fatigue through multiplied losses to despair. 1975 saw the publication of Bellow's *Humboldt's Gift* and Drabble's *The Realms of Gold*. (In 1978 I taught my first course on "The Literature of the Middle Years of Life" and included both.) Tyler's *Searching for Caleb* appeared in 1976, and her *Earthly Possessions* in 1977, along with Drabble's *The Ice Age*. Drabble's *The Middle Ground* came out in 1980, along with Tyler's *Morgan's Passing*. 1981 saw Updike's *Rabbit Is Rich*. Tyler's *Dinner at the Homesick Restaurant* appeared in 1982, and *The Accidental Tourist* in 1985. In 1987, Drabble brought out *The Radiant Way*.

There is nothing time-stamped about the philosophy and form of the midlife progress narrative, however (culture is not that monolithic). '75 was no magic date: Bellow's first, *Henderson the Rain King,* came out in 1958, and *Herzog* in 1964. Even more remarkably, Zora Neale Hurston's *Their Eyes Were Watching God* was published in 1937, during the Depression and at a difficult time in her difficult life, and when the norm for black fiction was (as Mary Helen Washington puts it) "tragically colored."[4] Even in oppressive circumstances, some spirits don't need extra empowerment: they learn how to stock their own inner supplies of hope and grit. They waive culture's passes.[5]

Such fictional events—and the rare progress narratives from the early twentieth century and before—revise the norm that we might call "pathetically or despicably aging." They can weaken the effects of the corrosive, powerful, negative ideology of aging we all grow up submerged in. To escape that ideology, one belief is necessary and sufficient: that life-affirming plots and thoughts can be given to midlife characters, because life energy can survive the encounter with adult vicissitudes. Some people may be "born" into such a hopeful belief and never lose it, despite poverty, lack of education, discrimination, bad luck, even illness. In many Eastern cultures, respect and value grow with the life course. But in our culture, for most of us (no matter how rich, well educated,

4. Mary Helen Washington, Introduction to *I Love Myself When I am Laughing . . .* , by Zora Neale Hurston (New York: The Feminist Press, 1979), p. 17. The expression "tragically colored" comes from an essay of Hurston's about her feelings about being black.

5. Studies showing how much harder it is for people who are economically and educationally deprived to achieve a sense of optimism are summarized in Margaret J. Lundberg, *The Incomplete Adult: Social Class Constraints on Personality Development* (Westport, Conn.: Greenwood Press, 1974). Age is not usually a variable considered in these studies, however. Growing up psychically could have benefits similar to those attributed to a rise in class—an increase in one's sense of power and control.

favored, and healthy) this belief has not been easy to attain, and once attained, it is possible to lose it again. Sadly, no special explanation is needed when a writer slips away from progress fiction and eases into a conventional plot of depletion, or—more typically—produces a progress narrative of bare survival, as Bellow and Updike have recently done. Aging has been so emphatically constructed as a no-win process that any counterconstruction (that there can be recovery and even *gains* in the middle years) may take considerable energy to maintain.

Possessing this belief, however, the progress narrative elevates members of a group we might call the once-poor-in-spirit. Rescuing them from a plot of depletion seems to be one of the genre's unspoken spiritual or ethical functions. They're not "heroines" or "heroes" in a classical way, but they have resistances, strengths, or sly timely weaknesses, ingenious mental feints. The author is free to choose their vicissitudes: financial hardship; loss of spouse, kin, and friends; psychic self-ravaging. In *Henderson the Rain King* Bellow found the genre suitable for a self-destructive male WASP millionaire, and William Kennedy (in *Ironweed*, 1983) for a violent social outcast, a homeless alcoholic Irishman. In *Their Eyes Were Watching God,* Hurston required it for a southern mulatto woman who through a tragic accident loses the love of her life after she's just found him on the third try at the age of forty. In *Foreign Affairs* (1984), Alison Lurie built her version of the genre around a self-pitying middle-aged white New England female academic who also loses a late-found love to untimely death. In *Other Women* (1984), Lisa Alther gave the plot of rescue to a lesbian whose self-esteem had been damaged in childhood. In *The Realms of Gold* Drabble chose a famous archaeologist whose sister has committed suicide and who thinks her own depressiveness comes from a family curse. Updike's *Rabbit Is Rich* helps along the rehabilitation of a man who, in archetypal decline fashion, has spent most of his life messing up and looking backward and knowing it. Tony Morrison's *Beloved* (1987) heals an escaped slave who has been forced to kill her own child. The genre can be very modest—merely letting a lively voice rise again after the worst is over (like Janie's in Hurston's novel) to say, in effect, "I'm still here to tell this story, and the next one too."

A close reader of the structure of these novels will learn strategies for constructing life stories as ameliorative sequences. In a special sense, as we'll see later, these are cure stories. The plot of a particular novel might move the evolving and sometimes consciously questing protagonist from randomness to meaningfulness, or from conflict to resolution, from pain to serenity, from stasis to activity, from defect to fulfillment, from drive to freedom, from loss to recovery. Of course, protagonists don't get everything they want—loss on some other dimensions of desire is not precluded. What the form implicitly—and sometimes explicitly—disowns, however, is a story of time balanced *more* toward loss than gain. Balanced, at times precariously, astride a judgment of what the life course brings, at a minimum such novels tip toward the positive.

A complete retrospective judgment about how our society came to permit the production of midlife progress narratives would want to include such factors as its will to overcome classism, sexism, and racism as well as generalized ageism; the degree of access "minority" voices have to publication; and the kinds of expectations of life various groups are encouraged to have. Relevant social factors would be the median age of the population, the number of children women have and the age at which they have them, and how free people are to change spouses or jobs or careers. Political factors conducive to the creation of mature adulthood would also be important: for example, the extension of the suffrage to "adults" regardless of gender and race,[6] and the expansion of employment opportunities. Such an account would consider the sexual mores and ideals of the tribe: how it overcame fear of "passion" and demythified sexuality and gender-otherness; how it deals with behavior that deviates from the norm; what acts it considers representable. Most crucial to this ideal account would be an evaluation of the literary tradition that has dominated midlife narrative for at least a century, the tradition of the decline story. Of related interest would be the culture's other fictions of adulthood, including the images that circulate in the media, in cartoons and jokes, and in psychology and philosophy. Reinforcing the whole ideology would be the culture's representations of the rest of the life course, especially myths of childhood, adolescence, and old age, if these are the alternative stages that the culture imagines and contrasts or (in the case of old age) elides with "the middle." Ideally, a thorough explanation would consider *all* the suprapersonal factors that must operate when a culture suddenly goes about producing a more complete and positive account of adult life, as is happening right now.

This little book—the first about midlife novels[7]—can do no more

6. How universal suffrage helped to weaken the binary division whereby "manhood and womanhood perceptually overrode adulthood" is one of the many topics addressed by Winthrop D. Jordan, "Searching for Adulthood in America," in *Adulthood*, ed. Erik H. Erikson (New York: Norton, 1978), p. 195. Through underemployment and unemployment, many adults are kept as "boys" and "girls," linguistically as well as economically.

7. A survey of medieval midlife literature exists; see Mary Dove, *The Perfect Age of Man's Life* (Cambridge: Cambridge University Press, 1987).

than adumbrate such a comprehensive explanatory position. While it develops some of these areas, it mainly concentrates on the individual trajectories that made midlife progress fiction possible in the careers of these four writers. Their midlife constructions offer persuasive examples of Victor Turner's contention that "culture is never 'given' to each individual but, rather, gropingly discovered, and, I would add, some parts of it quite late in life." These writers discovered unwritten territory in the "vast reaches" of midlife experience, and could not but give it "the impress of their own personality."[8] Because their personalities are so diverse, and because they continue to change as they age, they can give us an array of models of how to become in the middle years. To each his own life course, and to each her own.

What I want to return to here is the idea that *anyone who can identify with the psychological direction of the genre* can tell a version of the story. This identification is the fundamental *condition of possibility*. And I refer not only to professional writers when I say "anyone," but all of us who tell a story about our life. Many of us who have lived long enough are telling a story about our survivorship and growth—or would like to know how to tell one. To do this now, here, we must have rejected the prevailing decline version of adulthood. Rejecting one version and "discovering" (or "constructing") another can be profoundly liberating. According to Roy Schafer, who studies narrative and psychodynamics together, changing our story proves that our view of self in the past, the present, and even the future is "in principle modifiable. To accept this modifiability is itself a new action, and one of the most important a person can ever perform."[9]

Those of us who are trying to tell a progress narrative may have no name for it yet. We're not used to the idea that our own personal life story is likely to have a genre. Some scholars may want to call this particular genre a *Bildungsroman,* a term that has heretofore been used rather indiscriminately, to refer to written accounts about young people or adults, to progress narratives in general, and even (inaccurately, for want of a term) to decline narratives.[10] Some might be comfortable

8. Victor Turner, "Social Dramas and Stories about Them," *Critical Inquiry* 7, no. 1 (Autumn 1980): 144. Turner starts off by quoting from Edward Sapir's "The Emergence of the Concept of Personality in a Study of Cultures" (1934). This issue, devoted to narrative from many interdisciplinary points of view, is extremely valuable.

9. Roy Schafer, *Language and Insight* (New Haven: Yale University Press, 1978), p. 15.

10. For the history of the term Bildungsroman, and some characterization of the genre, see Martin Swales, *The German Bildungsroman from Wieland to Hesse* (Princeton: Princeton University Press, 1978), esp. pp. 3–7, 159–66. See also Jerome H. Buckley, *Season of Youth* (Cambridge, Mass.: Harvard University Press, 1974).

thinking of the genre (whether written or oral) in terms borrowed from philosophy or psychology: the telos of human striving, psychic aliveness, self-transcendence.[11] Whatever our vocabulary, we may not have a vivid sense of how bold we're being. We should keep in mind that the psychic *setting* that truly gives the genre novelty is one that has until recently been considered unpropitious however elevated its socioeconomic circumstances: the middle years.

II. Of Dead Dragons and False Fears

From one point of view, for writers to attribute psychic resilience to midlife characters might represent no more than a tiny shift of description. It might require only a different age attribution: make Tom Jones or Elizabeth Bennet or Huck Finn or Eugène Rastignac or Molly Bolt *forty* and you've got midlife progress narrative, no? Since the eighteenth century the *young* have been depicted as possessing India-rubber resilience in the face of obstacles, and faculties appropriate for self-development. But those characteristics have scarcely ever been attributed to the older protagonist. On the contrary. The plots that provided dragons for the young to conquer were our delight, and the discomfiture of the dragons—Lady Bellaston, Lady de Bourgh, and the Widow Douglas, to name a few—was our comic joy. Now that we peer more closely at such dragons, we notice how often they were *midlife* figures. The joy of seeing them defeated was in part a childish joy at vicariously overcoming parental oppression. Let's talk about the age of

11. Bernard Kaplan explains the development of developmental psychology as an outcome of various "speculative philosophies of history" that involve "the telos of human striving." See "A Trio of Trials," in *Developmental Psychology: Historical and Philosophical Perspectives,* ed. Richard M. Lerner (Hillsdale, N.J.: Lawrence Erlbaum Associates, 1983), p. 192. Other writers would give more weight to the paradigm of evolutionary biology. From an interdisciplinary viewpoint, nineteenth-century thought is full of parallel paradigms that prepare for the twentieth century's discovery of the middle years. In Chapter Seven I add the narrative precedent of autobiographical "crisis and cure" stories to the account. They seem a more significant precedent than some others, because the "setting" of some of the autobiographies is already the middle years. The phrase "psychic aliveness" is taken from the title of a paper by Dr. Arnold H. Modell, "Psychic 'Aliveness' in the Middle Years," delivered on March 7, 1987, at a conference on "The Middle Years: New Psychoanalytic Perspectives," organized by The Association for Psychoanalytic Medicine in collaboration with the Columbia University Center for Psychoanalytic Training and Research. This and other papers will be edited by John Oldham and Robert Liebert and will be published under the conference title by Yale University Press in 1989. Dr. Modell kindly made the paper available to me in advance of publication.

implied readers: no matter how old we are when we read these classics of the classroom, we are asked to be psychically adolescent, and accept the given, that our parents' generation represents the wicked world in its conventionality, vice, rigidity, or hypocrisy.

To write midlife fiction, however, both the author and the fictional protagonist have to *become* that generation. And to understand it, or at least to care enough to read it at all, readers must overcome the same mental difficulty. Can there be an equivalent plot of progress for the no-longer-young? Who or what would stand in for the dragons, now that many readers are conscious of being more or less the same age? And what would psychic triumph in the middle years consist of? How could it be represented? European and American literature has not left much space for writers to even ask these questions. The midlife image has primarily taken for granted a despicable or pitiable persona or an ironizing plot of decline. Aging past the courtship stage into adulthood has been represented in one way or another as "a terrible thing." [12]

One of the most effective reinforcers of the decline theory of life has been realism's typical plot of "systematic disillusionment," so well described by Harry Levin in *Gates of Horn*. [13] In this ideological system, the character is given false (defined as overly optimistic) expectations about the adult future, often based on reading romances: one thinks immediately of Emma Bovary, Anna Karenina, Jay Gatsby, Waugh's Charles Ryder, Stead's Henny Pollit. Inevitably, the ensuing adult "reality" requires a plot that contrives disappointments. Adult "knowledge" is only bought dear, and some (mostly female) pay the ultimate price.

It needs to be pointed out how regularly this standard emplotment has been given to adult characters, from the no longer quite young to the confessedly middle aged. For many people today, systematic disillusionment is *the* midlife plot. In critical thinking, we have, for the most part, abandoned the naive position that realism's conventions are true; they have now become visible as conventions. But not where decline narrative is concerned. Many readers steeped in decline's favorite con-

---

12. Kenneth Lynn, "Adulthood in American Literature," in Erikson, *Adulthood,* p. 245. See also Leslie Fiedler, "Adolescence and Maturity in the American Novel," in *The Critic as Artist,* ed. Gilbert A. Harrison (New York: Liveright, 1972), pp. 120–30. English and Continental literature has had its own ways of representing aging as a terrible thing.

13. Harry Levin, *Gates of Horn* (New York: Oxford University Press, 1966), p. 48. Also, "it has always been the method of realistic fiction to undermine a series of preconceptions" (p. 53). True, but the only "preconceptions" decline fiction wanted to undermine were what it called romantic or illusory preconceptions, not its own.

trastive strategy believe that no other plot of adult life is narratable or likely. Oddly enough, contemporary stage-oriented "self-help" guides often tell the same story, about how life is a process of losing our "illusions."[14] The myth still sells: that everyone starts off naive, anticipating that the next stage of adulthood is going to be rosy, harmonious, and delightful. We are being sold a story about our own presumed past innocence.

What these conventions ignore is that many people, on the contrary—women even more than men, now and in the recorded past—anticipate adulthood with some dread.[15] We fear failing in its tasks (or, considering what we think some of them consist of, succeeding in them). And then we experience actuality as dreadful because anticipations so often prove to be self-fulfilling prophecies rather than (as in fiction) set-ups for reversal. Fictionalized, this would be a decline plot, but one low in contrasts. Instead of either of these, we should consider the possibility that life can be constructed as a process of losing our false *fears,* our overly *pessimistic* anticipations. Such a shift would supply us with a radically new plot for the life course and for life-course fiction. And it would also provide a brand new evaluation of adult knowledge, no longer regularly identified with clear-eyed pain, but also, and perhaps primarily, with hard-earned relief.

The new plot would then have to record fatalism, disappointment, and anguish during the first encounter with adulthood "in all its length and responsibility."[16] Because of the way it gets treated in the novels I examine, I call this period, usually conceived of as occurring early after marriage, "the dangerous age."[17] In their varying registers, all four of my writers recorded it as such.

Safe at Last then shows that arriving at the *next* moment, true mid-

14. Roger L. Gould, *Transformations: Growth and Change in Adult Life* (New York: Simon and Schuster, 1978). Gould does tell a "safe-at-last" story, but one that requires "childhood demons" (chap. 1, passim) and "Major False Assumptions." The latter fill my category of optimistic illusions that I doubt many people hold after adolescence: for example, "Life is simple and controllable," "I am not like my parents in ways I don't want to be," "Threats to my security aren't real."

15. For interesting accounts from letters and diaries, see Ellen K. Rothman, *Hands and Hearts: A History of Courtship in America* (Cambridge, Mass.: Harvard University Press, 1987), esp. chap. 2, "The Scene is About to Be Changed."

16. John Updike, *The Witches of Eastwick* (New York: Knopf, 1984), p. 302.

17. Patricia Meyer Spacks refers to adolescence, in the eighteenth-century view, as "a dangerous age," because it was associated with "the Passions," especially sexuality; see *The Adolescent Idea: Myths of Youth and the Adult Imagination* (New York: Basic Books, 1981), p. 91. The dangerous age seems to have changed considerably.

life, allows some people to write some form of a happier genre. They are startled into a relative optimism.

Until we've read some midlife progress fictions with care—say, Bellow's *Humboldt's Gift,* Drabble's *The Realms of Gold,* Updike's *Rabbit Is Rich,* and Tyler's *The Accidental Tourist*—we probably can't imagine how a progress plot might be constructed for the middle years, or which culturally reiterated signs of aging would have to be discarded or overturned, or what new contrastive strategies would need to be invented, or to what extent the ironic mode would need to be revised in order to create midlife characters who grow.

No, for our culture, this "tiny" replacement of an attribute (the decision to make likeable characters "forty") has required immense upheavals in our systems of belief about aging and our sense of propriety about a kind of fiction that assigns "comic" outcomes to older figures. "We" are by no means yet sure that we generally approve of midlife progress narrative as a concept. The concept requires readers willing to identify with adult protagonists who are not ultimately daunted by their aging bodies, their inner dragons, their responsibility for creating their own lives, or the worst blows dealt by fate.

By contrast, midlife decline narratives, whatever else they do, put their surrogate adult in a victim's position—always too childlike-helpless against the dragons of the world, whether outer or inner: sometimes too vulnerable to live, sometimes unable to enjoy living, often brought to desire to end life, and, in every case, too helpless to be able to make the life in her or his charge a progress over obstacles. Keeping this alternative in mind will prevent us from objecting a priori to the relatively benign endings of progress narratives. Even when they end in remarriage or cohabitation, they evade the closed form and the shallowly optimistic prolepses of the marriage plot in youth narratives. They reach for open-endedness by endowing their idiosyncratic protagonists with plausibly personalized outcomes. And they do not necessarily construct a future with a particular content, but rather the characters' seasoned attitudes toward any future: out of patient curiosity or learned equanimity, all of them rely on their ability to shape it or to handle whatever it is likely to bring.

III. Midlife Genres and the Mitigation of Irony

Many midlife readers may not experience their own lives as progress narratives. Reading this book requires only that they admit the possibility of such a construction. As the philosopher Ronald Hepburn defines it, "an aesthetic education is an introduction to countless *alternative* possibilities for feeling: the options are shown to be immeasurably more diversified than the clichés allow." [18] It might be fruitful to hold in the mind the additional possibility that people truly grow in adult life, not just that some idealists crave to believe they do.

If the idea of adult growth is an illusion, the illusion seems to be taking over at the end of the twentieth century. The new consensus in serious psychodynamic theory is that development is probably a life-long process. This version of aging is trying to displace a persistent older myth: that some essence (sometimes called "human nature" or "character") gets *fixed* in human beings at a very early age. The progress fictions I describe and these theories have thus been developing along parallel lines. Indirectly at least, they must animate each other. [19]

The general model of growth I draw from the novels (in Chapters One and Two) is compatible with a number of psychosocial explanatory systems, such as interpersonal theory (Karen Horney, Harry Stack Sullivan, and Erik Erikson), object-relations theory (Otto Kernberg), self psychology (Heinz Kohut), integrated psychoanalytic/behaviorist theory ("interactionism"), family-based theory, and theories of normal lifespan development (Orville G. Brim, Jr. and Jerome Kagan

18. R. W. Hepburn, *'Wonder' and Other Essays* (Edinburgh: Edinburgh University Press, 1984), p. 93; emphasis in original. It may be useful to point out that *Safe at Last*, written to draw attention to a new discourse, should not be taken as implying that decline narratives are ipso facto aesthetically weaker, or stronger, than progress narratives. Presumably, the amount of craft is independent of genre.

19. It would be helpful to have studies of each writer's relationship, if any, to the post-Freudian theorists. Mark Shechner has written on Bellow and Reich, in a paper called "Saul Bellow: The Therapeutic Years," delivered at Northeast Modern Language Association, April 3, 1987, and in *After the Revolution* (Bloomington: Indiana University Press, 1987). According to him, Reich's theories had only a superficial influence on Bellow. Several of the novelists have been in therapy. All but Anne Tyler (married to a child psychiatrist) have expressed resistance to Freudianism in one way or another. On Bellow's explicit resistances, see Daniel Fuchs, "Bellow and Freud," *Studies in the Literary Imagination* 17, no. 2 (Fall 1984): 59–80.

and, in his different way, Robert Kegan). Although these theoretical accounts distinguish themselves from one another in many ways, and do not necessarily discuss the middle years per se, what they have in common from the viewpoint of midlife progress narrative is that they make it conceivable. They assert or assume that adulthood is a "developmental epoch" rather than merely "a product of [prior] development."[20] They have moved beyond the original, deterministic, "continuous" or essentialist, child-centered, id-centered, drive-driven emphases of traditional psychoanalysis. Erikson thematized his movement (and theirs) away from the erstwhile ageism of analytic theory: "I have, therefore, in recent years, attempted to delineate the whole life-cycle as an integrated psychosocial phenomenon, instead of following what (in analogy to teleology) may be called the 'originological' approach, that is, the attempt to derive the meaning of development primarily from a reconstruction of the infant's beginnings."[21]

Let us accept Roy Schafer's idea that psychological theories can be construed as telling a story of the life course—that such theories also produce a kind of "narrative structure."[22] Now these post-Freudian, post-Lacanian narratives are beginning to fill in or alter parts of the picture of adult life. The reevaluations this process entails can be staggering. Once looked at within the midlife context, sexuality (for example) proves to be less overwhelmingly dominant than at earlier life stages; it becomes one of many motives, not the central one or, in Freud's mythic agon, one of two. Eighty years after the death of Victoria and fifty years

20. Robert Michels, "Adulthood," in *The Course of Life: Psychoanalytic Contributions Toward Understanding Personality Development*. Vol. III: *Adulthood and the Aging Process*, ed. S. I. Greenspan and G. H. Pollock (Rockville, Md.: National Institute of Mental Health, 1980), p. 25. Michels's article both describes and exemplifies the transformation of psychoanalysis into a "developmental psychology," overcoming its "prejudice" toward equating "childhood" and "development." Because of the process he describes and other tendencies, I do not observe the old dichotomy "psychoanalytic/nonpsychoanalytic."

21. Erik H. Erikson, "Human Strength and the Cycle of Generations," *Insight and Responsibility* (New York: Norton, 1964), p. 114. The earliest move away from Freud's child-centered essentialism was apparently that of Karen Horney, *New Ways in Psychoanalysis* (New York: Norton, 1939); see especially the Introduction and the chapter, "The Emphasis on Childhood." (Horney's Introduction gives credit to Erich Fromm and Wilhelm Reich.) Donald P. Spence, in *Narrative Truth and Historical Truth* (New York: Norton, 1982), pp. 142–43, points out that Freud's use of "evidence" drawn from "the pregenital organization of the child" is inaccessible to proof or disproof. That "scientific" objection would not necessarily invalidate the myth. Some historians of analysis want to scapegoat Freud for this prejudice in his metapsychology; others want to deny he held it.

22. Roy Schafer, "Narration in the Psychoanalytic Dialogue," *Critical Inquiry* 7, no. 1 (Autumn 1980): 29; see also 30.

after the peak of the craze for orgasmic therapies, we are free to hear (from Otto Kernberg) that "the capacity for sexual intercourse and orgasm does not guarantee sexual maturity, or even necessarily represent a relatively higher level of psychosexual development."[23] Problems in one psychic arena may not contaminate other arenas: it's possible that we live in separate spheres, in some of which we are making progress, in others less or none. We may permit ourselves to be pleased by our progress in one area, and therefore relinquish despair about the other spheres and about the "incoherence" of the whole self as well. The old all-or-nothing neurotic self seems to be vanishing. Curing a piece of a self seems a much less monumental project than hauling a heavy old mechanism back along its developmental track after years of its being rustily stalled in place.

Developmental models are becoming kinder toward adult needs, much less likely to call them "regressive," much more likely to see regression as a preliminary to continued growth. "Kohut has emphasized that adults continue to require mirroring and self-affirmation as a kind of psychic oxygen."[24] "Healthy forms of heightened self-esteem," in Kohut's own formulation, are welcome both as aiding growth and representing growth.[25] Self-esteem strengthens the development of the ego ideal, the name given to the power to imagine a better future self and strive to become it. The superego (as a "structure" identified variously with patriarchy and patriarchal religion) is losing ground. For some it may still "exist," but it is attracting less discourse, losing justifications. "In contrast to the pressures and threats of punishment which we relate to the superego, the ego ideal seems to exert its pull by holding forth a promise."[26] Where superego was, there ego ideal shall be.

The most empowering of the new psychosocial theories emphasize how "natural" human development usually is. Freud himself once said,

23. Otto Kernberg, *Object Relations Theory and Clinical Psychoanalysis* (New York: Jason Aronson, 1976), p. 217. For a gendered perspective on this subject, see Ethel Spector Person, "Sexuality as the Mainstay of Identity: Psychoanalytic Perspectives," *Signs* 5, no. 4 (1980): 605–30. "In men, gender appears to 'lean' on sexuality. . . . In contrast, whether or not a woman is orgasmic has few implications for personality organization" (p. 619).

24. Modell, "Psychic 'Aliveness,'" p. 3.

25. Heinz Kohut, "Reflections," in *Advances in Self Psychology,* ed. Arnold Goldberg (New York: International Universities Press, 1980), p. 491.

26. Grete L. Bibring, "Some Considerations Regarding the Ego Ideal in the Psychoanalytic Process," *Journal of the American Psychoanalytic Association* 12, no. 3 (July 1964): 517.

"Let us start from the assumption that what analysis achieves for neurotics is nothing other than what normal people bring about for themselves without its help."[27] "Natural therapy," according to Robert Kegan in *The Evolving Self,* counts on "those relations and human contexts which spontaneously support people through the sometimes difficult process of growth and change."[28] Theorists are now interested in explaining how ordinary life—living with another person, helping children grow, doing useful work in the world, individuating from spouse and parents, telling one's life story—undoes old idealizations, fears, and resentments and frees people. As the culture gingerly embraces the concept that development goes on all through life, we can reappropriate for *adult* trials and goals the positive, not to say heroic vocabulary that used to be employed only for talking of childhood conflict ("a degree of stress and challenge seemed to spur psychological strength and competence"[29]). By employing a high-yield vocabulary, we're able to make larger and more exact claims about growth—to assert, for example, as analyst John Oldham does, that "the fullest and most enriched and rewarding autonomy achievable [develops] during the middle years."[30]

Are we curious about how all this might work itself out, attached to a specific individual behind an interestingly weathered face, in unduplicatable circumstances? A progress narrative shows it to us: the challenges in nervous-making detail, the dramatis personae offering tsuris and support and objects of care, the flick of luck, the waning of suffering, the irruption of energy for a task—the conflicts that theory

27. Sigmund Freud, "Analysis Terminable and Interminable," in *Standard Edition,* trans. and ed. James Strachey (London: Hogarth Press), 23:225 (referred to as *Standard Edition*).

28. Robert Kegan, *The Evolving Self* (Cambridge, Mass.: Harvard University Press, 1982), p. 256.

29. Arlene Skolnick, "The Family Revisited: Themes in Recent Social Science Research," *Journal of Interdisciplinary History* 5, no. 4 (Spring 1975), p. 710, quoted by Jerome Kagan, "Perspectives on Continuity," in *Constancy and Change in Human Development,* ed. Orville G. Brim, Jr., and Jerome Kagan (Cambridge, Mass.: Harvard University Press, 1980), p. 64. Kagan's article is intended "to provoke gentle brooding" about "the Western affinity" for the idea that variations in adult behavior are due to early childhood experience, and thus that over the life course continuity is more salient than change. He believes that this idea "is accepted for want of a competing account" (p. 68). Observing, in fact, numerous competing accounts of change, we can wonder only why the new paradigm is being accepted so slowly.

30. John Oldham, "The Third Individuation: The Middle Aged Child and His or Her Own Parents," delivered at the March 1987 conference on "The Middle Years: New Psychoanalytic Perspectives" (see n. 11 above). Dr. Oldham kindly made his paper available to me in advance of publication. Fullest autonomy need not preclude deep affiliations, generativity, and so forth.

separates, integrated into plots. Each novel possesses not a vocabulary or a theory that might be controverted by another, but believable people who can *own* a plot of recovery or mastery. A sequence of novels by the same author can just hand over to us, in a satisfyingly multi-stranded way, the conclusion cautiously emerging out of the scholarly particulars: that aging can feel like a cure.

In the most striking parallel to contemporary fiction, there has developed a new psychological discourse about "genres." This discourse might not have been introduced without the concept of adult development, which made a whole-life progress "story" thinkable and required that metaphors be borrowed from the newly flourishing field of narrative theory. "It may be helpful to think of the range of descriptive options open to the patient as comparable to the different genres open to the writer," writes Donald Spence, in his highly regarded *Narrative Truth and Historical Truth*. "In similar fashion, if the patient wants to speak in an ironical tongue, he [*sic*] will be forced to choose certain pieces of his experience and ignore others." [31]

The traditional psychoanalytic view values a "tragic"/"ironic" attitude because that matches its essentialism and determinism; it emphasizes how much of life is irreversible, and how unavoidable pain and suffering are. [32] The newer psychodynamic view may be called a shift or a revolution, depending on your taste in political metaphors. In any case, it regards irony toward the self's experience as a constructed and reiterated form of self-deprecation, another inhibitor of change. Patients initially offer as their own "truth" an ironic narrative, a verbal package of contrastive strategies to devalue the self, by concentrating on discrepancies between past dreams and present reality, by setting up unrealizable standards and berating themselves for not fulfilling them, by devaluing all present relationships, by telling their life story as a catalog of losses. Learning that they themselves are producing this ironic account may initially worsen the ironic gap and confirm their helplessness.

In the psychodynamic world, many tendencies are serving to take blinders off eyes bandaged by the tragic/ironic view, which may have had genuinely tragic consequences for women in particular and for all

31. Spence, *Narrative Truth*, pp. 127–128.

32. See, for example, S. B. Messer and M. Winokur, "Some Limits to the Integration of Psychoanalytic and Behavior Therapy," *American Psychologist* 35, no. 9 (September 1980): 818–27. In psychological theory, the notion of genres depends on the work of Roy Schafer, who introduced theorists to Northrop Frye's genre categories.

older people. Otto Kernberg argues that by unwittingly agreeing with "a woman in her forties" that "life has passed her by," the analyst may "feed into the rationalization of otherwise treatable character pathology." He goes on: "In particular, hysterical personality structures with masochistic features . . . may have a much better prognosis than is indicated by their 'tragic' list of long-standing disappointments and failures over many years."[33] Teaching people the role they play in creating lists of disappointments and accepting scenarios of failure—narratives of decline, in my shorthand—is crucial. Roy Schafer has defined the therapeutic enterprise for the analysand as one of taking responsibility for telling a life "history" (and presumably, also, leading a life) in which one becomes a main actor rather than a victim. "Thus, in the course of personal transformation, analysands [I would read "people"] . . . see that they have not been the vehicles of a blind repetition compulsion, but the perpetrators of repetition at all costs."[34] Many commentators write at times as if telling a complete and coherent narrative were by itself a therapeutic goal, but it should be clear from the preceding discussion that a decline narrative may be just as complete and coherent as a progress narrative, and perhaps even more compelling. (Certainly many readers find fictional decline narratives extremely compelling.) But in therapy such a self-presentation should not be final; and in life storytelling it need not be either.

To what extent *fiction* can be considered therapeutic discourse, and for whom, and what kinds of fiction, are fascinating questions. Most of them lie beyond my scope here. The Dutch novelist Harry Mulisch sagely points out the potential occasions of change when he notes that "in literature the actual happening takes place [for the writer] during the act of writing, and for the reader during the act of reading."[35] I came to believe that the "happening" of writing life-course fiction might particularly assist personal transformation: writers mull over their lives and stories just as we all do, but then they fix in print some version. In time, or even at the time, not every sentence in that version continues to sound "right," and all the sentences together may cease to be consonant. For these and other reasons, professional writers can do "self-analysis" in an intense, challenging, and changeable way. For the moment, the relevant point is that all four writers negotiated a shift in their

33. Kernberg, *Object Relations Theory*, p. 236.

34. Schafer, *Language and Insight*, p. 23.

35. Harry Mulisch, "Death and the Maiden," *New York Review of Books* 33, no. 12 (July 17, 1986): 7.

ironic practice from their most judgmental dangerous-age fictions to their most affirmative midlife fictions. Experimenting with alternative possibilities of feeling, they have revised irony the way they revised body image, the beginnings of plots, the endings of plots, and the idea of knowledge. (Irony, we should also remind ourselves, is not *fixed* in a text like a true trope: determining what counts as irony and to what degree it is withering or kindly is an interpretive act, a reader's story.)

On the spectrum of ironies, decline narratives often situate themselves toward the detached end, in realism's tradition of smart doom. Progress narratives call for the term "sympathetic irony," which used to sound like more of an oxymoron than it does today. We could say that these midlife novels are kinder cases of ambivalence.

And the reason is clear: some of the presuppositions of the harsher attitude no longer hold. These novels take lack of self-knowledge, which can be a terrible crime in decline narrative, as a given of the human condition: see the nearly novel-long bewilderments of Anne Tyler's heroine in *Earthly Possessions,* of Bellow's Herzog or Citrine; or, in Drabble's *The Radiant Way,* Liz Headleands's lack of suspicion about her husband's infidelity, or her "ignorance" about her mysterious absent father. Once we believe that growth goes on spontaneously, or that ignorance is never complete, or that people normally recover from the consequences of their ignorance, "blindness" need not be punished so devastatingly.

The novels don't find shortfalls from their authors' (presumed) values ultimately vitiating. Discrepant facts are to them local, not invasive ironies. This may be equivalent to the idea of "separate spheres" noted earlier. We can't help but notice how fate, in the form of the authors' plot-rewards, deals rather kindly with these imperfect people; and how at moments they are given "wisdom, poetry, virtue" that must be close to the best their authors can supply. It must be hard for writers to be ironic toward their best midlife characters.[36] These characters, with their sensitivity or resilience or composure or autonomy—with their quirks and kinks as well—stand much closer to their authors than their earlier unhappy young-adult characters were permitted to do.

My own reader's story in every case depends on having considered the novels in the order in which each author wrote them. How each one separately came to produce one or a few midlife progress narratives is

36. This revised midlife irony provokes charges that the novelists have grown sentimental or less intelligent about their characters. Ironic readings of the novelists considered in *Safe at Last* are plentiful, and some are referred to in future footnotes. Since *Herzog,* Bellow seems to be a primary object of such readings.

the heart of the book, the subject of Chapter Two and the four chapters that follow. I tell each story as a private adventure in *changing one's genre*. That means that I have read comparatively, deciding what features of narrative should count as fictional analogues of abstractions like "cure" and "growth," and then concentrating on the incremental signs of them in succeeding novels. No work is considered in isolation. My readings assume that more convincing analyses of irony, as of other interpretive aporia, are likely to come from such a longitudinal and contextual approach.

In our time, talking about "progress" or its component achievements still encounters a certain embarrassment. Erik Erikson gave instances of related linguistic difficulty twenty-five years ago, asserting that it arises because "we truly shy away from any systematic discussion of human strength. . . . In fact, we do our tortured best to express what we value in terms of double negatives; a person whom we would declare reasonably well is relatively resistant to regression, or somewhat freer from repression, or less given to ambivalence than might be expected."[37] The resistance may be higher when one applies a word like "development," such an orderly word, to a novel whose virtue may be that it encompasses vast amounts of the contingent, the random-seeming—the "unprofitable" days. But we are impoverished if we can't find a way to speak positively: to start with, we will not be able to recognize what's new in the genre. Likewise, knowing that readers are already adept at spotting decline motifs and patterns of loss, I have tried to balance my readings toward practice in revealing the *other* kind of change.

No writer's development in portraying adulthood reads like anyone else's. How long one writes young-adult fiction, what its problems are taken to be, at what age one starts to invent midlife forms, if and when one slips into a decline mode or a more restricted and sorrowful progress mode, how one expresses the benefits of growing older—I have tried to let each sequence speak in its own terms. In part, the authors were chosen precisely because they provided such variety; and with four such different trajectories, four seemed enough. I have been careful to contrast a writer's midlife work only with her own, or his own, earlier work. That decision required me to eschew comparing (say) Drabble's most confident midlife characterization with Updike's, even in narrow, apparently manageable terms: for example, Frances Wingate's image of her fortyish body and her sexuality, versus Harry Angstrom's image of

37. Erikson, *Insight and Responsibility*, p. 112.

his fortyish body and his sexuality. Inevitably, that kind of operation would imply that I was comparing the authors' own developmental outcomes. All four are still writing, and the best and worst of their descriptions of the middle years may be still to come. Updike was nearly fifty when he wrote *Rabbit Is Rich,* and Bellow was nearly sixty at the writing of *Humboldt's Gift.* At the least, we're going to have to disaggregate middle age and decline. Although no one can ignore a writer's return to an unhappier genre—*Roger's Version, More Die of Heartbreak*—we can't take these as final versions, either. When tempted to render judgment, we shouldn't be quick to mouth the most frequent cliché of decline, "Too late." In fact, it is too soon.

A first book on this new midlife genre has certain responsibilities that studies written in later moments will not necessarily have. The first duty, as I see it, is to illuminate the two phenomena: life-course fiction and the midlife progress narratives that grow out of it. Initially, I want to reveal the new creation's best points, clear a space for admiration before the *nil admirari* rushes in, and let readers decide what the benefits may be for them. Any gesture of standing beyond the writers—psychoanalyzing *them,* judging their ethical or emotional limitations on the basis of their characters' characters—would have proved not just a complicated and subjective gesture but also a distracting one. Judging their *characters* on these measures (although tempting and possibly unavoidable) I also tried to omit, for the same reasons.

Part of the complication is that a writer's limitations within the progress genre are never entirely personal, however responsible a writer may feel for them. A protagonist's worst faults may coincide with the author's, but a protagonist's failures of virtue or achievement may partly be our own. Given our cultivated readiness to accept decline scenarios, even a sage might be forced to cut down a character to fit our measure. The same restriction may explain why up until now the genre has not tried to contain even more sorrow—that too would require a nobler type to bear it than many readers find plausible. It's just possible that midlife progress writers are now offering us the highest idea of adulthood we can yet accept from fiction. If their concrete exempla fall short of the dignity or commitment or service or even heroism that some of us see, we should inquire carefully of our culture what ideals it will let its writers embody in narrative.

IV. Lifting the Dead Hand

Now that we have a number of progress narratives in view, the culture that practically forbade them from being produced earlier, and that may still be inhibiting their development, begs to be analyzed. If literary tradition were all, Charlie Citrine and Henderson, Frances Wingate and Kate Armstrong, Justine Peck and Macon Leary, Harry (the Rich) Angstrom and the others should never have appeared. Nothing much in earlier midlife fiction prepares for them: not the suicides and bourgeois failures mentioned earlier, and certainly not Rip Van Winkle (1820), Frédéric Moreau in Flaubert's *Education sentimentale* (1869), Trollope's fifty-year-old in *An Old Man's Love* (1884), Hurstwood in *Sister Carrie* (1900), Gustav Aschenbach (1912), Dick Diver in *Tender is the Night* (1934), George Orwell's thirty-five-year-old Flory in *Burmese Days* (1935), Simone de Beauvoir's Paule in *Les Mandarins* (1954), Humbert Humbert in *Lolita* (1955), Angus Wilson's Mrs. Eliot (1958), Graham Greene's Querry (1961) and other burnt-out cases, Joan Didion's Charlotte Douglas in *A Book of Common Prayer* (1977). A list that aimed at completeness rather than range and continuity over time would be unwieldily long and rather frighteningly familiar: as it is, it includes many of the great texts of humanistic education. Nor do isolated examples of earlier progress protagonists, many equally familiar, constitute a tradition sufficient to explain what I have been calling a "new" genre: Dorothea Brooke in *Middlemarch* (1871–72), Levin in *Anna Karenina* (1873–77), Theodore Colville in Howells's *Indian Summer* (1885–86), Lou Witt in Lawrence's *St. Mawr* (1925), Marcel in *A la recherche du temps perdu* (1913–27), Mrs. Ramsey in *To the Lighthouse* (1927), Fred Cornplow in Sinclair Lewis's *The Prodigal Parents* (1938).[38]

Invention is at least as mysterious as growth. Perhaps more so at the present time, when we overflow with paradigms for growth but are suspicious of the idea of invention—"invention, that vanishing marvel."[39] *Safe at Last in the Middle Years* will not clear up all the mysteries. Chapter Two does offer two kinds of theories about this particular invention.

38. The plot of *The Prodigal Parents* has some curious superficial resemblances to that of *Rabbit Is Rich*. Fred is a "motor dealer" in Sachem Falls, New York; his son Howard wants a job in the agency, but Fred says no because he wants Howard to finish his degree. Updike does far more than Lewis with this rich intergenerational material.

39. Berthoff, "The Way We Think Now," p. 600.

The first theory is that (within the right climate of possibility) the life course can be seen and reconstructed as a teacher of lessons about its own comparative benignity. The second theory has to do with the therapeutic advantages of living in a climate where one can write and publish and be rewarded for producing long fictions about the life course as it advances, and thus be encouraged to revise one's own sense of self and one's own formulations about aging and the middle years. In Chapter Seven and in a future volume called *Midlife Fictions: The Making of the Middle Years of Life* I discuss the obstacles to the development of the progress genre within Western culture, and in Chapter Two and more extensively in *Midlife Fictions* I examine the precedents and qualify to a degree the idea of the newness of the genre. Ultimately I will argue that the ideology that makes midlife progress narrative possible is as ancient as Western literature; but that the obstacles to the form—what were until recently many of the basic assumptions and values of Western civilization—prevented its emergence, except in rare cases, until the revolutions of consciousness of the last two hundred years, and prevented its becoming a multiplied event until the revolutions of consciousness of the late twentieth century.[40]

Let us give due weight to the effort required to become an adult telling a progress narrative within our own historical circumstances. (It may be easier if you don't know that's what you're doing.) The resistances are of a magnitude that hasn't yet been estimated, because we in the Western world have been too embedded in a decline mentality about aging even to ask why we are so embedded. Until we recognize that we have a midlife progress narrative for very nearly the first time in Western literature, we can't begin to explain the history of our erstwhile (un)consciousness and closed-mindedness. Psychic immaturity may turn out to be a mere fragment of explanation, weighted against the strategies that Western civilization has deployed—through aspects of myth, religion, philosophy, law, economic practices, popular imagery— that prevented individuals and groups of individuals from conceiving of a relatively continuous life course that could contain a well-integrated, sexually self-determined, subjectively valuable, self-responsible, and (finally) relatively satisfying adulthood. Not to mention achieving it.

Yet despite the thick contexts that the two books together are supposed to provide, I prefer to leave spots of perplexity in my account of

---

40. *Midlife Fictions* will provide the historical and theoretical background to *Safe at Last;* the theoretical issues that are latent here will be fully discussed there.

this development. I would like to leave readers impressed by the magnitude of the change that has been made, or could be made, in our image of the middle years; penetrated by the idea that the midlife progress narrative in itself constitutes an example of a psychic triumph over enormous cultural odds; and curious enough to go on speculating about what might be occurring in Emerson's heavenly days.

1

Safe at Last

I. The Kisser

Tooth decay. As soon as there are contemporary midlife novels, characters start having trouble with their teeth. Sitting jailed and supperless in the midst of Africa, in the belated middle of his road of life (he's fifty-five), in the middle of Saul Bellow's story of his search for meaning, Eugene Henderson finds himself additionally beset. "And now one of those things occurred which life has not been willing to spare me. As I was sitting waiting here on this exotic night I bit into a hard biscuit and I broke one of my bridges. . . . I felt the jagged shank of the bridge and was furious, disgusted, frightened; damn! I was in despair and there were tears in my eyes."[1]

Henderson copes with the mishap and others a good deal worse. As his exuberant and rather hyperbolic despair suggests, his story is an energetic philosophical midlife comedy: it even turns out that his teeth break for a heartening reason, although some woman has said it's because he grinds his teeth. "Or maybe I have kissed life too hard and weakened the whole structure" (p. 129), he theorizes. His embrace of reality—whom he sexualizes as "the old bitch"—has been, if anything,

---

1. Saul Bellow, *Henderson the Rain King* (New York: Viking, 1959), p. 120. Subsequent quotations from the novel are identified by page numbers in parentheses. This will be my regular procedure with each novel quoted.

too passionate and eager. "Me? I love the old bitch just the way she is and I like to think I am always prepared for even the very worst she has to show me. I am a true adorer of life, and if I can't reach as high as the face of it, I plant my kiss somewhere lower down. Those who understand will require no further explanation" (p. 150).

Margaret Drabble's Frances Wingate, a lonely archaeologist in her early forties, eating a solitary alcoholic dinner, also—no coincidence— traveling far from home, dislodges a whole filling while picking a fish-bone out of her mouth. Frances takes her loss in stride with a lot of codeine; she recites some of her favorite poems, consoles herself with the thought that nobody ever died of a toothache, recalls Dr. Johnson, and finally has the tooth extracted. Then she heads for home and eventual reconciliation with the man she had foolishly left six months before. If her own lost tooth is negligible, her lover's teeth are precious, talismanic. "When he got some new false teeth (he had two on a bridge) she made him give her the old set. She carried them around for ages, then put them in a drawer by her bed with his letters. Later, when she had left him, she got them out again, and when she returned from Africa and started again upon social life, she had taken to putting the teeth down the front of her brassiere. She liked the feel of them, Karel's teeth resting gently and delicately and wirily against her soft evening breast, they kept her company."[2]

How are we supposed to read this new but instantly familiar midlife sign, the broken tooth? It depends on the kind of novel we are in. An anxious forty-year-old worrier in Bellow's *Seize the Day* thinks he can size up an old man's sorry life by counting his porcelains. "Each of those crowns represented a tooth ground to the quick, and estimating a man's grief with his teeth as two per cent of the total . . . it came to a sizable load."[3] The dentist in Updike's *Couples* handles the hermeneutics of teeth with doom-filled glibness. "Losing a tooth means death to people; it's a classic castration symbol," Freddy Thorne declares flatly. His assertion occurs, reliably, as the introit to what we have to call the classic midlife discourse, about whether life is to be conceived as a progress story or a decline story. The limp, castration-concerned dentist gets to enunciate the decline theory of life: "Carol, you're right about the nifty machine we begin with; the trouble is, it runs only one way.

2. *The Realms of Gold* (New York: Knopf, 1975), p. 18.
3. *Seize the Day* (New York: Viking, 1956), pp. 31–32.

Downhill."[4] "We don't die for one second out there in the future," he says pedantically, "we die all the time, in every direction. Every meal we eat breaks down the enamel" (p. 370).

A progress novelist of the middle years, however, would not let a dentist interpret tooth decay any more than the ancients let butchers interpret entrails. Right interpretation requires priests of the imagination, who turn out to be those articled to the guild of survivors. Almost all have experienced tough times in the past: they want to tell us about these, but as retrospects. What we see first-hand is the way they can cope with a "last-straw" kind of trial in present time. In their novels, what they think about lost teeth and kindred matters is controlling. Henderson's view, which doesn't disguise his erstwhile aggressive side, is that he has kissed life too hard. Karel's teeth for Frances are the "guardians of her virtue," and they work like magic to rescue her from promiscuity while the lovers—eventually to be spouses—are apart.

Maybe there's an erotics of teeth hidden in the midlife progress novel, or at least an anatomy of love. Our sample is full of characters who though no longer young are capable of loving and inspiring love; and this state seems normal to them. (The privileged state of mutual love used to be reserved in fiction for the young alone.) Love arrives via many plots in the middle years, not just in the standard first-time-around marriage plot; and it comes for characters who are not all charm. Tyler's timid armchair traveler, Macon Leary in *The Accidental Tourist,* reduced almost to automatism by the murder of his son, risks falling in love for the second time—and his sister, close to him in age, risks it for the first time. When Frances Wingate marries the man with the bridge, both her reasons for doing it and the prognosis for happiness are better than they were her first time around. At forty-seven, and a large sloppy man at that, Harry Angstrom (of *Rabbit Is Rich*) discovers how much he values his long-term wife and many other people and things besides. Justine Peck, the wispy seeker of *Searching for Caleb,* she of the Breton hat and nearly new clothes, also discovers late in a long marriage that it has been the *right* situation for her, not just one she desperately wanted for the wrong reasons when young. In another departure, love does not have to be sexual or marital: friendship may be the kind of love the protagonist feels most, just then.

If we want to measure how radical successful midlife love is in fic-

4. *Couples* (New York: Knopf, 1968), pp. 241–42.

tion, we can look at a few decline figures whose love (and teeth) fail them. Freddy Thorne's decline theory arises, Updike lets us know, from impotence and his professional deformation. When we meet Vronsky at the end of *Anna Karenina,* he is a man who has failed to commit suicide in the self-imposed way, and is going to war to put himself in the way of someone else's bullet. This could be read as a romantic picture of fidelity, if Tolstoy did not, rather cruelly, give him a toothache. "Men through the ages, for all their reverence before the magical potency of teeth and all their admiration for the beauty of teeth, still find something grotesque, ridiculous, and degrading about toothache," comments one scholar.[5] Our present context suggests that Tolstoy must have disliked so weak a will to live, so passive a will to die.

Updike's hero in *Couples,* on the other hand, the only man in town who really loves sex and fears death, opts for an antidecline theory. It's worth quoting in full.

> "Freddy," Piet said, tenderly, wanting to save something of himself, for he felt Freddy as a vortex sucking them all down with him, "I think you're professionally obsessed with decay. Things grow as well as rot. Life isn't downhill; it has ups and downs. Maybe the last second is up. . . . What impresses me isn't so much human self-deception as human ingenuity in creating unhappiness. We believe in it. Unhappiness is us. From Eden on, we've voted for it. We manufacture misery, and feed ourselves on poison. That doesn't mean the world isn't wonderful." (p. 242)

When Henderson is willing to kiss life low down, and Frances hides Karel's teeth in her cleavage, and an adulterous builder expounds the idea that decline theory arises from *misreading* the world, we know that however much trouble besets these protagonists, we can expect from the novels they inhabit the surprise-pleasures and affirmations of progress novels—Bildungsromane—of the middle years of life. To *prize* something that is usually treated (in myth, folklore, and modern literature[6]) as a bad sign of aging—that is what a lover or a good friend does. In fiction, this is one of the human services of the Bildungsromane of the middle years. Its assured and savvy advocacy of a neglected or maligned stage of life belongs at the beginning of any characterization of the

5. Theodore Ziolkowski, "The Telltale Teeth: Psychodontia to Sociodontia," *PMLA* 91, no. 1 (January 1976): 15.

6. "In myth and folklore, teeth have long symbolized sexual vigor as well as wisdom" (ibid., p. 11).

genre. But that function scarcely suggests the cultural audacity of the genre. It dares to prize the middle years *more* than earlier stages of life. (In time, this may seem less audacious, as more of us come to believe we invented the value ourselves.)

Bellow, Drabble, Tyler, and Updike have been creating this genre in the course of producing more or less traditionally mimetic fiction about personal life: fiction about characters marrying and married, having children and raising them, working, thinking, and—remarkably—aging. They have thus provided for themselves a context out of which midlife discourse has developed, and has become visible as such. This context I call "life-course fiction." These authors are brought here together because, unlike as they are in so many other ways, they came via similar roads to similar midlife literary forms and some friendly conclusions about aging.

My dental disquisition has thus eased us into some of the assertions of this book, which is about the remarkable phenomenon of the contemporary midlife progress narrative and its relationship to life-course fiction. Supposedly, trouble with teeth has to be a dreary, "natural" sign of aging—a dreary coordinate of debility, ugliness, impotence, pessimism, and the increasing closeness of death.[7] Midlife *Bildung* (the term emphasizes process and positive change) turns this entire system upside-down. If writers can reverse conventional notions about losing teeth, they have the power to reverse or discard *all* the negative images and metaphors that the decline theorists and novelists associate with aging. They can even wind up saying—to the astonishment of some readers— that it is better to be older than to be younger. This is roughly what I take these four writers to be saying at certain moments in their careers, and the rest of *Safe at Last in the Middle Years* is an attempt to explain what this saying means for each of them and how they came to write the peculiar genre that lets them say it.

Making the middle years seem like a beneficence is rather a noble achievement, and one that will draw credit and gratitude to this group

7. Tooth decay won't be useful as a natural sign of aging much longer, at least in the First World: because of advances in hygiene, decay is vanishing. Adults are getting good dental care, "toothlessness has almost been eliminated in middle-aged adults," and the next generation is getting scarcely any cavities, according to the National Institute of Dental Research. Their report may be read as a sign about such signs. See Daniel S. Greenberg, "A dental report that gives something to smile about," The Boston *Globe,* March 28, 1987, p. 11. It has always been possible to see twenty-year-olds or even children in poor areas who had missing or decayed teeth.

of novelists and others doing similar work, for a long time to come. But it should be said that, although their invention of the genre was no accident, it was certainly not their original intention.

II. The Dangerous Age

She remembered how [her ex-husband's] knees and elbows had jabbed her in bed those early years when nightmares twitched him; she had rather loved him for those nightmares, confessions as they were of his terror as life in all its length and responsibility loomed to his young manhood.

—Updike, *The Witches of Eastwick*

Midlife is a "contrast-gainer" (to borrow a phrase from Bellow at his sixtyish wittiest).[8] To feel good about the middle years it is helpful to have had a miserable young adulthood and, in particular, a trying time in the early years of marriage. This is such an easy requirement, according to the representations of all four novelists, that it's a wonder we don't all praise the middle years. Since we don't, the earlier stages of life-course fiction force us to suspect that it may be in part because our memory has prettied up our past. After all, few of us have produced records of how we actually felt then with which to confront the retrospective construction of what some people like to call "the happiest years of our lives." These novelists *did* produce such a record. They all published young, and quickly started writing about characters more or less their own age and over the threshold of marriage. Bellow's first protagonist was two years married and of draft age; Updike's second (his first protagonist was ninety-six) was married and twenty-six; Drabble's second was married with two small children; Tyler's third gets married and pregnant.

In their early novels young adulthood is depicted, from the viewpoint of young protagonists (from within, as some critics say), as a dangerous age—a tense, threatening, crowded, and overwhelming time. And the novels that are written later, in the safer middle years, often

---

8. *Humboldt's Gift* (New York: Viking, 1975), p. 61.

"So I was merely a contrast-gainer," I said.
"I thought contrast-gainer was just your term for married couples. You like a lady because she's got a husband, a real stinker, who makes her look good."
"It's one of those portmanteau expressions."

regard young adults with detached sorrow, pity, and compassion—as if, yes, alas, we now understand how the young are obliged to navigate a perilous crossing with rudimentary equipment before getting to the other side. At the time, terror, dread, anxiety, dismay, anger, hurt, and resentment are words that describe what characters feel in Updike's *Rabbit, Run* and *Rabbit Redux;* in many of Drabble's novels (*The Garrick Year, The Waterfall, The Needle's Eye*); in Tyler's *A Slipping-Down Life, The Clock Winder,* and *Celestial Navigation;* and in Bellow's first two novels, *Dangling Man* and *The Victim,* and in *Seize the Day. Rabbit, Run, Seize the Day,* and *Celestial Navigation* record a considerable permanent worsening of the protagonist's situation over time (that would be another way of identifying a decline narrative), but even those that end relatively well report long moments of desperate feeling.

We see in these novels the first shock of concussion as "life in all its length and responsibility" looms. There's no buffer of pleasantness, such as love might provide, because almost no love is represented. Marriage gets picked up as a topic of fiction in circumstances of such alienation and difficulty that no reader expects to hear about the honeymoon, or, for that matter, about any marital joys. The only first-hand view of the honey-mood is in Tyler's *A Slipping-Down Life,* where the groom is soon found, by the pregnant bride, with another woman, in their marriage bed, on the night her father has died. In Tyler's novel about true love between cousins, *Searching for Caleb,* their affection and desire to marry is treated as a disaster by Justine's father, who deserts his wife and all her family in protest; after he dies of a heart attack, Justine's mother walks in front of a car. There's no room right then—in the young-adult part of the novel—to be glad about being married. A Drabble heroine recalls (for completely other reasons) "the sad despairing communion of dismay that had marked the first years of their marriage."[9] Bellow's Augie March, the only person in all the young-adult novels who is both in love and unencumbered by parental solicitude, gets called up for service right after the wedding.

Their motives for marrying are always in some way mistaken. Even Augie thinks he's getting someone who will help him run a kind of orphanage, when what she wants is a career as an actress and other incompatible things. If Justine marries her cousin to stay in the same family, most young people marry to get away. Drabble's Emma Evans in *The Garrick Year* comments on her own success in that line. "And we did

9. *The Needle's Eye* (New York: Knopf, 1972), p. 220.

achieve an exile, of course. We could hardly have achieved less."[10] Up-dike tells the same story of empty youthful "romance": in *Rabbit, Run,* Rabbit (Harry Angstrom) says laconically, "Actually . . . she can't stand her parents any more than I can. She probably wouldn't've married me if she hadn't been in such a hurry to get away from 'em."[11] Even fear of otherness can seem like a good motive in that early stage of stupidity. One young-married doesn't want her husband-to-be to tell her about himself: "All I wanted was this feeling of terror with which he inspired me" (*The Garrick Year,* p. 30). That desire doesn't last long. The best thing that can be said for marriage as it is described in these novels is that when it appears to have destroyed affection, it hasn't killed any-thing that was especially healthy.

Yet these plots are not fronts for diatribes against marriage (as many nineteenth-century fictions now seem to be), as much as they are repre-sentations of radical unreadiness for it. It's as if making a permanent connection with someone of the opposite sex were some awful impera-tive of life. As a setting for this resistance to the imperative, writers can now choose either the courting period or the early-marriage stage. The women write novels describing the dread that women experience in the courtship stage. "The game of sexual selection seemed to me, as I em-barked upon it, to be the most savage game in the world," says Jane Gray in *The Waterfall,*[12] and Tyler's *The Clock Winder* and Drabble's ear-lier *The Millstone* dramatize the dangers and the avoidances of this pe-riod. Marriage is not a bad situation only for women—men too write about the miseries of the early years, with Updike's *Rabbit, Run* the *locus classicus* of unreadiness. (If anything, Tyler's and Drabble's female protagonists handle the phase more adroitly and rationally.) Why is this life-course imperative—whose desirability, until quite recently, has often been taken for granted in our culture—seen as so dreadful?

From the young-adult novels themselves, it's hard to disentangle pre-cisely what frightens young people when they find themselves com-mitted to another person. What gets rendered faithfully is the chaos of experience as it is lived without much clarity. A character's motives for behavior sometimes seem underdetermined, but more often they are overdetermined, so that young-adult novels can support many and sometimes conflicting interpretations. (Explanations often come later, in the same writer's midlife novels.) Of course, to generate plots, mid-

10. Margaret Drabble, *The Garrick Year* (London: Weidenfeld and Nicolson, 1964), p. 33.

11. *Rabbit, Run* (New York: Knopf, [1960] 1971), p. 133.

life protagonists have to have problems too. But chaos gets *represented* in midlife progress narratives; it's not as much the medium in which they are written. Charlie Citrine in *Humboldt's Gift* describes his life as disorderly in a controlled tone that Tommy Wilhelm couldn't muster and would certainly envy.

At the simplest level, youthful characters seem to experience the period after the wedding, without remedy, as a confused set of deprivations. One of Drabble's most chipper early protagonists bluntly lists them.

I could hardly believe that marriage was going to deprive me of this, too [a good, steady, lucrative job]. It had already deprived me of so many things which I had childishly overvalued: my independence, my income, my twenty-two-inch waist, my sleep . . . a whole string of finite things, and many more indefinite attributes like hope and expectation. (*The Garrick Year*, p. 11)

This is a woman's list, and as far as she's concerned, her husband hasn't lost anything. But Rabbit's list, if he could make one, would be just as likely to start with Emma Evans's first item, and end with her last.

The basic problem may derive from feeling oneself, by one's own agency, no longer independent. Solitary self-centeredness or individuation, goals that have barely been achieved in adolescence and are supposed to be the "natural" condition of the unmarried, abruptly cease or threaten to. "The great astonishment of this state," according to Augie March deep in love, "was that the unit of humanity should maybe be not one but two. Not even the eagle falconry [his girlfriend's loony idea of a career for the two of them] distressed me as much as that what happened to her had to happen to me too, necessarily. This was scary."[13] In myths, the fear of merging with another was objectified in a plot in which one party attempts a rape and the other person flees: the myth of Daphne and Apollo is a woman's version of the story, Venus and Adonis a man's.

In novels, the story is more complex and not exclusively sexual. Marriage is represented as a humiliating or terrifying or (in the best case) rather empty dependency. The other person has few resources for one to draw on and is either critical or indifferent or just as helpless as oneself. In Bellow's first dark early novels, the wife is an absence: at work or

12. Margaret Drabble, *The Waterfall* (London: Weidenfeld and Nicolson, 1969), p. 132.

13. Saul Bellow, *The Adventures of Augie March* (New York: Viking, 1953), p. 323.

out of town; in *Seize the Day,* as an estranged wife, she's a malicious, goading, sapping harpy. When women and men are shown interacting, except in Tyler's novels, they're often afraid of each other. Updike's protagonist, Rabbit Angstrom, is scared of his wife Janice. "He feels frightened. When confused, Janice is a frightening person" (pp. 10–11). Several of Drabble's heroines are afraid of their husband's anger, with good reason; and Bellow's Tommy Wilhelm (in *Seize the Day*) cringes under his wife's scorn.

If satisfying sexual activity had once been a goal of marriage, the event does not justify the anticipation. Updike and Drabble show this in present-time novels, and Bellow presents sexual foul-ups (in later novels) as a past source of unhappiness. (Ejaculatio praecox is alluded to in Bellow's *Herzog* and in *The Middle Ground* as having once been a problem.) "The total disaster of her sexual life" (*The Waterfall,* p. 44) is one of the subjects Drabble's Rosamund Stacey in *The Millstone* and Jane Gray in *The Waterfall* both spend pages reviewing. The plot of *Rabbit, Run* is organized so that Rabbit never has sex with his (pregnant) wife; his blind resentment finally drives him out of the house and precipitates the catastrophe. The plot of *Rabbit Redux* is organized so that Rabbit has intercourse with his wife once. A divorced protagonist in another Updike novel, *Of the Farm,* recalls that he feared coition with his first wife because of the "claustrophobia" of the "descent." "I felt in danger of smothering in her. She seemed, like me, an adventurer helpless in dark realms upon which light, congested, could burst only with a convulsion."[14] If this is the convulsion we guess, then an initial dread (and dislike) of sexuality may be more widespread, for both men and women, than we usually think.

But the curiously tense and constricted relationships depicted in these novels make us think that sexual malfunction (which is not a problem for the protagonists of midlife novels by the same writers) is a sign of some deeper disorder. Looking at the way characters talk about the surface disorder of their lives can show us how authors construct the idea of their psychological disorder.

One of the signs of male-female enmity, comic when one first starts noticing it, is dislike of the other person's clutter. Good guys are neat; their spouses are not. Or vice-versa: in bad situations either dichotomy can mimic and magnify the basic gender division. "I hated the way David would throw his clothes all over my neatly folded garments when

14. *Of the Farm* (New York: Knopf, 1965), p. 47.

he undressed for bed," Emma Evans complains in *The Garrick Year* (p. 33). "It seems to [Rabbit] he's the only person around here who cares about neatness. The clutter behind him in the room . . . clings to his back like a tightening net" (p. 14). The more we look at this imagery of "congestion" and "nets" and mess the more serious it gets. Unused to otherness, protagonists feel trapped. "For what made him mad at Janice wasn't so much that she was in the right for once and he was wrong and stupid but the closed feeling of it, the feeling of being closed in" (*Rabbit, Run*, p. 271). The epigraph to this section, written out of a peak of midlife tranquillity, gently recollects symbolic restlessness and kicking in the semiconsciousness of the early matrimonial night. At the time there were terrible struggles and resistances at the extra presence in the double bed.

But no matter what you're kicking at, of course, if there's another person in the bed she or he gets kicked. It's not just the scariness of the other unit that makes young people feel trapped. Bellow's novels use similar imagery—"His high, thick chest felt intolerably bound and compressed, and he lifted his shoulders in an effort to ease his breathing"[15]—and his first two plots are not about evading sex (directly), but instead are about being drafted into war or being victimized by anti-Semitism. All the plots would seem to be the outside garment that prior feelings of constraint (and weakness in the face of constraint) use to express themselves. Aside from marriage, writers invent plenty of plot circumstances to explain why young people feel intolerably constricted.

Young protagonists react to their sense of marital entrapment, these novels tell us, by flight or fight—sometimes both. Plots of alienation and painful separation are common: both men and women write them. Rabbit leaves his wife twice in *Rabbit, Run* and she leaves him in *Rabbit Redux* (where, speaking to his son, he describes his earlier desertions as "a vacation"). Jane Gray forces her husband to leave her in such a way that he'll feel he deserted her. A bit of bleak dialogue between Jane and her cousin Lucy about the absent husband represents an attitude belonging to this stage (not usually stated so calmly) about the way characters can come to regard their spouses. "'You're better off without,' said Lucy, calmly, abstracting the toast, burning her fingers, picking it up from the floor where she had dropped it. 'Yes, of course,' said Jane" (*The Waterfall*, p. 28). Tyler's *Earthly Possessions,* about a woman married many years who hangs on to her young-adult image of herself too

15. *The Victim* (New York: Vanguard Press, 1947), p. 79.

long, opens with the sentence, "The marriage wasn't going well and I decided to leave my husband." [16] In Drabble's *The Millstone* (1965; later known as *Thank You All Very Much*), after the plot has put the woman and man together once for the purpose of conception, the woman goes through the entire process of pregnancy, including the birth and a grave operation the baby requires, without ever calling him, and they meet only once again, by accident, after she has weathered the entire experience alone.

The extra presence in the double bed feels like a crowd already, but it's nothing to the extra presence in the crib. Babies mean trouble, in Updike, Drabble, and Tyler. (There are no babies in Bellow's young-adult novels, where we'd expect them—perhaps because his men scarcely have wives. *Dangling Man* has an adolescent niece whom Joseph detests, and Leventhal in *The Victim* has nephews he hasn't been close to until one of them gets sick.) In the dark young-adult narratives of the others, the birth of the baby results in an actual or symbolic divorce between women and men, and grindingly hard work for women. The children absorb all their mothers' love, which turns out—at least in the novels of Tyler and Drabble—to be more ample and available to them than it ever was to their fathers. The men dislike and resent the intrusion. Rabbit clears out the second time partly because he can't visualize getting anything he wants from an infant: "somewhere there was something better for him than listening to babies cry and cheating people in used car lots" (p. 271).

Tyler twice tells the story of men fleeing babies, first with the man's motives a muddle, in the present-time frame of *A Slipping-Down Life* (1970), and fifteen years later, in *The Accidental Tourist* (1985), as a clearly understood retrospect. Macon's friend Muriel tells how her marriage ended after her baby Alexander was born sickly. "'I adjusted better; I mean pretty soon it seemed to me that that was what a baby *ought* to look like, and I hung around the hospital nursery but Norman wouldn't go near him, he said it made him too nervous.'" [17] "Norman said, 'Muriel, won't we ever get our ordinary life back?' Well, you can see his point, I guess. It's like I only had room in my mind for Alexander. . . . And *Norman* was no help, I think he was jealous. He got this kind of stubborn look whenever I had to do something, go warm a bottle or something" (pp. 176–77). The typical young husband in

16. *Earthly Possessions* (New York: Knopf, 1977), p. 1.
17. *The Accidental Tourist* (New York: Knopf, 1985), p. 170.

Drabble is not jealous but indifferent. "It was his rejection of the role of ordinary English father that had made her, forcibly, making a virtue of necessity, draw the children to herself, take them entirely upon herself, set up, even while he was still there, a solitary life with them, in which she took sole charge, sole responsibility" (*The Needle's Eye*, p. 134).

Because the plot of the earlier *Thank You All Very Much* similarly found ways (as in Tyler, involving a sickly baby) for a woman to take "sole responsibility" for her child, we may be forgiven if we conclude that the fantasy of crowding out the husband is a desirable one in the dangerous age. In her original mood of ambivalence about the situation, however, Drabble called the book *The Millstone* when it was first published. In it Rosamund Stacey is presented as jealous of her own experience of pregnancy, birth, and mothering, wanting to possess it wholly on her own, as a kind of narcissistic unshared monologue. This situation does not seem much different from the narcissistic unshared monologue of Bellow's *Dangling Man*, written in diary form, except that Rosamund is happy. The men's plots in Bellow's novels and *Rabbit, Run* also crowd out spouses, as we've noted, but not in favor of children.

The ambivalence of women about motherhood gets expressed later on, as usual, in a midlife novel. The *second* time an author uses a situation, we look for signs that it has been consciously analyzed and understood: one of these is that it's told in a shorter, more explicit way. The first time, it may take an entire novel for the writer to work the character out of the fog; when the fog recedes, the work can be done in a sentence. Mimicking the unconscious, a midlife text may enunciate the character's most irrational fear only after it has been completely cured—like Justine Peck's strange idea that she was likely to die prematurely, as her mother had done, out of some inability to combine the roles of wife and mother. "And now what? Justine had raised her daughter without dying after all; she was freed from her fears."[18] We can hear rapture in Drabble's lines about "sole charge, sole responsibility," but the same protagonist recalls "hardship" too. "It was no wonder that she had ended up alone with the children: she had been forced to take them on alone, she had strengthened herself on those hard years, she had developed the muscle to deal with them, she had learned to love the hardship of dealing with them" (p. 134). The early plots suggest that if women feel resentment against young children, that feeling gets turned against men. Only in the direst case of male-female extremity could it also be

18. *Searching for Caleb* (New York: Knopf, 1976), p. 188.

turned against the children—at least this is the way I read Drabble's passage about Rose Vassiliou's disliking, at times, her first-born son: "there had been a time when she had ceased, almost, to love him" (p. 141).

As if the explosive mixture of husband-wife-child were not enough to explain the images of crowding and pressure, many novels of the dangerous age stir in the protagonists' parents. These are portrayed (at least at the beginnings of novels, and sometimes all through) as remaining sources of anger, or neglect, or adverse judgment, just as they were in their children's fictional childhood or adolescence. And the parents are still the objects of their adult child's fear, resentment, hostility, or incomprehension—the children haven't changed either. Anne Tyler has portrayed two older mothers, Mrs. Emerson in *The Clock Winder* and Charlotte Emory's mother in *Earthly Possessions,* who tried to give their first child back to the hospital at the time of its birth. In novels about reluctantly taking on mothering, these characters are images of women unprepared for motherhood, projected onto the prior generation. But long after the mothers stop expressing doubt about whether the children are theirs, their adult children can't get rid of the idea that they are unwanted. Sometimes they're right. Wilhelm in *Seize the Day* cries out to his father, "When I suffer—you aren't even sorry. That's because you have no affection for me, and you don't want any part of me" (p. 54), and his father doesn't deny it.

Some plots describe the relationship with parents in terms of making obligatory and long-deferred visits to them. A visit is all one can stand, because the parents voice the protagonists' own continuing inner sense of failure and worthlessness. A visit literalizes the protagonists' fear that they can't put a permanent distance between themselves and their own despicable self-evaluation. (The parents objectify the disapproving super-ego, Freudians would say. If so, they represent it as something that should be *past* but somehow is not.) Sometimes the visit confirms that the parent hasn't changed: Rose Vassiliou's father is described as "stubborn and angry . . . clearly a mean and rude old man" (pp. 308–9). "Rose, herself, was thinking that nothing had changed. It was all as it had been, dreary, oppressive, painful beyond belief" (p. 315). This sort of vision could be a confirmation that it is the *child* who can't change. But some of these novelists doubt the Freudian hypothesis that the super-ego remains a punishing implant. Freedom may be slow in coming, but it can begin. Rose leaves her father's house as soon as she can. She does make a self-punishing decision soon after, but she feels hopeful that it will be only temporary. If a novelist forces his protagonist to *live* with his unloving father, as Bellow situated Wilhelm, then it may be a sign that he has (for the time) accepted the deterministic view that an adult who is a loser will always be a loser. But Charlotte Emory lives with her mother in a novel that ends as a midlife Bildungsroman, and there Tyler subverts the fatalism of *indwelling*. Charlotte misreads the sign.

Images of feeling pressed, crowded, and claustrophobic—suddenly we see what must be the basic psychological situation, and it's the same whether the plot trouble is sex or parents or children or war. Whatever it is, the characters fear that for some reason they don't understand, they can't create a self-chosen, more self-confident, happier future—they can't progress in the life course as they must and want to. In these young-adult novels, unloving parents are seen—like spouses, like children—as closing it off. Fictional parents who don't change mirror their adult children who feel they themselves can't change. Falling into the psychology of determinism and the tropes of misdirection, those who can't imagine progress for themselves can only imagine regress. The following is from Drabble's *Jerusalem the Golden*. "And these visits managed to reduce her to exactly the same stage of trembling, silent, frustrated anxiety that she had endured throughout her childhood; she felt, each time, that she had gone back, right back to the start, and that every step forward must be painfully retraced." [19] This state of mind can be attributed to a woman still in college, as in *Jerusalem the Golden*, or to a man of forty, which is the age Wilhelm is given. Wilhelm feels as if buried underground, not even as smart as a "woodchuck," who "has a few exits to his tunnel" (p. 54). Such characters say they can't go forward or up, which are the privileged directions in the travel metaphors of life-course fiction. And escape, which, whether as inner withdrawal or physical departure, gives an illusion of progress, also is not possible for everyone. Wanting to change, without being sure you are able to change—this is the story inscribed in the darker narratives. The dangerous age is the age when one still fears *reversibility*.

For this reason, I believe, dangerous-age novels contain more than their share of shrieks, blows, accidents, and death. Incidents of inexplicable anger—overreactions and violence—break out in Bellow's first two novels and several of Drabble's. The violence in early Tyler and Updike, almost more frightening, comes unpremeditated, out of a more

19. Margaret Drabble, *Jerusalem the Golden* (London: Weidenfeld and Nicolson, 1967), p. 90.

neutral surface. The most shocking image in any of these novels is that of the young drunken mother putting her newborn baby in the sink to wash it—to drown it, every reader can anticipate—in *Rabbit, Run*.

Bellow's protagonists live in a constant state of irritation, and Drabble's heroines' husbands have a short fuse. The dangling man viciously spanks his niece when he feels insulted, makes a scene in which he sarcastically proclaims his "shame," and yells at his wife when she becomes upset at the whole episode. He publicly taunts an old acquaintance who has cut him and sneers irascibly at old friends. He punches his landlord for not providing heat: "A pistol would not have deterred me." [20] In *The Garrick Year*, Emma's Welsh husband punches a hole in the wall in anger at his wife, and drops a marble pedestal down a flight of stairs, barely missing a child at the bottom. Rose Vassiliou lives in terror of her husband's violence: when they were married he beat her, and after they were divorced he raped her.

Death, so far away from these protagonists in its natural form of old age, threatens them unnaturally. Props that rarely appear in midlife fiction come into perilous focus: gas ovens and guns. Props that are innocent in other contexts—sinks, streams, cars—become treacherous. Joseph, about to go to war, is certainly "justified" in fearing death, but many others are targets. Waking accidentally from a dream, Leventhal finds his apartment broken into; his enemy has turned on the gas, apparently trying for a combined suicide-murder. Tidying up the garden in her habitual way, Elizabeth in *The Clock Winder* finds herself facing "a little steel pistol whose eye was pointed at her heart"; [21] it is held by a man who thinks she is responsible for his brother's suicide, a man whose hostility she has never taken seriously—but he shoots. Charlotte's kidnapper in *Earthly Possessions* keeps a gun on her. In the second volume of Updike's trilogy, neighbors set fire to Rabbit's house. In *The Waterfall*, Jane Gray's lover drives sports cars recklessly, and eventually, while driving with Jane and her children, has an accident in which he almost dies. Although she says, "He's dead, you know," to the first witness who arrives, he isn't. "The accident, it seemed, had given shape and form to my guilt," she concludes (p. 208). Rabbit could say the same thing after the wife he deserted drowns their baby. All the writers inventing death, at this stage, connected it with guilt. Or perhaps they simply felt fragile and invented threats from outside to prove it and guilt to justify it.

20. Saul Bellow, *The Dangling Man* (New York: Vanguard Press, 1944), p. 145.
21. Anne Tyler, *The Clock Winder* (New York: Berkley Books, [1972] 1983), p. 251.

At this moment of vulnerability, paradoxically, a protagonist suddenly acquires power to cause immense harm to others as well—or the belief in this power. Both men and women are shown fearing the harm they can do or cause others to do. In fear of this power, Jane Gray had tried to make herself small. "She had once thought herself a dangerous woman, and it was in fear of such knowledge that she now lay where she was, in the bed she lay in, lost, harmless, weak, her shadow falling nowhere, occupying no space, blotting out no light," Jane explains (pp. 29–30). In *The Clock Winder,* the man courting Elizabeth courts suicide because he has destroyed his fledgling career, but threatens it— and commits it —when she refuses to break an engagement to go away for the weekend with another man. Most plots (except Bellow's) link danger with the passions evoked between men and women: their infatuations, revulsions, wounded pride, sexual frustrations. In short, they blame "love." What Rose thinks about this natural urge, Emma, Elizabeth, Wilhelm, and Rabbit and his wife Janice could also think, in their own way. "And she had a strange sense . . . of love as some huge white deformed and not very lovely god, lying there beneath the questions and the formality, caught in a net of which points alone touched and confined him—points, blows, matrimonial offences, desertions, legalities, all binding love down though he shapelessly overflowed and struggled—and necessarily bound, the net being entirely necessary, because without it there was violence and terror and warfare" (p. 84).

How dangerous can a young person actually be at this stage? Not very. Most don't do much harm; but harm occurs, and they're confused in it. Of all four writers, Updike gives the most frightening answer to this question. At the end of a story that is in part about Rabbit's nature—is he as harmless and lovable as he'd like to think?—the woman he's decided he loves says to him, "Boy, you really have the touch of death, don't you? . . . I see you very clear all of a sudden. You're Mr. Death himself. . . . No, you don't do anything. You just wander around with the kiss of death" (*Rabbit, Run,* p. 304). This is an angry woman talking: he has made her pregnant and left her after a particularly humiliating moment in their uneasy connection. He hasn't in fact killed anyone: it was his wife who drowned their baby. But allowing for hyperbole, his "kiss" is death. His randiness brings sheer misery to both women: the one who doesn't kill their baby tells him she's going to abort their foetus. And, in a sense that the novel doesn't question, his neediness *is* his nature.

A lot of young-adult fiction records this moment, when one feels forced to believe that one's identity as an adult is primarily sexual. Sex is the new power, given by the life course for as long as any young person can imagine, so that if it seems overwhelming they can think they'll be overwhelmed forever. Even Rabbit's sexual whims get executed, and then punished. The only woman who doesn't turn away from him angrily is an ancient widow, past her vulnerability, who tells him that he kept her alive one more year. Sex gets presented in these novels as biologically uncontrollable too. Three young-adult plots depend on conception resulting from characters having had intercourse once: Updike's *Rabbit, Run* and *Couples,* and Drabble's *The Millstone.* In this plot, generative power is certainly magnified—as part of the punishment, because in none is a baby intended, or initially wanted. Again, it's their own absence of control that most terrifies the young. Why so many novels in which young people neglect or even scorn contraception? The young are shown as yielding a control they might exert, and proving with the resulting embryo how far-flung the consequences are.

Children whom the protagonists are responsible for are most at risk in these fictional milieux. The infant in *Rabbit, Run* is not alone. In an argument with her husband, Rose Vassiliou hurls one of their children at him. In *The Garrick Year,* two small children as well as the heroine's husband and an au-pair girl (all the accoutrements of her adult life) are almost asphyxiated by gas from a jet accidentally left open when Emma is out. Later in the same novel, the little daughter slides into a stream and almost drowns. In Bellow's *The Victim,* one of Leventhal's nephews dies of a neglected fever. Charlotte Emory has a miscarriage and fears that her body "did this on purpose" (*Earthly Possessions,* p. 126) because another baby would have tied her once again to her family unhappiness. The contexts of risk suggest several related ideas. At a minimum, children are a sign of the hardship that adulthood entails, since they require unremitting care. They interfere with their parents' freedom. They bind the responsible parent to an unloved spouse, or are associated with marital grief. At worst, they are a sign of adulthood's enormous, terrifying powers, because we can have "so much effect on [them]" (*The Clock Winder,* p. 11).

All this young-adult misery—which readers have perhaps forgotten or not suspected—is hard to take. I've put us through it because our ability to recognize that the middle years can be welcomed as a relief by some people may depend on our traversing the dangerous age imaginatively, in however truncated and inevitably detached a way. These novels (and many others like them by other writers) offered hitherto unspeakable statements about the over-the-threshold period of life. Not so much about marriage in itself, whose appalling sides have been presented in excruciating detail in the novel since Flaubert focused on the Bovarys at dinner and Tolstoy pictured Karenin coming in to Anna at midnight all washed and combed, saying "It's time, it's time." The nineteenth-century novel amply deconstructed the spousal relationship.

Most of the new bad news came with babies and parents. The taboo topics in our cultural self-representations for this era of life have been the resentment fathers feel toward their infants, the ambivalence of mothers, the relative indifference of both women and men to those they have freely married, and the anger both men and women continue to feel in adulthood toward their parents. But literature proceeds—as sociological document and subjective expansion—by making discourse out of taboos, as Tolstoy did when Kitty's family makes much of her pregnancy in *Anna Karenina,* or when Anna finds she can't love her daughter Annie.

Whatever fictional precedents we may find for these situations separately, three aspects taken together seem contemporary: making characters with domestic problems like these relatively sympathetic, rather than "bad"; giving these characters the whole set of relational problems all at once; and correlating all these sexual and generational problems with the early years of marriage and adulthood. It's the dangerous age that should be called the middle years; that's when the real squeeze is on. Forget the so-called midlife crisis. It's the "young-adult crisis" we ought to be commiserating with.

Sometimes readers living through similar moments can be grateful for seeing their plights described so starkly: they may be able to see themselves not necessarily as less unhappy, but as less peculiar or deviant. On the other hand, our fiction may now provide too many pictures of young-adult unhappiness. To the convention that describes marriage as nearly unworkable we have added images of intergenerational conflict that could almost make "life" seem impossible as one is barely entering into it. We receive full in the face from decline narratives the implication that life has played a rotten trick on us by letting us get old enough to sink into adulthood without having given us the inclination or the power or the ability to be adult.

But decline writing makes a mistake—a human and a literary mistake—in treating the first period of adulthood as if it were the pattern for the whole life course, as if no amelioration were possible. We've noticed the many images of changelessness in young-adult novels (or in midlife novels that continue the imagery): traps and nets and compulsion and culs-de-sac; or, on the other hand, physical sensations, of impeded breathing and aimless running and helpless prostration. The first set of images represents the impediments as coming from outside toward the self; the second set locates them within the self. Each set is also an explanation of what is wrong: the first says, "It's the world," the second, "It's me." The final images of decline novels often emphasize sensations of inner powerlessness: they are of tears or escape or stasis. Wilhelm cries at the end of *Seize the Day*, Rabbit runs, Jeremy in Tyler's *Celestial Navigation* drifts in a circle. Coming where they do, before the blank page that every reader knows to read as the future, these images imply that a person can weep, or run away, or stand still, for the rest of his life. Not so. Only madness and death (the endings of the most dire decline fictions) can be imagined as permanent conditions. It speaks hopefully for our four writers that they ended their darkest early novels in conditions that no one can imagine as having duration. If change were not a law of life, it would still be a necessity of life-course fiction.

III. Looking Back

Not so very much later—in Bellow's case it was in the very next novel after *Seize the Day*—every one of them wrote a Bildungsroman of the middle years, expressing indirect gratitude for no longer feeling that young and pressed. Each new-stage novel puts a distance between a now mature protagonist and a character or two still in the dangerous age. Henderson has a son who wants to get married and a (fourteen-year-old) daughter who wants a baby without having a husband. He is presented as being so ostentatiously detached from the stage of family formation that his children scarcely seem like his. "Can this be the son of my loins?" he wonders (pp. 125–26), looking at this "practically faceless" boy out of his own monumentally sculpted face. "I felt like the Pharaoh at the sight of little Moses" (p. 36), he says about his daughter's stolen child and, if that's ambiguous, makes her give back the baby. "And moreover a man wants to protect his children from the bitterness of things if he can" (p. 124) is the explanation he gives for advising his son not to marry but to go to medical school (Henderson's own belated dream). *Henderson the Rain King* offers a mere snippet of what youth is like at the very beginning of the tale, just enough to sharpen our sense that what Henderson wants—celibacy, Africa, and a new start—is somehow more original, appropriate, sane, and potentially satisfying.

In *Earthly Possessions,* after forty-year-old Charlotte Emory is kidnapped just as she's getting money out of the bank to leave home, Charlotte watches impassively as her young kidnapper and his girlfriend go through the throes of making a couple together. Mindy is pregnant, and Jake intends to leave her but finds he can't. At the moment that he accepts the adult ties to Mindy that he has already formed, Charlotte tells him she is leaving, to do (we know) the same thing herself: accept her own adult ties. The difference between them is that Jake is panicky and can't bear to lose her comforting maternal presence, while Charlotte has been calmly taking things in stride for years. In their externally similar circumstances, she recognizes that she is no raw runaway, but a long-time resident of her adult life. Recognizing the contrast between Jake and Charlotte is one of the pieces of learning that the novel needs in order to end—as the Bellow novel needs the contrast between generations in order to begin.

For Rabbit at forty-six, two novels of Updike's trilogy onward, it's his college dropout of a son, sleeping with two women, who provides the contrast; and for Frances Wingate, in Drabble's *Realms of Gold,* it's a young second cousin with a runny-nosed baby and an odiously superior husband. Because these contrasts are so central to the major midlife novels in which they occur, they are more fully treated in following chapters. Here it's enough to speak generally about the point of these encapsulations of the dangerous age.

Harry, Frances, Charlotte, and Henderson are very different midlife figures, but all are shown to be broader people, and readier to face life than the young. They are relatively competent at life's tasks, where the young are doing harm to themselves or others. They know better who they are and what they want or don't want: they are individuals, sometimes to the point of eccentricity. They don't fear love, and if they don't want it, it's not because they unconsciously equate it with dependency. If they start off stuck in situations, they see how fully these are of their own making. Their own desires, rather than anger and evasion, produce plot. They're more hopeful than the young.

None of them looks back with longing to the dangerous age, or would wish to be that younger person. On the contrary, the benefits all seem to be on the elder's side. They look on the unhappiness and confusion of the son, the cousin, the kidnapper, and the children with a detachment that has no hint of identification. The women manage a mature, commemorative compassion. Even Harry, who talks as if his son were a threat, sees that the young are no threat. The novels themselves don't find the young as interesting or as productive of discourse as the midlife characters who have moved beyond that stage. (And why would they? Is Telemachus as interesting as Odysseus? Is Lily Briscoe as interesting as Mrs. Ramsay?) Midlife progress narratives see with understanding and no terror the ways in which the young afflict themselves. The dangerous age has been boxed, marked, shelved, and put behind.

2

Healing Fictions

*It was so difficult, looking back, to remember how things had
ever reached such an extremity.*

—Drabble, *The Needle's Eye*

I. Writing Through the Life Course

The starting point of *Safe at Last in the Middle Years* is
that these writers—and their characters—grew out of the dangerous
age. Many of the problems of young-adult novels turn out to be peculiar to those stages and somehow disappear, and the problems that replace them turn out to be more manageable—or the "managers" more
competent to deal with them. Even some representations of early-adult
trouble assure us that people grow out of it. Many of the Tyler and
Drabble novels mentioned in Chapter One are at bottom young-adult
Bildungsromane, if only squeakers of hope. The typical form of the narrative is compressed by one of Drabble's hyperbolic storytellers thus:
"But somehow, after [some good event], and this again is a common
story, I am proud of its commonness, things improved out of all recognition. We changed. I can see now that it is as simple as that: we
changed."[1] Well, change is not simple. How complicated it is we are

1. *The Garrick Year* (London: Weidenfeld and Nicolson, 1964), p. 33.

23

about to examine in the present chapter and in those that follow. Change is multiple even in Emma Evans's case: her formula—that one good event (the birth of a baby) changed her life—is simply untrue. Much more was needed to effect the improvement in her from furious resentment of her husband (and marriage) to patient wise forbearance and acceptance of responsibility and marital fidelity.

One is never, of course, absolutely safe: there are no guarantees against calamity. "Safe" refers to a state of mind, comprising skills and powers and certain attitudes toward time. As an attitude toward time, safety is always comparative—but then, so must be all conclusions about "life," starting, as Piet Hanema noticed, with the decline story told in Genesis about Adam and Eve, where a putative Golden Age in Eden is the prior term of comparison. Until recently, the decline version of the midlife story has prevailed. We have been mysteriously—masochistically—eager to accept bad news about middle age and aging. Even now, enormous numbers of the no-longer-young have personally let themselves become melancholy comparatists, contrasting their present existences with a vague but presumably happier past, looking fondly but myopically back, feeling somehow sure that life is a diminished thing. And literature presenting this state of mind has often been called "realistic," as if only a pessimistic view of the life course could be called real. The difference in the late twentieth century is that the more optimistic minority view of the life course is beginning to appear, in the reiterated and gradually more self-conscious way that lets any new vision become visible. We are seeing the new paradigm—the new ideology—about the middle years shape itself under our reading eyes. My own willing (although once skeptical) voice is stating the paradigm and thus contributing in some small way to the shape it takes as well.

Literature now possesses this paradigm because our four writers continued to write fiction, and, as they have aged, their characters have aged also. Updike's three-volume sequence about Harry Angstrom offers the clearest illustration of the pattern. In the first novel Harry was twenty-six; Updike was twenty-eight when it was published (1960). In the second (1971), Harry was thirty-six; Updike was thirty-nine. (Presumably Updike started off by giving Harry his own age exactly, and then refrained from altering it as the manuscript went through revisions and publication.) With a few interesting exceptions, to be discussed in their place, the protagonists' ages all trail their authors' in more or less this way—a rather skimpy disguise for spiritual autobiography. Thus, we have developmental sequences not only within some individual Bildungsromane but also, more importantly, in each writer's oeuvre over the life course. The sequences give us something like the literary equivalent of what in social-science research are called longitudinal studies, with the writers themselves providing the research materials and interpreting them at the same time. Even the youngest of our writers—Anne Tyler and Margaret Drabble—have written a double handful of novels, more than enough for noticing the repetitions and contrasts on which *Safe at Last* depends.

The existence of the life-course sequence is not unprecedented in literature. George Eliot's dangerous-age novel was *Mill on the Floss*, written when she was forty; ten years later, she was writing one of the earliest midlife progress narratives, in the second half of *Middlemarch*. Tolstoy wrote *Childhood, Boyhood* and *Youth* early, and then the two great early-adult/midlife novels, *War and Peace* and *Anna Karenina*. Lawrence wrote one novel of troubled late adolescence, *Sons and Lovers*; *Women in Love* is his extraordinary young-adult Bildungsroman; and *St. Mawr* his even more unusual midlife starting-again book. Like him, but with a more serene appreciation of the middle years, Virginia Woolf portrayed survival through the dangerous age, as we can appreciate by contrasting Rachel Vinrace in *The Voyage Out* and Mrs. Ramsay in *To the Lighthouse*. (Could Woolf, confined in Hyde Park Gate unable to change into a tree, have imagined the husbandly irascibility that would comfort queenly Mrs. Ramsay? Could Joyce, as an insolent adolescent, have thought he had Bloomlike serenity and Mollybdenum felicity ahead of him?) Maya Angelou has written autobiography as a safe-at-last sequence, but the first volume, about her childhood and adolescence, came out in 1969 when she was nearly forty, and already conscious of being "bodacious enough to invent my own life daily."[2]

This short list could be expanded. But until now, few writers have had the experience of "writing through" their lives, at least past the early marital stage, and fewer yet have seen the life course as a progression. My four novelists were chosen from a tiny group of living life-course novelists who fit these two conditions. In addition, they are all excellent writers, whose works many readers have been avidly consuming, as they appeared in sequence, for years. For comparative purposes I also needed two women and two men. As for cohorts, this small sample gives me representatives of three, with one writer born in 1915, another in 1932, and the two others in 1939 and 1941. (Nonetheless, I have been cautious about drawing gender contrasts, or generational ones, with so small a sample and so close an age spread.)

2. Maya Angelou, Dedication to *Gather Together in My Name*.

Perhaps, to have life-course sequences of a progressive kind in any numbers we had to wait until several favoring circumstances combined in the second half of the twentieth century. Confessional literature became acceptable, while the novel form provided the illusion of privacy for authors who might otherwise have been reticent to appear more confessional even than the poets. (Updike has offered the opinion—never more true than in contemporary Anglo-American narrative—that "the autobiography of a writer of fiction is generally superfluous, since he has already, in rearrangement and disguise, written out the material of his life many times."[3]) A demographic boom provided an audience getting readier, as it aged, to relinquish its original cult of youth; and thus prepared to hear better news about its anxious aging. Indeed, like Juggernaut, some part of the midlife cohort is happy to crush old stereotypes of aging beneath its future-breasting cart. A postcard, a sweatshirt, and a mug keep before us a progressive slogan: "Never trust anyone over 3̶0̶ 3̶6̶ 4̶0̶ 45." Where economic decline would have placed an intolerable strain on the reading public's willingness to assent to stories of midlife improvement, the postwar years have been a period of economic boom. Divorce laws and the sexual revolution have expanded the choices and attitudes open to adults, and the feminist revolution those open to women. Like any major cultural change, this one is overdetermined.

The individual stories are told in the following four chapters. In the remainder of this chapter, I want to describe and as far as possible explain the remarkable common experience that these four sequences taken together represent—nothing less than healing through time.

II. "Time" Heals

We might be tempted to take this healing for granted, as a kind of miracle. Santayana neatly phrased our human tendency not to inquire too closely into the origin of the good: "if anything is well, we

3. "Alive and Free from Employment," in *Picked-Up Pieces* (New York: Knopf, 1976), p. 485. Updike would, however, no doubt want us to observe the following caution, expressed here by Bernard Paris: "We must be careful, of course, when making inferences about an author from his [*sic*] fictions. We must allow for artistic motivations, for the requirements of the genre and of the *telos* of the individual work." Bernard J. Paris, *Character and Conflict in Jane Austen's Novels* (Detroit: Wayne State University Press, 1978), p. 169. I suggest that in life-course fiction, genre and *telos* depend on subjective factors.

neglect to ask why it happens. The inner connivance and peace of our will explain it sufficiently."[4] Yet despite inner connivance, people are now intensely curious about health in general, and mental health and health in adulthood in particular. From their overlapping points of view, many disciplines (not just psychology) have been speculating about cure. This reflects a sanguine change in the object deemed worthy of study. Joint curiosity used to focus on the disease entity; now these allied heads have swung around to peer more closely at the inner sources of health and recovery. The medical metaphor behind this new activity is a hopeful one: physicians point out that most illnesses heal themselves, so researchers want to investigate. Sure, time heals—but how?

The first part of the explanation is that time brings "relief from prior suffering": this theory was exemplified in Chapter One and will be amplified in this one. (This is a negative theory, and such theories by themselves, however powerful, come to seem inadequate, particularly with regard to the fictive middle years, where clearly something more than mere relief is represented. Negative theories need to be supplemented by positive, goal-oriented ones, as they will be later on in the present chapter.) Sociologists support and historicize the relief theory: they recognize the stresses of young adulthood in our highly age-graded culture. The deans of historical demography tell us that "growing up, as a process, has become briefer, more normful, bounded and consequential—and thereby more demanding on the individual participants."[5] Another scholar describes "the age distribution of . . . life strains": "Young adults simultaneously face the formidable tasks of having to establish themselves in their occupations, having to accommodate to marital relations that probably are not yet crystallized, and having to take responsibility for young children who of necessity are heavily dependent on them. Thus chronic hardships and conflicts that can be found within these major social roles are much more likely to invade the lives of young adults, and to have been reconciled or left behind by the older adults."[6] Calm language for the dangerous age.

The middle years, so often talked about as more full of responsibility

4. George Santayana, *Platonism and the Spiritual Life* (New York: Scribner's, 1927), p. 6.

5. John Modell, Frank F. Furstenberg, Jr., and Theodore Hershberg, "Social Change and Transitions to Adulthood in Historical Perspective," *Journal of Family History* 1, no. 1 (Autumn 1976): 30–31.

6. Leonard J. Pearlin, "Life Strains and Psychological Distress among Adults," in *Themes of Work and Love in Adulthood,* ed. Neil J. Smelser and Erik H. Erikson (Cambridge, Mass.: Harvard University Press, 1980), p. 182.

and care than "youth," can actually feel less pressured, less anxious, freer. For couples, one reason may be that they are having fewer children: the hectic child-raising years end sooner; the released feeling (a happy alternative to the "empty-nest syndrome") comes earlier. This probably still means more for mothers than fathers. One team of sociologists, asking questions of couples at marriage and twenty years later, found that "women on the follow-up study showed a statistically significant shift toward greater self-confidence." Another study of "work-centered mothers, who were the lowest in energy and the least satisfied with their lot during early adulthood" found that the same women "were marked by high energy, good health, and life satisfaction in their aging years. Radical changes for the better were seen in those mothers."[7] Tyler and Drabble, after writing early novels about intense and exclusive and anxious bonding with children, went on to write about the children growing up and growing away—Drabble with blithe brevity in *The Middle Ground*, Tyler (in *Searching for Caleb*) as a complicated set of stages, in which the adult child's first divergence from the parents' way of being feels like a repudiation but can eventually be understood and sympathized with.

The psychodynamic literature also corroborates and elaborates relief theories. Freud's theory of cure was from the beginning a story about release from suffering or freedom from unconscious inhibitors. The shift to analyzing normal health—the strengths of the self, its adaptive mechanisms, its ability to grow—starts to fill out the story of how we overcome psychic weaknesses, like anger, guilt, and jealousy; solve issues of dependence, commitment, and autonomy; and distinguish better between inner and outer. But young adulthood is not the first time some of these conflicts have arisen, and any of them may recur at later triggering points. The difference between feeling pressure at one time of life and relatively less later comes via aging: in analyst Arnold Modell's words, if these conflicts recur as we grow older, they are likely to get worked through at "increasingly higher levels of mastery."[8] The idea that practice can make perfect, psychically speaking, can restore content to words like "healing" and "experience." The narrative part of the

7. Howard A. Moss and Elizabeth Susman, "Longitudinal Study of Personality Development," in *Constancy and Change in Human Development*, ed. Orville G. Brim, Jr. and Jerome Kagan (Cambridge, Mass.: Harvard University Press, 1980), pp. 578 and 583. Moss and Susman are reporting on studies by E. L. Kelley, and by Maas and Kuypers, in that order.

8. Arnold Modell, "Psychic 'Aliveness,'" p. 4. See Introduction, n. 11.

therapeutic story—that a conflict gets worked through over time—provides the fixed reference points (before and after) that enable a person to judge that she or he has experienced "release from suffering" and permit someone to call the feeling "self-mastery," or even "progress."

In short, the old life-course essentialism and determinism have been loosened. For midlife Bildungsromane, for midlifers in general (and for older people, whose fictional turn has not yet come), that may be the most important consequence of all these developments in intellectual history. Once the culture questions "the traditional idea that the experiences of the early years . . . necessarily constrain the characteristics of adolescence and adulthood,"[9] a momentous liberation in itself, then it can even leap ahead to believe that the midlife can break free from adult constraints as well, and change becomes possible throughout the life course.

To my mind, the fictional life-course sequences are way ahead of other aspects of the culture in embodying these beliefs. It is not finally the psychologists or sociologists or philosophers of whatever stripe who have been delivering the most persuasive and individual stories of "cure" to you and me, but novelists like Bellow, Drabble, Tyler, and Updike. It is they who may prove to us, as Karen Horney asserted long ago, that "life itself is the most effective help for our development."[10]

III. Cure Stories

Safe at Last has tried to tease out of the works of these writers their own models of development and cure. These models are available to us in two different ways. The traditional way would be to examine the theory of development inscribed in each novel that presents itself, however timidly, as a Bildungsroman. The unorthodox

9. Brim and Kagan, *Constancy and Change,* p. 1. Karen Horney argued a similar point earlier: "It is one of the great scientific merits of Freud to have vigorously stressed the tenacity of childhood impressions; yet psychoanalytic experience shows also that an emotional reaction that has once occurred in childhood is maintained through life only if it continues to be supported by various dynamically important drives." See "The Problem of Feminine Masochism," in *Feminine Psychology,* ed. Harold Kelman (New York: Norton, 1967), pp. 221–22.

10. Karen Horney, *Self-Analysis* (New York: Norton, 1942), p. 8. She admonishes later (p. 232), "But when treatment is endowed with such omnipotence it is forgotten that life itself is the best therapist."

way—the way employed in Chapter One—is to look at the giant magical leaps of life-course fiction as it represents one "age" after another. (As most readers will have observed, these ages have no set chronological division.)

Curiously, the two methods tell two different stories about cure. Individual progress narratives convey what writers believe about cure at that particular time of their lives. Each conveys the narrative illusion of that cure, and the cures all operate according to conventions of our time that determine how much a character can change within the bindings of a book. Thus, even in *The Realms of Gold* or *Humboldt's Gift,* the cures are relatively modest. (These are still wonderful and welcome stories, for which a reader can be extremely grateful.)

Life-course fiction, on the other hand, which cannot be planned and has never been theorized and thus has no ruling conventions, tells us (once we learn how to read it) about big sweeps of growth (and about occasional regression), but the leaps of development that it describes would be unimaginable (unacceptably inverisimilar) in a Bildungs-roman except as a retrospect: "It was so difficult, looking back, to remember how things had ever reached such an extremity."[11]

Let's see how the difference emerges.

All narrative fiction tells us what it is like to become "older," if only a day or a few hours older. It has to carry the protagonist from the first page to the last, and this usually means from younger to older. Whether the protagonist is better or worse off as a result of this trajectory—a gross measure but to a reader an inexhaustibly interesting and deeply important one—is the decision a writer makes very early. Even novels told entirely in flashback have to tell us whether the character is better or worse off in the "present"—meaning, the moment at which he or she is oldest. All Bildungsromane by definition plump for "better." (They thus fall under the broadest, simplest, definition of comedy, as an action that produces improvement in the state of the main character, but individually they vary so much from gaiety to caution that the comic rubric doesn't take us far.)

For every writer, there's the next problem, usually neglected in theories of fiction and ignored even by writers talking about their works: to wit, what of the next book? Is the next main character to be older or younger? This is one decision affected by convention: before there was midlife literature, the character could not continue to be the same age as

11. Margaret Drabble, *The Needle's Eye* (New York: Knopf, 1972), p. 82.

the aging author. If older, is the next character better or worse off than the last one ends up? And how does the writer decide? How does the writing of a cure story affect the next set of choices? Is the writing of Bildungsromane an inoculation against the writing of decline stories? (As it happens, it's not. But why not?) The total set of decisions of this kind that a writer makes produces the life-course sequence.

At the beginning of a contemporary adult Bildungsroman, the (un-written) formula requires that the writer set up a developmental prob-lem of adulthood.[12] There are so many available, contrasted to the stan-dard problems given youth—whom to marry, how to escape. Not wanting children, not knowing what one wants to do with one's mean-ingless life, not being able to recover from divorce, having become too much oneself (too fixed, or too distractable), living with one's mother-in-law—these are some of the given problems. "For plot starts (or must give the illusion of starting) from that moment at which story, or 'life' is stimulated from quiescence into a state of narratability, into a tension, a kind of irritation, which demands narration," Peter Brooks has sug-gested, in uneasy metaphors.[13] Modern adult progress narratives are stimulated into narratability by the desire to show a character overcom-ing an inner block. Some idea of what good development requires is of course presupposed. By the end, the character can perform an action or think the kind of sentence that was impossible before. The ending of the Bildungsroman signifies that no more effort is needed, for the moment, along this particular line of development; this character has reached a place where she (he) can rest.

The girl in Tyler's *The Clock Winder* who fears that babies are too vulnerable to be borne winds up slinging her own on her hip and taking care of an entire family of less warmly generative people. Jane Gray in Drabble's *The Waterfall* recovers from agoraphobia and the fear of her own powers; she can fall in love and take the children outdoors. "I was saved, I was released from my enclosure. I was able to go out now with the children into the sun, because I was no longer bending upon these

---

12. "Adult Bildungsroman" here includes both the young-adult and the midlife prog-ress novel.

Some novelists may find sentences in this section puzzling, if my language seems to imply more intention on their part than they like to concede. My use of words like "choices" and "decisions" is intended, in this context, to be compatible with varying de-grees of consciousness. In my way of thinking, writing a progress rather than a decline narrative requires any writer to make a set of complex interrelated choices.

13. Peter Brooks, *Reading for the Plot: Design and Intention in Narrative* (Oxford: Ox-ford University Press, 1984), p. 103.

trivial fears and excursions the whole force and weight of my ridiculously powerful passions."[14] Bellow's Henderson loses that voice that constantly shouts "I want, I want" without providing a direct object for the verb, and by the end wants to go home; and Herzog is able to stop writing manic letters and feel "intensity, a holy feeling."[15] Charlie Citrine wakes up from a sleep longer than Rip Van Winkle's.

Even drastically schematized, these are by no means trivial stories of self-cure. But the life-course sequences tell more radical stories yet: as we have seen, they show how someone grows out of the dangerous age. The big cures occur, as it were, between the novels. A (young) early character with two children is torn between caring for them and having an affair, and renounces the affair; a later (naturally, older) one winds up handling four of her own, the affair with the new man, and his children too, in a plot that is about some other problems altogether. Between *The Garrick Year* and *The Realms of Gold*, of course the children got older and easier (that isn't even mentioned), but also Drabble developed an enhanced idea of what midlife female energy can cope with. An early couple with one eccentric and self-enclosed member splits because neither can say straight out that the other is necessary; a later novel matches (in what is a second marriage for each) a pair of oddballs who have just enough ability to express their need for each other. From *Celestial Navigation* to *The Accidental Tourist* Tyler has become ready to trust differentnesses, and the power of (older) people to get what they want. An early character thinks he loves women and procreation but winds up running away from one woman and her baby and another woman and her pregnancy; twenty years later he's bought a new house to live in with the selfsame wife, and is scrambling up hill and down dale looking for that long-lost daughter. What has Updike learned about the powers of normal growth? One early novel treats the despair of a man whose avaricious father won't lend him money at a critical juncture in his life (*Seize the Day*); in a later novel (*Herzog*), the same incident is treated in a single scene, which blames the son for his past egotism and insensitivity to the father's fear of death. Bellow has no more thunderous small claims to press against male parents; he has become almost too generous.

The comparison of early with later novels shows that some important original incapacities—fear, guilt, anger, sense of risk about life-course tasks, hesitation about believing in change, sense of stagna-

14. *The Waterfall* (London: Weidenfeld and Nicolson, 1969), p. 172.
15. Saul Bellow, *Herzog* (New York: Viking, 1964), p. 340.

tion—have been noticeably resolved. The writers may still be struggling with related or different issues, but the degree of resolution they have donated to their older characters would certainly have amazed them when they were writing the earlier work. The later novel in each case repairs the earlier situation and goes well beyond it. Book answers to book, plus. Why bother writing out the better state of being? Later on, this chapter speculates about the dissatisfactions that cause revision: one must be the pressure to keep the fiction more or less up to what can be said about the state of the self. *Pruritus anni* we could call it, a developmental itch. Writing a novel about young people over again—a conventional "rewrite"—never turns out to be the salve for the itch. The larger cures come through creating a new discourse about the older, more interesting characters: representations of relatively mature and rational people—precisely the kind of midlife adult that eighteenth- and nineteenth-century fiction writers relegated to secondary roles, almost unable to imagine them as creators of plot and centers of subjectivity. In the middle years, theirs is the state of being (with its concomitant genres and tones of voice) that our four writers mainly want to spend time with.

IV. Toward Modern Conventions of Cure

Every Bildungsroman comprehends some theory of development: the authors of the *Odyssey* and the story of Joseph in Genesis already had ideas about development in which aging played a large, necessary part. If we think about Odysseus's original tears, we are tempted to say that even the many-sided hero needed to be cured of weaknesses revealed by the dangerous age. His tale too is a recovery story.

In any particular Bildungsroman, change can be presented as either the work of an instant or as a developmental process. If a process, it can be simple and monocausal (brought about by love and learning, most often), or complex and irreducible. It can rely on a theory that some privileged speaker, character or narrator, enjoys stating, or by means that are covert and unknown or unstatable. For reasons that should soon become clear, midlife Bildung has come to be presented as the result of complex processes, rather than a single or monocausal moment of change, and (for reasons that perhaps can never all be known) the processes are shown as depending on long periods of time.

This is true even in the most penurious grant of amelioration—Bellow's in *The Victim,* in the few sentences that conclude that paranoid fantasy made literal. Leventhal's troubles simply vanish. "Things went well for him in the next few years. The consciousness of an unremitting daily fight, though still present, was fainter and less troubling. . . . And, as time went on, he lost the feeling that he had, as he used to say, 'got away with it,' his guilty relief, and the accompanying sense of infringement." [16] Brief, mysterious, and superficial as these lines are, they too, coming at the end of a novel in which we see a man overcome an inner sense of unworthiness that has been exacerbated by an outer attack, suggest a theory—of the crisis that tests, that seems beyond one's powers yet ultimately strengthens them. This passive agentless theory gives no credit to the subject self ("Things went well for him"), but it contains a grudging admission ("as time went on") that growth and relative satisfaction can accompany aging.

Progress narratives also find a way of picking out that part of the self that needs to grow, in order to raise the question, "How serious is this trouble?" The most comic novels emphasize cognition; darker ones, not surprisingly, emphasize parts of the self that can be imagined as difficult of access, like self-image and will. The Bildungsroman of youth began by treating the long middle of the novel—the space of suspense—as a field for the display of mistakes, which were the result of ignorance or miseducation or moral weakness. What ended error, for Tom Jones or Elizabeth Bennet, was new learning (new values) produced by "experience"—that is, whatever happened within the space of suspense. The simplest idea of learning is that it can come readily from new information, as exemplified in the letter Elizabeth Bennet receives from Darcy in *Pride and Prejudice* that completely changes her notion of his character and alters her view of her own. If a little *learning* is all characters are shown to need, and the worst you can do is make a *mistake,* and a change in *values* can alter your behavior, then life does not have to provide much in the way of therapy. Narratives based on this frame of reference have typically been called novels of "education." We can now judge how few novels fit this plot. Intelligent contemporary adult Bildungsromane never do. Learning (or better, reinterpretation) may still play a part in some progress stories, but not the pivotal dramatic part it could once play. The scene of revelation—Dorothea Brooke or Isabel Archer in Rome—so admirably epiphanic to an earlier generation of critics,

16. *The Victim* (New York: Vanguard Press, 1947), p. 285.

would seem quite inadequate now. Both Charlotte Emory (*Earthly Possessions*) and Clara Maugham (*Jerusalem the Golden*) learn something important, suddenly, from photographs of their mothers, but the learning is embedded in a long process. Revelation counts for little when what is needed is cure.

The idea of cure is not an exact opposite of the idea of learning. "Cure" covers a lot of psychic ground: cuts need to heal, as well as deep wounds. In the twentieth century, however, the strongest example—the best known and the most unrepeatable—of the progress narrative of the middle years may be a story about a particularly difficult, long-deferred, and last-minute cure. Proust's *A la recherche du temps perdu* expands the space of suspense (which he makes synonymous with the whole life) as far as it can go in fiction, partly to show the repeated failures of mere learning. Marcel's inability to do what he wishes in life—to write—is too complicated a failure to analyze here; but its persistence and intricacy are precisely what make a mysterious liberating cure the only solution Proust could imagine for ending the novel. (The cure depends, of course, on discovering "inner riches." Maybe that discovery *is* the cure.) From one point of view, the three thousand pages of Proust's narrative can stand as the phenomenological equivalent of the idea of midlife belatedness, or, in other words, deep resistance to cure.

Fiction apparently had no idea of midlife latency until then. Decline novels of the middle years had shown people like Lambert Strether in James's *Ambassadors* for whom it is already "too late." At the opposite pole, the rare Bildungsroman of the middle years had paid no attention to belatedness. (Homer, however, gives us the facts that show how slow Odysseus was to mature; now we're likely to tssk about his staying with Calypso so long that he misses his son Telemachus's whole early life.) If a contemporary progress novel were to take seven, or twenty, or in Marcel's case over forty years to change its character's fortunes and give him his desire, it would be giving us a dire view indeed of the possibility of change. The more drastic or slower the required cure, is one logical implication, the more serious the "disease." In Proust's imagined circumstances of delayed development, only a miracle can save Marcel. Although his whole life has prepared for this miracle, it is no less transfiguring and sudden than an Ovidian metamorphosis or a Christian conversion story.

Now, in our realist, post-romantic, psychoanalytic age, those who manage to believe in positive change are equally far from both innocent beliefs: either that better information will change a life or that a last-minute miracle can. That's why our midlife novelists had to imagine cures, and particularly in-between kinds of cures, involving more radical psychic changes than most youth Bildungsromane propose, and change more gradual (illness less serious) than Proust devised.

We are all vulnerable to fears of belatedness, theories of lingering neurosis, and the dread that cure to work on us has to be drastic—not necessarily because of Proust, but because of the traditional weight of decline stories in fiction, religion, orthodox analysis, and popular culture. In their young-adult novels, our four writers had to work away from such pessimistic received opinions. Indeed, getting over the fear of permanent illness turns out to be one stage of what a writer has to do to believe in natural healing.

This stage is tricky, because, while in it, writers don't consider the problems of their characters as "illnesses." There's not much point in looking for images of disease; and where they exist, they would be misleading. Rarely did the troubled young-adult characters we looked at in Chapter One have "symptoms": they had something worse, "natures." In the grimmest of them, it's a moral question, about an "evil" nature. Tyler's Jeremy in *Celestial Navigation* starts off with agoraphobia, presented as an oddity derived from his secluded childhood and reinforced by his artistic sensibility, not as an illness. Drabble's Emma Evans describes herself as shallow *in essence*. Her Jane Gray suffers from a long self-erasure, which in its turn is presented as a characteristic she has formed in response to her fear of her self and life. Bellow's Dangling Man is choleric. Rabbit fucks and runs, frightened and confused. "How can anyone be cured of his or her 'nature'?" is the way these novels set up the question.

Only later, in midlife Bildungsromane, can characters finally have kinky noticeable (initial) symptoms. Frances Wingate starts off with inexplicable crying jags, and Malcolm Leary sleeps in a homemade body bag and mangles his laundry under his feet while showering; Henderson shoots bottles on the resort beach and Herzog writes letters he doesn't send. These are not treated as moral or intrinsic problems. Pessimistic younger writers give their characters obstinate natures because, as we've seen, they doubt change so much. Essentialists always do. Essentialism was part of their characters' disease and, in the worst cases, perhaps their own. Optimistic midlife writers give their characters, at worst, discardable symptoms. From a superficial point of view, the midlife characters may look "sicker," but only because the writers are now able to foreground their symptoms: conscious of them as passing moments, their creators can finally present them as such. We are finding in midlife novels conventional signs of illness after the idea of being incurable has itself been discarded.

Basically our writers came up with two theories of cure, both of course dependent on time. The easier cure assumes that illness was a passing moment—this is a homeostatic or recovery theory. A secondary character in Drabble's *The Middle Ground* epitomizes the recovery theory when he "decides that he is merely going through a phase, like [the heroine] Kate, and that when he emerges, everything will look quite different and much more alluring. This cheers him up no end. 'There's life in it yet,' he says to himself, aloud, and smiles vaguely at the wall."[17] The other theory (far more widely used) requires change, gradual change. As Jeremy says wistfully in *Celestial Navigation,* "Gradually, wasn't that the key? Oh, if there were any god he believed in, it was gradualness!"[18] As it happens, the god of gradualness fails Jeremy, but smiles benignly on many midlife Bildungsromane.

It wasn't nature, after all, from which the young were suffering. It was (in a word) youth. We must turn now to the life-course sequences to discover what the cures are for that.

V. Survival

Toward the end of *Herzog* (1964), Bellow names the first prerequisite for growth—or for midlife narrative. *"But for this higher education survival is necessary. You must outlive the pain"* (p. 319, italics in original). Survival over the short span of a Bildungsroman may mean outliving pain. Over the longer span from early adulthood to the more secure middle years it means literally that we don't die. This observation gets recorded by some of our writers as an astonishing fact. "Still no shot rang out. I saw now that it never would. I released my breath, marveling at my slipperiness: I had glided through so many dangers and emerged unscathed."[19] Anne Tyler, here in *Earthly Possessions,* has created a whole plot to express relief at the ending of what must be a widespread superstition of adolescence and early adulthood, that we won't live to make old bones. Looking back at past troubles, a fortyish Drabble

17. *The Middle Ground* (New York: Knopf, 1980), p. 186.
18. *Celestial Navigation* (New York: Knopf, 1974), p. 104.
19. *Earthly Possessions* (New York: Knopf, 1977), p. 183.

heroine confesses the same superstition: "in those early years . . . she could not contemplate them as calmly as she does now. *Her life was at stake*" (*The Middle Ground*, p. 35; emphasis added).

We can estimate the dreadful strength of the original superstitions, and the degree to which they have vanished, by looking at the more detached way in which violence is portrayed in midlife Bildungsromane. Midlife plots still contrive death, and even the death of children. Macon and Sarah Leary's son Ethan is gunned down by a holdup man while away at summer camp, in Tyler's *The Accidental Tourist*. Bellow's Herzog attends the trial of an unmarried couple who battered her three-year-old daughter to death; Herzog then rushes off to Chicago to protect his own little daughter, picking up his father's gun along the way. In Drabble's *The Realms of Gold*, the heroine's nephew kills himself and his newborn infant and an old woman dies of starvation; in subsequent novels characters get mutilated, burned, imprisoned, decapitated. In Updike's *Rabbit Redux*, Harry Angstrom's house is burned down by racists and his childlike girlfriend is burned alive in it. In Bellow's *Humboldt's Gift*, the hero's car is battered with baseball bats and he himself is threatened with a gun by a gangster whose "honor" he has offended.

A case could be made, in fact, that the violence is worse (say, from the point of view of criminal justice) in midlife novels than before. Tyler never earlier imagined a holdup man shooting "each and every person through the back of the skull"[20]; her earlier holdup man had a gun but wound up begging the heroine to stay with him and his girlfriend and look after them. Drabble's earlier books are full of vulnerable children who almost get gassed or drown or die in operations, but she had never before imagined infanticide. Updike had done *that*, but had never before imagined the murder of a sentient adult. Bellow had drawn earlier heroes who were belligerent with their weight and fists but never one who wanted a gun for killing another human being.

Nevertheless, for good reasons, none of these episodes (even the Updike arson-murder) colors the entire book that surrounds it, blending its tone of terrible extremity into the tone of the whole, as happens in *Dangling Man, The Victim, Rabbit, Run,* and in the first half of *The Clock Winder* and *The Needle's Eye*. In a midlife Bildungsroman, the violence is in some way detached from the master consciousness of the book (the hero's, the narrator's, and ultimately the author's). The strategies for distancing violence are immensely various. First of all, no

20. *The Accidental Tourist* (New York: Knopf, 1985), p. 18.

violence is committed by a protagonist. Herzog doesn't use the gun. All the other willing-of-harm is projected onto very distant others: holdup men or gangsters or terrorists (professionals in evil); people deranged by racism (in *Rabbit Redux*), or simply deranged (*The Realms of Gold, The Radiant Way*). Not-us. Insofar as we identify with these protagonists, we too are in the relatively safer position, finally only spectators of harm. We may empathize, and suffer through loss, as the bereaved parents do in *The Accidental Tourist,* but neither we nor they are any longer the agents or the targets of violence. Violence is now contingent rather than projected—a description of the way the world works rather than an emanation of our guilts and fears.

What this evidence suggests is that death enters young-adult fiction as a deep, personal, perhaps only half-conscious anxiety, whereas in midlife Bildungsromane it is a topic—a serious, absorbing topic, but no longer an obsession. "Fear of death does not increase with age," one study finds;[21] indeed, death anxiety may be greatest in the young. Thomas J. Cottle takes this so much for granted that he warns against drawing too large a conclusion from it. "One cannot say that *only* the young contemplate or fear death. This is not true."[22] It may be that some markedly felt decrease in the intensity of one's fear of death is the major precondition for being able to write midlife progress narratives. In one of the earliest American examples of the genre, William Dean Howells's *Indian Summer,* this alleviation forms part of a list of subjective reasons for valuing the middle years. An elderly man of "original" ideas is speaking.

"At forty we have enlarged our perspective sufficiently to perceive things in their true proportion and relation; we are no longer tormented with the lurking

21. A. M. Downey, "The Relationship of Sex-Role Orientation to Death Anxiety in Middle-Aged Males," *Omega* 14, no. 4 (1983–84) : 357. She is reporting on a review of literature by J. M. Pollak. The conventional view is that "the most reliable conscious indicator of entry into midlife is death anxiety"; see Solomon Cytrynbaum et al., "Midlife Development: A Personality and Social Systems Perspective," in *Aging in the 1980s: Psychological Issues,* ed. Larry W. Poon (Washington, D.C.: American Psychological Association, 1980), p. 467. Statements like this unveil the biases according to which our culture has constructed the so-called midlife. What of five-year-olds and seventeen-year-olds struggling with death anxiety? I am reminded of a cartoon in which one young pro athlete says to a group of others, "In my neighborhood, you better have your mid-life crisis by seventeen, or you won't live long enough to have one" (Jeff Millar and Bill Hinds, *Tank McNamara*).

22. Thomas J. Cottle, "The Time of Youth," in *The Personal Experience of Time,* ed. Bernard S. Gorman and Alden E. Wessman (New York: Plenum, 1977), p. 184.

fear of death, which darkens and imbitters our earlier years; we have got into the habit of life; we have often been ailing and we have not died. Then . . . we have learned to smile at many things besides the fear of death. We ought also to have learned pity and patience. Yes," the old man concluded, in cheerful self-corroboration, "it is a beautiful age."[23]

The original superstition may reflect a death-wish arising out of the sufferings and constraints of the dangerous age, or a fear that in our emergence as willful adults, conflict with others may cause them to desire our deaths. Freudian analysts might say that the death-wish or death-fear is a hangover from childhood guilt. Erikson believes it is a despair (varying from mild to extreme) involved in the maturation of identity: he would regard it (to put Ernst Kris's words in his mouth) as "regression in the service of the ego."[24] Or it may be that the difficulties of adulthood strike us at first with such force that we simply fear we may not have the ability to endure or may fear that we won't want to live. A historian rather than a psychologist might hypothesize that in our time marrying or having children or both together are so clearly signs of beginning the aging process that by themselves they can trigger images and fears of dying. For writers, writing about over-the-threshold material, rather than about childhood and adolescence, may be the trigger. It may bring on a "crisis of finitude"[25] that we commonly think of as occurring much later.

Is it the "habit of life," as Howells's Mr. Waters suggests, that ends "the lurking fear of death"? Simply that we haven't died? One of Updike's protagonists (at thirty-eight) also thinks we just need time, to confirm our "right to exist" as a separate and self-centered being. "So many of Alexandra's remarkable powers had flowed from this mere reappropriation of her assigned self, achieved not until midlife. Not until midlife did she truly believe that she had a right to exist, that the forces of nature had created her not as an afterthought and companion . . . but as the mainstay of the continuing creation."[26] Many of us may consider the "reappropriation" of the self as the outcome of tremendous effort, but in midlife progress fiction, the new "right to exist" appears as another ample, firm gift of the life course.

23. William Dean Howells, *Indian Summer* (Bloomington: Indiana University Press, [1885–86] 1971), p. 128.

24. Erik H. Erikson, *Identity and the Life Cycle* (New York: Norton, 1980), p. 143; see also pp. 136–37 and 144.

25. Downey, "Death Anxiety," p. 357.

26. John Updike, *The Witches of Eastwick* (New York: Knopf, 1984), p. 14.

In this context, even dreadful strokes of misfortune will not irreversibly undermine the protagonist. They become *episodes,* bracketed from the general tenor of the novel by verbal signs. A year after Macon Leary's son dies, his wife leaves him. Yet early details hint that this is to be a story of his survival. He is listening to a bird singing "what sounded like the first three notes of 'My Little Gypsy Sweetheart.'"

> "Slum . . . ber . . . on . . ." it sang.
> Macon wondered if even this moment would become, one day, something he looked back upon wistfully. He couldn't imagine it; he couldn't think of any period bleaker than this in all his life, but he'd noticed how time had a way of coloring things. That bird, for instance, had such a pure, sweet, piercing voice.
> (*The Accidental Tourist,* p. 15)

Decline narratives imply that we never can recover: they naturalize a kind of panic about time. What midlife Bildung assures us is not that we become stupidly impervious to tragedy, but that even the bleakest event is a "period." The future retrospect—"one day I will look back"— is the tense in which life's worst events sooner or later get viewed. It's the survivor's tense. Using it detaches the sufferer from his or her suffering—not instantly, but as the beginning of a process. It helps to produce a more cheerful comparatist, starting with a person who has lived long enough to estimate human tenacity. As Updike at thirty-four pointed out to an interviewer, "We do survive every moment, after all, except the last one." [27]

VI. The Magic of Aging

Because we survive, other major problems of young adulthood disappear of themselves. If there is any universal magic in aging, this is it. The problems of young adulthood that we saw identified were infants, parents, and spouses. (Let us bracket same-age "significant others" for the moment, noting only that in the history of Anglo-American culture, adultery, divorce, remarriage, loving someone of your own gender, and even celibacy have become easier in the postwar period, and particularly since about 1970. When you feel freer, un-

27. "One Big Interview," in *Picked-Up Pieces,* p. 519. This part of the interview took place in 1966.

tangling your sense of personal achievement from the changed conventions of culture can be hard.) That leaves infants and parents. And then, in the natural course of life-course fictions, infants grow up and parents age, weaken, or die.

If this sequence of events seems like a mean joke as a foundation for developmental fiction, it could nevertheless be the fierce truth of a desperate situation. Getting what you want is a thrilling experience. After a certain point of misery, how can people in the dangerous age not wish—with some part of their being—for these outcomes attributable to normal aging? But the life course, in its immense generosity, gives us these outcomes without our needing even to wish for them. An early analyst describes how adults may change toward their children. "The hostility which a parent may harbor towards his child . . . will, under happy conditions of individual and family development, tend naturally to diminish as time passes. . . . More especially of course, the feelings of hatred and jealousy . . . will usually be overcome, or at least adequately held in check, by the feelings of parental love which are brought into play by contact with the child and by the process of providing for its needs."[28]

When the death of parents occurs in midlife, it leaves the characters innocent. Establishing their innocence is not difficult. Charlotte Emory observes, as her dreadful unloving mother is dying of cancer, that in fact she doesn't want her to die, as her mother's death in no way frees her. We've seen this to be true: it was years earlier that she was conscious of wanting other less embarrassing parents. Our deepest gratitude toward the life course may come from its giving to us things that we didn't know (or dare) to wish, as if we didn't wish them. Or it may be that the timing of parental death and filial growth teaches us that we no longer *have* such guilty wishes.

Whatever the explanation, the fact is that the protagonists' parents, like children, confront death more in young-adult fiction than later fiction. (In midlife progress novels, either parents are back again, "revived," aging but hale, and at last minor in importance, or they die more easily, as in *The Radiant Way*. Or, if the idea of parents is still too difficult, members of their generation, like mothers-in-law and older friends, serve as likable representatives.) Three of our novelists (Drabble, Tyler, and Updike) describe a powerful parent's wrenching last illness in present time—something that has to be lived through as it happens—in novels in which the adult child is slowly recognizing herself or himself

28. J. C. Flügel, *The Psycho-analytic Study of the Family* (London: Hogarth Press, [1921] 1950), p. 167.

as an adult. Where fear of personal survival is great, parent figures may die as surrogates in place of young adults, dying in fiction to prove to the next generation that it can outlive them. Before the twenty-five- or thirty-five-year-old child can feel separate, different, free, a parent faces death.[29] The more deterministic the novel (that is, the harder the child finds it to grow), the more crudely this liberation is presented. Drabble is often the boldest in psychoanalytic echoes, as in *Jerusalem the Golden,* where the mother's death threatens the daughter's life too. "Her mother was dying, but she herself would survive it, she would survive even the guilt and convenience and grief of her mother's death, she would survive because she had willed herself to survive, because she did not have it in her to die. Even the mercy and kindness of destiny she would survive; they would not get her that way, they would not get her at all."[30]

Unexpressed feelings toward parents can come after hostility (at the ends of novels or in later novels), or after their deaths—in short, when characters feel secure in their liberty. Reconciliation scenes occur either on the mother's deathbed (as in *Earthly Possessions* or *Jerusalem the Golden*), or after the parents' death, in memory (*Rabbit Is Rich, Herzog*). *The Radiant Way* finds room for a woman's guiltless resentment toward her mother. But now at last there may be room for longing, tenderness, regret, understanding—tones from sentimental schmaltz to sober filial piety to reverence for all the dead. One thinks of Henderson squawking on his violin to the father he had always disappointed. "Also down there in my studio I sang as I played, 'Rispondi! Anima bella' (Mozart)."[31] Or

29. A writer does not have to have lost a parent to use these themes. Much of our psychological work goes on with internal representations of the important people in our lives. We may work through "anticipatory orphanhood and anticipatory grief," also anticipatory freedom and risk taking. See Miriam S. Moss and Sidney Z. Moss, "The Impact of Parental Death on Middle Aged Children," *Omega* 14, no. 1 (1983–84): 71–75.

Guilt about "leaving" parents is intimately intertwined with attitudes toward aging, as the following interview material makes painfully clear. Updike at thirty-five (1967): "The sense that in time as well as space we leave people as if by volition and thereby incur guilt and thereby owe them, the dead, the forsaken, at least the homage of rendering them." He thought as he was writing "Flight," where the feelings are given to an adolescent, that there was "irremediable grief in just living, just going on." See Charles Thomas Samuels, "John Updike," in *Writers at Work, The* Paris Review *Interviews,* 4th ser., ed. George Plimpton (New York: Viking, 1976), p. 433. Drabble at the same age actually used the word "survival" in this context: "So I think there's a conflict between feeling a loyalty to one's past and a desire to escape from it and I think that this is why one feels a bit guilty about the survival issue." See Iris Rozencwag, "Interview with Margaret Drabble," *Women's Studies* 6 (1979): 339–40. The interview was conducted in 1974.

30. *Jerusalem the Golden* (London: Weidenfeld and Nicolson, 1967), p. 224.

31. *Henderson The Rain King* (New York: Viking, 1959), p. 30.

Harry Angstrom running on the earth that now feels more sacred because his parents are beneath it.

In all our writers, the dangerous problem of male-female relations is also mitigated in their later midlife Bildungsromane. Whatever they do or however much they may suffer, characters are no longer victims: they are no longer blindly fleeing or hitting or resenting or merely enduring their spouses. Those who feared merging find that merging isn't a fate. Contentment is no longer seen as so rigidly dependent on the one variable of sexual or marital success.[32]

Updike has written a remarriage novel that marries Harry to the same wife, in a relationship full of cooperation, devoid of passion and pain. In *Rabbit Is Rich*, the old sex war slowly concludes, tailing off into amiable separateness in some areas of life and amiable agreement in others. After all, the narrative discloses without disappointment, it *isn't* Harry's nature to be a stud; he manages to take disappointments to his sexual desires calmly.

Bellow has no convincing novel of "remarriage." Henderson after Africa heads back to his wife Lily, but the novel ends before Bellow had to write their reconciliation scene. The new marriage in *More Die of Heartbreak* is an instant failure, but exiting from it is a cinch. After *Seize the Day*, however, Bellow's novels began to contain warm, likable women who aren't sexual or marriage partners but friends: Penelope-like listeners, alert and well disposed.

Drabble, in the easy flexibility of the middle years, writes one narrative about true love leading to (second) marriage, and later ones about women who have given up on marriage, but who find outlets for affection, as Kate Armstrong does, in "friendship[s] of a most intimate nature."[33] A specifically sexual problem that had been cured in a dangerous-age novel later gets replaced by an affirmation of the joys of sex. An early heroine had "feared the wetness"; a later one, without any to-do, celebrates "the least sensible, the messiest and the most amazing of mysteries."[34]

---

32. It is decline novelists who never loosen this connection. For them the misery of life may begin at menarche (as in Jean Rhys) and end only when all sexuality or desiring does, as in Hardy's *The Well-Beloved*, with Jocelyn saying, "Thank heaven I am old at last. The curse is removed." The line is quoted in J. Hillis Miller's *Fiction and Repetition* (Cambridge, Mass.: Harvard University Press, 1982), pp. 150–51.

33. *The Middle Ground* (New York: Knopf, 1980), p. 183.

34. "Fearing the wetness" occurs in *The Waterfall*, p. 48. "One of the things she had always most feared in love had been the wetness. It had dismayed and haunted her, that fatal moisture, and she had surrounded herself with towels and tissues, arid, frightened,

Tyler probably rehabilitates marriage with more conviction than anyone except Drabble in *The Realms of Gold*. In Tyler, leaving your spouse and selecting another mate, as a Morgan and a Macon Leary do, is done in an atmosphere of gentle accommodation very different from the wrenching separation of Mary from Guy or Mary from John or Mary from Jeremy in *Celestial Navigation*, or the glue of responsibility that prevents Charlotte from leaving her husband in *Earthly Possessions*. All four writers tell midlife stories in which unlikely characters are attracted to each other, but she is probably the most sanguine about the unions of such people. In the same novel in which her shy sedentary forty-two-year-old, Macon Leary, embarks on a new commitment to a flouncy sociable bustling dog-trainer, the outgoing businessman marrying Macon's even more backward sister states enthusiastically, "God, Macon, isn't it amazing how two separate lives can link up together? I mean two *differentnesses?*" (*The Accidental Tourist*, p. 206).

In the middle years, sexuality recedes relative to other interests. To reach this equanimity, writers have come a long way from the moment when sex seemed an all-encompassing identity. One stage of the process seems to be writing stories about celibacy. All four wrote I-denied-and-I-survived stories. Drabble produced the one about the woman who after having had sex once never calls the man again (*Thank You All Very Much*). Sometime after *Couples*, his most energetic bed-hopper, Updike wrote *A Month of Sundays*, about a clergyman punished for his promiscuity by having to spend a month in an all-male religious center for addicts of all kinds. With abstinence not thus a choice, the oversexed priest spends his days over his diary, recording his agile past. No day without a fantasy of orgasm. Bellow's midlife novel about a hero ostentatiously evading sex is *Henderson*, in which he imagines a much older man than he was, having the simple will to lead an absolutely celibate life. Tyler's characters have phases of celibacy, represented in her fiction by going back to the family of origin: it's safe, but only a moratorium.

This is the moment—after having followed life-course narratives to

---

fighting like a child for the cold flat dry confines of a narrow bed, superstitiously afraid, like a child, of the body's warmth: and now she lay there, drowned in a willing sea." When Freud was nearly seventy he talked about similar feelings indirectly in a footnote. "All neurotics, and many others besides, take exception to the fact that '*inter urinas et faeces nascimur.*'" See "Civilization and Its Discontents," in *Standard Edition*, 21:106n. Freud assumes that this squeamishness can never change, but Jane Gray is cured by love and cunnilingus. The passage about the messiest mystery comes from *The Realms of Gold* (New York: Knopf, 1975), p. 67. "Messy" is no longer a pure pejorative.

the point where the parents have died and been resurrected, the children have grown up and turned out well enough, and the second marriages have been consummated or evaded—to focus again on time: not time the boring abstraction, or time the destroyer, but time the purveyor of benefits. All progress narratives trust time: Bildungsromane of youth trust time to bring the heroines and heroes the "good gifts" (in Bruno Bettelheim's phrase) of spouse and fortune. But in midlife progress novels, time proves to be beneficial first against the young-adult fear posited earlier: that we may be dangerous to ourselves and others. It proves beneficial next against the gravest suffering that can be inflicted by the world. And finally, it grants some of our deepest wishes without anyone having to state them. These are better gifts than youth gets; and every other gift of effort or luck in the middle years depends on these three.

VII. The Writing Cure

Appreciating that we survive, and enjoying the psychic liberations that may accompany survival—these are part of what I mean by normal healing. It explains many of the changes between early adult and midlife fictions. We all may experience this kind of healing, because even as nonwriters we constitute ourselves by telling our personal narratives as we go along—and, given appropriate circumstances, some people will give personal accounts of being "safe at last." Novelists are blessed through a special, though related, experience that they themselves may not know to tell—to wit, the healing that comes from *writing out* these narratives, one after another.

Cures can seem to happen "between" novels, as I said earlier that they sometimes seem to do, because the writing process aids a person's understanding of human muddles (E. M. Forster's pre-Freudian word for neuroses: a "muddle" can be more easily smoothed out, cleared up, and left behind). Writing life-course fiction facilitates a constant revisionary process that is psychological (and potentially therapeutic) as well as stylistic, as the writer meditates on the adequacy of a work as it is being written, revises as reflection and other less conscious motives dictate, and critically contemplates what has become a past performance in a procedure that may lead to the construction of the next. Of course, autobiographical events also occur: actual divorces and remarriages and the deaths of parents; hitting the best-seller list or not selling as well as expected; reading; having to change one's eyeglass prescription or finding the first gray hairs. On the evidence of the novels, the most disturbing of these events is divorce, which three of the four (not Tyler) have experienced, and all have written about. A different kind of account might want to juxtapose the published fictions with whatever else can be known of such events. Years hence, such an account might use diaries and biographies—associated subjectivities. Meanwhile, these writers cannily protect their psychic intimacy, releasing information selectively about their pasts and trying to set the terms in which they prefer to have their books read. Committed readers of novels are in any case wont to give primacy to the more considered and extended texts— the novels and short stories—over the other self-presentations in interviews and diaries. And, all our other hesitations aside, while writers live it seems presumptuous to speculate too closely about their secrets.[35] Fortunately, even without having much biographical information, we can deduce this second healing process from the body of works themselves—in fact, from relatively short sequences within a single writer's oeuvre that enact particular resistances or cures.

Relatively early in his career, Updike wrote an exemplary fable about how the process of telling a psychic conflict in the wrong way injures the storyteller. In the short story, "Should Wizard Hit Mommy?" a father tells his four-year-old daughter a bedtime fairy tale about a boy skunk who goes out into the world to get a wizard to make him smell like roses so that all the other little animals will be willing to play with him. But when he returns home transformed, his mother objects, saying authoritatively, "You smelled the way a little skunk should have,"[36] hauls him back to the wizard, and gets his bad family smell restored— without any objection on his part. The storyteller's daughter, already at four no doubt thinking about getting along with the little animals of her own social world, calls the mother skunk "stupid." Seeing her resistance to his version, the father pulls his prerogative as the main giver of stories, and ends by telling her that "the little skunk loved his mommy more than he loved aalll the other little animals and she knew what was right" (p. 82). He then goes downstairs, where his wife, pregnant with

35. The American Psychiatric Association's Task Force on Psychohistory has set up strict guidelines for analysts writing psychobiography of living subjects. See William McKinley Runyan, "The Psychobiography Debate: Ethical Issues," in *Life Histories and Psychobiography* (New York: Oxford University Press, 1982), pp. 232–39, esp. p. 236.

36. *Pigeon Feathers* (New York: Knopf, 1962), p. 80.

their third child, has begun a woodwork-painting project they have decided to do jointly. There he is overtaken with incredible revulsion from his wife: "he did not want to speak with her, work with her, touch her, anything" (p. 82).

No special literary or psychoanalytic expertise is needed to see that this is a story about a man's difficulty moving from his mother's sphere of influence into a world dominated by the likings and needs of his nuclear family. But it is also about regressing through storytelling.

I take this short story very seriously as a way of understanding fiction, regression, development, and genre. "Should Wizard Hit Mommy?" is a tale of adult decline, a dangerous-age story (written when Updike was not yet thirty) in which a man's conviction that he sides with his mother (against his daughter and his wife), far from helping him, in the frame story sickens him.[37] The utterance, far from being cathartic, is harmful. The penultimate word of the story is not that his mother "knew what was right" but that her power to control his "smell" and other intimate self-identifications has left him feeling "caught in an ugly middle position" (p. 82).

We can assume that Updike's ability to write both the daughter's skeptical lines and the father's self-conscious lines ("she realized he was defending his own mother to her, or something as odd" [p. 81]) comes from the next larger frame story, his life—which of course includes his writing life. In *this* story, verbal expression leads not to sickening reality and silence but to more, and better, verbal expression. That is, having written this blunt, adumbrated, striking version of pure and potentially permanent illness, Updike went on not much later to write an extended piece of fiction, the novella *Of the Farm* (1965), in which he literally places a man between his mother and his wife, in the realistic setting of a couple visiting the husband's mother, and works out in dramatized detail the mixed attractions and repugnances of his middle position.

What Updike taught himself by writing "Should Wizard Hit Mommy?" is that it was *the wrong genre* for dealing with this complex young-adult conflict. First of all, it was too short. And the embedded fairy tale made the conflict too binary: the little male taking his first journey into the world to form his identity can be *only* a skunk or a rose. That had to be too narrow and incomplete a description of maturation.

37. But cf. Albert J. Griffith, "Updike's Artist's Dilemma: 'Should Wizard Hit Mommy?'" *Modern Fiction Studies* 20, no. 1 (Spring 1974): 111–15. The wife is taken (rather misogynistically) as representing "the prosaic responsibilities that circumscribe his creative imagination" (p. 115).

Saying out loud, through a (fairy) story, that he has chosen one of the two does not make this storyteller feel right; on the contrary. Finally, the tone was too bitter. In an actual case similar to this told by Karen Horney, a woman who was doing self-analysis and had been left by her lover found herself disgusted by the way she had been choosing to tell herself stories about how miserable and lonely she was. "At this point she suddenly saw the grotesqueness of her way of arguing. . . . She recognized that a tendency must be at work which made her talk herself into an exaggerated misery." "She had an expectation that great distress would bring about help. And for the sake of this unconscious belief she made herself *more miserable than she was*" [emphasis added]. "From one point of view the whole development she went through could be described as a growing freedom to feel what she really felt"[38]—that is, less miserable. We have many prejudices about art and suffering, art and neurosis. Greater torment is not necessarily the truth about one's life, nor does it necessarily produce more powerful art. Writing out anger or misery may produce relief not because it "purges" those feelings (as we are so used to saying), but because it reveals their degree of falseness.

Updike needed a form, and a symbolic image (of the farm) that could make a more mixed and many-sided (and indeed somewhat blurred) statement about Joey's relationships to women. Moreover, the mother skunk inside the fairy tale, with her know-it-all tone and unilateral action, had not been able to meet or talk to the pregnant, nest-building wife, who existed only within the frame story, and who in that version had no utterance of her own and didn't know anything about the husband's state of mind. Some genre is needed (or at least, *Of the Farm* supplies it) where the two women talk to each other—indeed, where they argue over their views of him and his needs. On the next to last page, the mother, who is dying, describes herself as an "old witch" in a statement that pulls out of her son a verbal concession to her. On the last page, both women praise him, and he and his mother both admire his wife, and his mother authorizes him to leave her to go home with his wife. "I want you all to go back to New York where you belong."[39]

38. Horney, *Self-Analysis*, pp. 233, 234, 234, and 249, respectively. Horney here anticipates Roy Schafer's work, and her account (I believe) improves on his in using language like "felt what she really felt." If we don't retain some notion of "accuracy to" (the patient's changing feelings) rather than "competing versions of" (stories), we sound as if a preferred story is one that matches the analyst's idea of what a healthy account should sound like.

39. *Of the Farm* (New York: Knopf, 1965), p. 172.

This form (not definitive either, in the sense of being the last version of the triangle that Updike told) enabled him to imagine a considerably happier outcome to the story of a man in the "middle position," and led to the separation-and-remarriage story of *Rabbit Redux* in 1971.

Eventually Updike lost the need to write about this midlife triangle: it ceased to generate stories for him. At the end of *Redux,* when Harry admits to his wife under cross-questioning that he loves their son better than her, and his mother more than either, and she says, patly, "You are a sick man,"[40] their exchange is almost a comic routine, because no sickness of this kind has been enacted in the novel. For Updike, moving along in the life course, the next predominating midlife triangle— again, he'd begun with short stories about them—came to be the ones between a man and his wife and his lover (or her lover), or between a man and his wife and their son.

Many intricate geometries are available in the young-adult and middle years, given (by definition) that a protagonist exists potentially in the middle of a three-generation family with gender differences in each cohort. (Indeed, when we think how long adulthood was regarded as an undifferentiated, static period of life, the proliferation and variety of stories in the second half of the twentieth century seem staggering.) What seems undeniably personal, autobiographical, is a writer's decision to repeat, for a time, among all the possibilities, stories of a particular conflict. Updike's texts could only be Updike's: no one else could have written "Should Wizard Hit Mommy?" and the rest of the sequence; to no one else could belong the trenchant, big-boned, dryly humorous, and verbally dominating mother who appears in the earliest Olinger stories and in the Rabbit trilogy as well.[41]

Patterns of repetition and variation suggest that some writers have a powerful need or even obsession to deal with psychic problems in their art. This has long been understood in literary biography. But the existence of different *versions* of the psychic situation *over time* forces us away from the typically static analytic statement about a writer's unresolvable "problem": instead, we are urged outward toward the bigger and ultimately more useful hypothesis that for some writers, whether

40. *Rabbit Redux* (New York: Knopf, 1971), p. 399.

41. Bellow (to take a counterexample) doesn't tell the mother-self-wife story, perhaps because his mother died when he was in his teens. But he once told a story about blaming someone else to divert attention from some basic trouble between a man and a woman who are having trouble forming a new couple: "A Father-To-Be" (1955), in *Mosby's Memoirs and Other Stories* (New York: Viking, 1968). Rogin's mother does come into the story briefly and ludicrously.

they know it or not, writing fiction over time helps to solve problems. Some critics may have difficulty getting "behind" any single text to identify some authentic particular problem, but most readers, following a set of grouped texts chronologically, should have no difficulty recognizing change.

Major changes in genre—from dangerous-age structures and motifs to the affirmations of midlife literature or from midlife affirmation to midlife depletion—taking place as they do over a writer's lifetime, cannot be arbitrary fictive games. In a long form like the novel, a whole year's work at the very least and often much more, no one chooses genre arbitrarily: if a genre is distasteful, most writers cannot force themselves to stay in it for as long as it takes. The short story offers more play; it's no surprise that within an oeuvre some of the more peculiar regressions and the more eccentric stylistic inventions and other anomalies surface in short stories. At the margins, the mind can fool around, practice, and discard. When a whole novel indulges a fantasy—as in Drabble's *Thank You All Very Much,* or Bellow's *Henderson the Rain King*—that degree of captivation, or captivity, makes us stare.

Genre derives at any given moment from temperament responding to circumstances, and temperament cannot be forced (or concealed) for long. When Bellow got his Guggenheim and went to Paris, he tried to write a third "sad" book, but *Augie March* bubbled out instead. Drabble wrote Bildungsromane right out of Oxford, but then had a period of holding hard on to the form as her heroines' early brittle confidence disappeared and the narratives darkened. Tyler edged her way toward Bildung, writing rather gloomy progress stories and even one decline story until her sixth novel, *Searching for Caleb.* Updike came to Bildung late and reluctantly where Rabbit was concerned: he made Rabbit undergo a long sorrowful apprenticeship toward life mastery. There was Angst-room enough for several books.[42]

Abstractly and generally, is there a way of explaining why people change their attitudes toward their own lives and (as one hard-pressed writer, Isak Dinesen, phrased it) reevaluate "[their] qualifications for, [their] difficulties in achieving either development or happiness"?

42. Here and elsewhere, *Safe at Last* focuses mainly on the Rabbit trilogy. The trilogy is Updike's masterpiece; his sticking with Harry for more than twenty years has made him his most substantial alter ego and most relevant character of all for my purposes.

I will not begin to divide them into those arising from outward circumstance and those that may be said to originate from my own temperament, for I think that in reality these two categories form part of each other. If, for instance, I am cold, it can be said that this is a result of my own constitution or of the surrounding temperature, but whichever is the case my feeling is the same, and figuratively it would take a very clever man to decide whether I ought to take a tonic or light a fire.[43]

Pursuing Isak Dinesen's metaphor, I would add that what is needed for development is the desire *not to be cold*. People who really want to be warm (and who own the wood and the mixings) probably both light the fire and take the medicine. The writing of life-course fiction, for some, turns out to be a way of warming the inner self. Not everyone can change like this. There are plenty of writers who find ways of telling decline stories again and again: they never learn to describe reality in any other way; this way never comes to seem false to them; it never accomplishes catharsis. Change can be fearful, we know—even positive change. The insightful therapist in Alther's *Other Women* inquires seriously of her patient, at a crucial point in the process, "But now can you face the terror of feeling good?"[44] No matter how much we know about a particular writer as a person, some mystery may always remain about this fundamental bifurcation.

The happier genre seems to come, for lucky writers, from producing a sequence of narratives each of which progressively better satisfies their private sense of accuracy and their culturally conditioned sense of appropriate form; this seems to involve describing developmental advances. The proof that the later narrative is "right" can be (like the proof of cure in structured therapeutic situations) that it ends some compulsion to repeat.

Tyler tells within *The Clock Winder* a story of a cure that comes about this way, when the heroine, Elizabeth, retells her friend Margaret's story correctly. Margaret is in a crisis in which she cries constantly, remembering the way her young first husband "let her go" when her mother came to "take her away" after their elopement. All Elizabeth does to force the reinterpretation is to say incredulously, "But took you away! She's so little" (p. 192). Tyler ends the chapter by having Margaret's tears end; Margaret admits to herself that it was she who left him, and she knows that "if he ever came back it would be dimly, for

43. Isak Dinesen, *Letters from Africa, 1914–1931,* trans. Anne Born (Chicago: University of Chicago Press, 1981), p. 281.
44. Lisa Alther, *Other Women* (New York: Knopf, 1984), p. 223.

only a second, in the company of others whose parts in her life were finished" (p. 204). Telling the story "correctly" emphasizes Margaret's adult agency in separating from an unsuitable husband, rather than her childish yielding to her mother's will. It was she who was cruel. Subtly purveyed in Tyler's interpolated short story about interpretation, endings, and adulthood is the notion that adults should (even) accept the cruelty built into satisfying their desires rather than believe that they were once innocent victims. Having revised Margaret's script this way, Elizabeth goes on to call off her own wedding at the altar. She has learned the lesson that one must be the agent of one's own life, even though it involves exerting momentarily cruel power. (Many midlife Bildungsromane—like the personal narratives of nonwriters[45]—accept the risks of agency in the actions of willful adults; they do this as a way of overcoming dangerous-age determinism.) Having accepted the revision of her script without having changed anything in her external circumstances, Margaret willingly goes back into her contented second marriage, which when she saw herself as a victim had seemed like a *pis aller* forced on her by her mother's notions of marital suitability. She discovers that she is a free agent leading a self-chosen life. Like Macon Leary making the same discovery, she could say, "I'm more myself than I've been my whole life long" (*The Accidental Tourist*, p. 249). In this simple assertion of feeling are packed a lot of ideas (about reality and change in self-recognition) that remain difficult to state abstractly.

Presumably this is the way revision in sequential texts works. The writer has to play the roles of both Margaret and Elizabeth, of course, to produce the necessary "dialogue." Or perhaps it would be clearer to say that the dialogue goes on between the first text the writer produces—let's call it for the moment the "Margaret script" (about a victim with an unhappy outcome)—and the writer, who takes the de-

---

45. Many studies of "personal narrative" find that "agency"—feeling in charge—is extremely important, important enough to be exaggerated. "Good stories . . . are aligned with the distortions that memory normally makes in creating personal history." See John Kotre, *Outliving the Self: Generativity and the Interpretation of Lives* (Baltimore: Johns Hopkins University Press, 1984), p. 223. "Depressives appraised their degree of control over probabilistic outcomes more accurately than did normals, *with normals frequently overstating their extent of control,*" according to a well-known study by L. B. Alloy and L. Y. Abramson (1979) cited in Anthony G. Greenwald, "The Totalitarian Ego: Fabrication and Revision of Personal History," *American Psychologist* 35, no. 7 (July 1980): 614 (emphasis mine). Greenwald goes on to suppose that "the likelihood of effective performance may be greater for a person whose efficacy expectations are generally inflated . . . than for one whose expectations may be more objectively accurate." "Normals" do for themselves what analysis tries to get analysands to do. For Bildungsromane, agency is the true story; for these psychologists, it's a distortion, an overstatement, or an inflation.

tached, incredulous, critical, revisionist, *curative* role of Elizabeth. Although the writer may believe the revision deals with "style," it may also resemble the dialogue between a therapist and a patient (as, say, Roy Schafer or Karen Horney might describe it). "Elizabeth," the friendly ghost-writer, helps "Margaret" to a more active story of her past, not one that is faithful to the original version.[46] The new version matches an adult definition of self, substituting "I" for "she" (the mother) and the active voice for the passive voice. "Margaret," the new self, accepts the new version not only for those reasons but (I would add) because it permits her to return to the life she likes. The story gives her a future shaped to her present possibilities and desires.

Let's say that the Bildung impulse includes the psychic ability to invent Elizabeth-the-interpreter-of-experience. Afterward, it becomes much easier to conjure up "what Elizabeth would think about that." Building her up with a gender and a vocabulary and a tone of voice amounts to creating an ego-ideal (handier than a living therapist, and more influential than unwritten words in one's head might be). Afterward, the dialectic can continue between the writer and this Elizabeth. And the Bildung impulse is also the urge that allows a writer to give Elizabeth-as-protagonist her own script of change. This aspect of the impulse judges the (character's) desire and, finding it good, appropriate, and able to be made fictively plausible, rewards it. (It's like a benevolent super-ego.) Broadly speaking, this kindly judgment determines the ending, and the ending the genre.[47] From this point of view, genre represents a degree of not just empathy but goodwill toward the character who stands in for the self. Drabble has told a curious anecdote about how writing a happy ending for a character felt like a gift to *herself* of a happy future. "But when I wrote my first novel and decided that it was going to have a funny ending, I thought, 'I'm really going to be a different kind of person: This is wonderful,' I felt. Life is going to be good, not bad."[48]

46. Apparently there is no clear consensus about what Meredith Anne Skura calls "the status of psychoanalytic explanation" ("Is it explanation, or is it merely a parallel version of the experience it claims to explain?"); in any case, it has been observed that even untrue (or "inexact") interpretations can effect cures. See *The Literary Use of the Psychoanalytic Process* (New Haven: Yale University Press, 1981), p. 22 and n. 33. The question itself, however, begins to seem unsatisfactory.

47. "Many of the most suggestive analysts of narrative have shared the conviction that the end writes the beginning and shapes the middle: Propp, for instance, and Frank Kermode, and Jean-Paul Sartre." See Brooks, *Reading for the Plot*, p. 22.

48. Barbara Milton, "Margaret Drabble," *The Paris Review* 20, no. 74 (Spring 1978): 56–57.

If this were the whole story of progress narrative, then once writers had safely appropriated the Bildung form, their tendency might be to continue writing Bildungsromane of the middle years, and perhaps even progressively happier ones. Or to stop writing. Drabble may have succumbed to this second tendency when she stopped writing fiction for about five years after *The Middle Ground,* explaining recently that she had "come to the end of a certain style or *kind* of novel."[49] It was as if she had come to the end of a successful analysis. But silence from such a cause must be rare during the enormously crowded, dynamic years of adulthood, when major life events occur, and a writer's responses to them leak into fiction.

Both decline and progress narratives need obstacles to happiness— decline narratives to justify plots in which people don't get what they want, and progress narratives to justify the reward when they do. Narrative necessity, within an ambitious midlife novel, may thus require many vexatious triangles and dyads, with the result that, if the most threatening situations vanish after the dangerous age, others still amply challenging take their place. Yet it seems (so far, for these writers and others like them) that once the worst life crisis has been inscribed—a period they have somehow labeled "the worst"—none others that follow can require rhetorics so savage, structures so perilous and punishing, tones so full of suffering. A reader has only to contrast *Roger's Version* with *Rabbit, Run,* or *More Die of Heartbreak* with *Seize the Day* or *Herzog,* to realize that when Bildungsromane have intervened, certain repetitions cannot occur. In life, you may realize that the shot will never be fired at you; in fiction you find you can't write ironic fable or self-pitying melodrama or fairy tale, victim literature or grotesque fantasy or lachrymose comedy, or whatever your antique form used to be. As with crumbling teeth, skunkiness, or a domineering mother, so with other painful vicissitudes: you have developed your midlife attitude, and the old modes have become phony genres.

VIII. Praising Aging

Here is one last paradox, for those who still loathe the middle years and believe that only youth can honestly be presented fa-

---

49. Miriam Berkley, "PW Interviews: Margaret Drabble," *Publishers Weekly,* May 31, 1985, p. 60 (emphasis in original).

vorably in literature—or for those who are enchanted with the new world to which our investigations have taken us. Some of our midlife Bildungsromanciers have praised aging explicitly, through the mouths of protagonists who have earned the right to be listened to. It's not as if they were praising aging from the viewpoint of people who are twenty-one, rich, in love, and on the threshold of marriage. When *midlife* Bildung is being celebrated, Tom Jones and Elizabeth Bennet are joined by Harry Angstrom, Charlie Citrine, Frances Wingate, Malcolm Leary—an experienced crowd. The bold simplicity of Howells's Mr. Waters could not, one hundred years later, be theirs. When characters like these praise aging, a lot of complicated calculations contribute to that bottom line. "Middle age is a wonderful country, all the things you thought would never happen are happening," says Harry in *Rabbit Is Rich,* referring obliquely to his survival in a context that refers to his acquiring both an old man's smell and a wise man's sense that the meaning of life is close up and all around, not, as in his youth, frustratingly distant and vague and unattainable except with guilt.[50] Looking at a hacked and graffitoed cement lion that she likes "very much," Rose Vassiliou, not unhacked herself, likens it to a person who has been developing since birth. "Mass-produced it had been, but it had weathered into identity. And this, she hoped, for every human soul" (*The Needle's Eye,* p. 389).

Progress narrators know that aging carries a body closer to death even as it produces a self that we rather like to live with, at last. Many things remind Harry that "he's suffered another promotion, taken another step up the stairs that has darkness at the head" (p. 171). How do writers who trust time enough to scoff at tooth decay manage to maintain trust in the face of this last extremity? For some, the head of the stairs is simply still too far away to worry about (a rational perception, actuaries would agree). Others have invented an idea of death that suits them. All have narrative techniques that reveal how they have come to terms with the contradiction. Maintaining faith in the processes that accompany aging may be the crucial factor. (Readers tempted to call these modes of faith "mystifications" should realize that that temptation is tantamount to telling a decline story about adjusting to aging.)

The first amounts to appreciating change—Bellow calls it "strangeness." Henderson argues that "the strangeness of life . . . makes death

---

50. John Updike, *Rabbit Is Rich* (New York: Knopf, 1981), p. 231.

more remote, as in childhood" (*Henderson,* p. 84). But for another kind of novelist, we sense, strangeness is terrifying and brings death closer. Only Bildungsromane slyly praise it.

Tyler's Macon Leary makes this explicit: that we need the idea of change per se because it makes living—with all its vicissitudes, including banality and disaster—seem a nonstop series of "adventures." Macon wants to give his dead son his own human advantage.

And if dead people aged, wouldn't it be a comfort? To think of Ethan growing up in heaven—fourteen years old now instead of twelve—eased the grief a little. Oh, it was their immunity to time that made the dead so heartbreaking. . . . The real adventure, he thought, is the flow of time; it's as much adventure as anyone could wish. And if he pictured Ethan still part of that flow—in some other place, however unreachable—he believed he might be able to bear it after all. (*The Accidental Tourist,* p. 354)

Some would say that what seems heartbreaking is the egocentric difference between us and the dead—our own vulnerability to time contrasted with their invulnerability. But imagining an afterlife in which they continue to live and age forbids self-pity as well as softening grief. Charlie Citrine, reading to his dead, has almost convinced himself that the funeral doesn't end it all; what comes after is the ultimate tutorial. For most of us, death is the end of change, and just by the logic of antithesis, in opposing death we would be forced to embrace time. We want more from time, though, than change; as our midlife novels show, most of us want progress.

Progress sweetens aging in one familiar way, and one curious, superstitious way. Progress means not just an increase in well-being, desirable as that may be, but also access to the intangibles that philosophy used to permit the wise in the days when becoming wise was assumed to require climbing lots of rungs on the Ladder of Ages. Bildungsromane don't try to prove that we become perfect in this process, but they hint that characters—all of us—are improving within our means, and collectively they validate the idea of *perfectibility:* that's what Jeremy means in *Celestial Navigation* when he says that gradualism is his god. (Indeed, validating process might imply that even turning the pages of Bildungsromane is improving.) Bellow, speaking here in some irony, suggests one final, irrational but intuitively satisfying reason why (some) writers might want to write life-course Bildungsromane and why (some) readers read them avidly. In trying to understand his gnomic saying, I have had recourse to Zeno's paradox, in which motion is conceived of as perpetual and progressive and yet never able to end. By "tirelessly" improving ourselves, he says, "we deny the power of death over us because as long as we're getting better there's no reason we should die."[51]

51. Saul Bellow, "Distractions of a Fiction Writer," in *Herzog,* ed. Irving Howe (New York: Viking Critical Library, 1976), p. 372. Bellow, writing in 1957, was mocking this attitude: "We are not perfect. We must perfect ourselves, we must exhaust ourselves." By 1975, when he had more energy, trying to improve did not seem so exhausting to him.

3

John Updike: Rabbit Angstrom Grows Up

The miracle of it: how things grow, always remembering to be themselves.

—Updike, *Rabbit Is Rich*

I. Money and Riches

"Hearty and huge" and "serene in his middle years" is the way Updike describes Harry Angstrom at age forty-six. "For the first time since childhood Rabbit is happy, simply, to be alive."[1] He knows that sentimentality about the past is an enemy: "Reminiscence. Sad to see it rotting Charlie's brain" (p. 27). Harry has a memory accurate enough so that complacency about his past is not a fault he is liable to commit. He remembers—and has finally named—"the stifled terror that always made him restless" (p. 97). He doesn't have a model of growth, he doesn't know that what has saved him from himself is change. But in his innerly perceptive way, he feels himself to be a different person. Crucially, he has different, and less fierce, desires; he is not so driven by desire. "He wants less. Freedom, that he always thought was outward motion, turns out to be this inner dwindling" (p. 97). There are elements of Stoic or oriental philosophy (unknown to Harry)

1. *Rabbit Is Rich* (New York: Knopf, 1981), p. 10.

in this quite un-American idea of midlife freedom. A bad self has dwindled—a wanting, craving, selfish, angry, violent self of young adulthood. Confusion, passion, and tragedy resided in the past that that self created or imagined, and Harry has lived long enough to survive it. Once he does regret the loss of "keen dreaming," but the perspective of the whole book—in which he manages an active fantasy life akin to that "dreaming"—makes that regret minor, fleeting. It's submerged in the gratitude for having moved on, into another state of being. As long as you avoid mirrors (and Harry gave it up "since at about the age of forty he came out of that adolescent who-am-I vanity trip" [p. 377]), life is sweet. "He sees his life as just beginning, on clear ground at last" (p. 97).

Rabbit Is Rich starts off with clichés of decline, but they are a typical Bildungsroman ploy: the establishment of decline motifs for the sake of creating contrasts. The first words of the novel sound at first like a modern metaphor for middle age, an expectable, bathetic metaphor. "Running out of gas," Rabbit thinks, looking out on the world; and the traffic looks to him "thin and scared compared to what it used to be." He's looking at the world through "summer-dusty windows" (it might be a definition of "realism" about the life course that it sees summers as dusty), but he's safe inside the car dealership that since *Rabbit Redux,* when he lost his job as a linotyper, has given him affluence beyond his early expectations. These metaphors connect Rabbit, long known as Harry, to his earlier self and his early certainty of decline, but only to show how far he has come.

Money alone will not produce midlife ease, although it's true that all four of our novelists have projected into fiction images of poor or deprived childhoods, and that at some later point they imagine a main character who is by the earlier standard quite respectably or even phenomenally rich: Bellow's Henderson (1959), Drabble's Rose Vassiliou (*The Needle's Eye,* 1972), Tyler's Justine Peck (*Searching for Caleb,* 1976). Harry isn't rich by this standard, compared with Tyler's Roland Park Pecks with their genteel money, or Drabble's manufacturing heiress, or Bellow's millionaire from an aristocratic family. Harry Angstrom is the only one of them who has never had a chance to live on unearned income, and the only one who likes his money ("having enough at last . . . has made him satisfied all over" [p. 49], he exaggerates).[2] The other

2. Updike and Bellow were both born early enough, and into poor enough families, to have been affected by the Depression, but my sense is that Bellow came to romanticize his childhood, including its poverty, whereas Updike experienced his as a series of humili-

writers produce novels padded with inherited wealth mainly to show how little the characters care for it. All three feel rich enough to disparage riches. (Updike feels rich enough not to.) The other three have managed to create a new stock figure for the midlife Bildungsroman: the remarkably rich protagonist who renounces wealth and comfort and thrives on the choice. This figure is not inevitable—Updike hasn't produced one—but it makes a lot of sense, thought of developmentally. Perhaps we can assume that many adolescents or young adults worry about earning "enough." Some learn they can't. Eventually most find they can, and a few find they can earn a good deal more. The fictional image of the mature rejecter of riches arises, we may speculate, at that point in life where authors see themselves as secure, as if (like the characters they depict) they have had money a long time.

Updike identifies with the working stiff grateful for unexpected financial security. Money matters more in *Rabbit Is Rich* because of the ways in which Harry values it. Updike shows how he uses it to measure his distance from his family's sad, impoverished life: the poor people's holidays in Jersey that always made his father throw up, the household smell of hard deprivation. His father could never have imagined him living so well. In such thoughts there's a softened edge of competitiveness, as well as a sense that his father would have approved of him, even admired him, for being a big, solid clubmember and landholder. The way he thinks about money makes it an antinostalgia strategy, an *aide-mémoire* for writing a progress narrative about his life. Harry thinks frequently about products, profit margins, and investments, but—except when he's showing off to Nelson how much he knows, or hoping to impress Janice with their gold—in an uninvested way. Money is not one of the things he needs to *want*. As a result, it can generate scenes—conversations with his older friend Webb, the roll in the gold with his wife Janice—but it can't generate plot, which is based on fundamental needs and desire. In this novel, the many plots (the Nelson plot, the "daughter's" plot, the Cindy plot, even the house plot) are connected to people.

The passages about Harry and his kinky gold are not where Updike's most good-natured book lives; gold is a necessary but not sufficient cause for satisfaction. Harry's "expanded resources" are not primarily

ating deprivations. Moreover, he used to link his birth year, 1932, with the year in which the family lost ground in the struggle, as if his coming into being had been a marker for decline.

material, and it is a person—an unexpected person—whom he finally calls his "treasure" and his "prize." The world itself may run out of economic goods—many characters talk about America's decline as something fairly certain, and feel sorry for the young—but Harry agrees with the radical voice he has internalized on such subjects, that "the world was never a pleasant place" (p. 176). Harry could have gotten rich and stayed sour. But in the (comic) novel of psychological advancement, inner resources count more.

Although Harry doesn't dwell on the misery of his past, his forgetfulness is not treated as a crime; it seems like a favor of recuperation. When someone wants him to suffer from his recollections, he declines. "He is sick of these allusions to his tainted past" (p. 123). Time (the fictive ten years since Updike last visited him), as manipulated by his creator, has dealt him some compassion, vastly increased appreciation, a portion of contentment, even gold-capped teeth that enable him to enjoy eating more than before. Finally, it has given him the pleasures of friendship, in contrast with his earlier overheated worlds of family or strays. Within the space of cure the novel provides, "time" imperceptibly undoes some of his resentment about his son, settles an old bad account from the long-gone past, secures him in a less driven sexual identity, and lets him attain a symbol of freedom he hadn't before been able to choose. Unless a reader dislikes him for not suffering more (his son Nelson's view) or scorns him for appreciating his state of being as much as he does, these goods Updike gives him seem plausible and just. "Rabbit is rich" is not to be taken, at the deepest level, as an ironic statement.

II. The Grateful Age

The big surprise of the book is love. That's what Updike calls it, and he explicitly connects Harry's ability to love with his aging and the acceptance of the deaths he has witnessed.

Now the dead are so many he feels for the living around him the camaraderie of survivors. He loves these people with him. . . . Harry loves the treetops above their heads, and the August blue above these. What does he know? . . . He loves Nature, though he can name almost nothing in it. . . . He loves money. . . . He loves men, uncomplaining with their pot bellies and cross-hatched red necks, embarrassed for what to talk about when the game is over, whatever the game is. What a threadbare thing we make of life. Yet what a marvellous thing the mind is. (p. 139)

These thoughts echo Piet Hanema's speech to Freddy Thorne (*we* make life threadbare), but Harry gets beyond Piet in admiring not just the world but the mind that contemplates it. And Updike manages to make his contemplating mind if not marvelous, continuously interesting.

In the context of Updike's oeuvre, this unexpectedly awed passage hints that love (a new kind of midlife, post-romance, impersonal love) inscribes it all, all 467 pages of writing, all the minute descriptions, all Harry's observation of acid-green Corolla SR-5 liftbacks, shrouded gas tanks, the suburban sprawl of Mt. Judge. Closeness of observation, which Updike has almost always demonstrated, has been transformed, from a Nabokovian fetish of formal decorativeness to a sign of affectionate engagement with the world. Unlike most Americans including his creator, Harry has stayed in one place all his life, and he possesses it minutely. He, and all of Updike's younger characters, and generations of "young" European and American protagonists, used to be irritably dissatisfied with the provincial woodwork. Now, in the I-Been-Moved world, that kind of dissatisfaction isn't automatically chic. Loving the familiar, the quotidian, what endures (and is yours to endure), even without knowing it, is becoming acceptable, and even comforting. Comfort—the little comforts almost everyone can invent and procure—was always one great secret discovery of the middle years. Maybe that too will come to be less despised.

Updike springs a related secret—one quite alien to his own earlier novels (including his adulterous "romances" like *Marry Me* and *Couples*). Somebody whom he is not in love with falls genuinely in love with Harry—turns out to have been loving him (listening to him) all along—and her unreciprocated and unasked-for praise of him, startlingly, reveals him as lovable. The circumstances could have been treated as grotesque or sordid: Thelma has lupus, and is not the woman Harry wanted to sleep with, and giving him devotion skirts (vicarious) narcissistic wish fulfillment. Moreover—upsetting the usual plot of male extramarital relations—nothing more in the amative or retributive vein comes of it. The point is that Thelma has been established as the most intelligent person in Harry's set, and she is put face to face with dying in a way fiction often associates with truth telling.

"Uh—not to, you know, milk this, but what is it about me that turns you on?"

"Oh darling. Everything. Your height and the way you move, as if you're still a skinny twenty-five. The way you never sit down anywhere without making sure there's a way out. Your little provisional smile, like a little boy at some party. . . . Your good humor. You *believe* in people so—Webb, you hang on his words where nobody else pays any attention, and Janice, you're so proud of her

it's pathetic. . . . See? You're just terribly generous. You're so grateful to be anywhere, you think that tacky club and that hideous house of Cindy's are heaven.
It's wonderful. You're so glad to be alive."

"Well, I mean, considering the alternative—"

"It kills me. I love you *so much* for it." (p. 418)

Thelma smacks his lower-middle-class tastes, but her praise for his
character and value feels acceptable. Rabbit can be singled out as lovable, ultimately, because he's "so glad to be alive." This wasn't true at
twenty-six or thirty-six. That root feeling is what makes him himself—
humble, comical, grateful, and observant. Noticing how observant he
is, readers have suspected that he was Updike with different similes.[3]
Perhaps he always had been, in another sense—that he may have embodied an anarchic, egotistic, antisocietal side of himself that Updike
admitted, feared, defended publicly,[4] condemned fictionally, and has
now finally altered and reevaluated through Harry. Now, despite Harry's
dumbness both verbal and human, Updike likes him better, and lets
him like himself, giving Harry "a sense of miracle at being himself, himself instead of somebody else" (p. 419).

For many people, only a "realist"—a person with sound credentials
as a decline novelist—can bring a message like this of love and well-
being, precisely because he brings it cautiously, dryly, and either spo-
radically, so that a reader may overlook it, or so overtly that it can be
dismissed as ironic. For such readers, the idea they think they have of
life now that they are over thirty requires that fiction about a Harry Angstrom should not depart too much from the decline conventions: that
the self is not of much intrinsic interest, even to itself (but must be
puffed up through art); that ordinary life is drab and empty of meaning; that work is repetitious; and that relationships do not provide
much in the way of satisfaction, being mainly hollow forms.

Harry's relationship with his wife Janice conforms to this convention
up to a point. The signs occur, as so often in Updike's work, in the sex-

3. "I think it's possible to have a character who isn't very verbal but who nevertheless
is very sensitive," Updike said, arguing how alike he and the Rabbit of *Redux* are (Josh
Rubins, "The Industrious Drifter in Room 2," *Harvard Magazine* [May 1974]: 44); he
defended a similar point in the 1971 section of "One Big Interview," in *Picked-Up Pieces*
(New York: Knopf, 1976), pp. 508, 509, 510: "Intellectually, I'm not essentially advanced over Harry Angstrom. . . . Like Harry, I try to remain open. . . . Like Harry, I'm
hog fat, reactionary, passive. I'm a plugger."

4. In a self-interview in 1971, Updike described himself as "by disposition an apolo-
gist for the spirit of anarchy—our animal or divine margin of resistance to the social con-
tract." See John Updike, "Bech Meets Me," in *Picked-Up Pieces*, p. 12.

ual realm: impotence or selfish orgasm, increasingly pornographic fantasies of another woman. But the other realms, especially that of discourse, elevate her, as Thelma was jealously quick to notice. As in other midlife progress narratives, sex is not central enough to be symbolic; it's only a component of a relationship, and not a large one. In their conversations, Janice, the "dumb mutt" of the earlier books, shows some midlife wisdom, easiness, and energy ("middle-aged friskiness," he calls it) that Harry feels he lacks. When he thinks about her as an individual, he accepts her superiority without anger. He *is* big and serene. "She has had a lot of lessons. The decade past has taught her more than it has taught him" (p. 138). "Janice waves away his complaint with a queenly gesture she wouldn't have possessed ten years ago" (p. 77). Their relative positions have changed: not only can't he "put her down," but often she has mature answers: "It sometimes startles Harry, how smooth Janice can be in her middle age" (p. 158). When they talk about their son Nelson or any other personal matter, he is the ignorant questioner, she the one with the answers. When he tries to sound adult, affectionate, paternal—tones Janice now manages easily—he thinks he sounds like an "impersonator." He even admires her physically. Updike gives her more hair and a better figure than she had as a young woman: in 1960 he had described her, newly married, as an aging woman who was losing her hair and looks, but now he gives her signs of youth as well as a way of being that Harry defers to.

Having taught himself, like a reader of midlife decline novels, to expect nothing much from matrimony but burdens, Harry is surprised to be soothed by their "connivance" (p. 177). If the word conveys that they have played some trick on the world, it also conveys that they have done it together. At one level Harry trusts her so much that he confides in her one of the few things about him that she can't accept. "He had mistaken the two of them for one. . . . A mistake married people make" (p. 72). On her own, she guesses his other pitiful longings, and forgives them. There's something maternal (in the way kind teachers are maternal) about her responses to his backwardness. They have real conversations; Updike has filled the novel with spousal discourse, as (I think) no other novelist has done. (But I think of the talk between Kitty and Levin in *Anna Karenina* when she brushes his hand with her lips to explain, "Won't bite.") Updike has not only enriched the conventions of midlife dialogue, but has also shown how much the long-married have to talk about, and how important the dialogue is to them. In the Rabbit trilogy, his long-term marriage frees Harry so that he can finally feel "not for the first time in twenty years plus . . . a furtive rush of loving her, caught with him as she is in the narrow places life affords" (p. 373). "She is his fortune," he admits plainly. The book feels right ending when it does, soon after Harry in effect admits that he is married to her for good. Adolescents and young adults run, in the trilogy's view of the ages of life; but adults pretty much stay put, and with equanimity.

Once when she got like this [flustered, frowny, grieved], her fear contaminated him and he ran; but in these middle years it is so clear to him that he will never run that he can laugh at her, his stubborn prize. (p. 455)

As soon as Harry recognizes his marriage, the book's tense changes. It has been present tense all the way through, as in the two earlier books. But the present has a different tonality here—juicier without being crisis ridden, even but deeply attentive. The change to the past ("And it was true, [they] did come over last night." [p. 456]) comes as a shock. After a few pages, Updike reverts to the present tense and ends with it, but we have registered that the end is near. Exactly what is ending? It seems (although it surely won't be: Updike certainly has a fourth and not necessarily final Rabbit in his hat[5]) like the end of Harry, our last night with him. We knew we appreciated him, and now by giving us this sense of dislocation and loss, Updike forces us to realize the degree of our involvement. If midlife Bildungsromane are not reintroducing "heroes," they are bringing back the welcome companionship of much nineteenth-century literature—characters whom we find, in the reading at least, that we like to live with.

Updike goes one better. He conveys to the reader the attitude toward death that Harry has arrived at after the terrors of his early years. This attitude is connected with Harry's long-deferred acceptance of marriage. He had earlier, with a sinking heart, linked monogamy with dying. Monogamy had been the "known road" (p. 347) and to the adolescent mind (in a body of whatever age) the known road has to be shunned as a living death. Novelty and sensation are the values of this stage, and these can be had within the affective life only through adul-

5. In private conversation in 1982, Updike said that he "promised" an interviewer to write another volume. In 1974 he said, "I kind of committed myself with the first revisitation. I have the opportunity—if I live a few more decades—to do a man's life by revisiting him every ten years or so. I would like to be able to write a kind of Victorian tetralogy" (Rubin, "Industrious Drifter," p. 44). The third was originally going to be a short, pastoral book called *Rural Rabbit* (see "Bech Meets Me," in *Picked-Up Pieces,* p. 13).

tery, as Piet Hanema said in *Couples* (1968), defending adultery when one of the women described it as "silly" and "so much trouble." "It's a way of giving yourself adventures. Of getting out in the world and seeking knowledge."[6]

It turns out that what Rabbit feared was not actual death or monogamy the living death, but what then felt, erroneously, like hated routine without the possibility of change. Now on every page, Harry's sensibility sees change even amid the familiar—"For years nothing happens; then everything happens" (p. 392). In any case, life has taught him that there are worse things than being bored. "On Earth, when you look up from being bored, things have changed, you're that much closer to the grave, and that's exciting. Imagine climbing up and up into that great tree of night sky. Dizzying. Terrible" (p. 181). For a man who used to like being scared, his idea of death provides just the right amount of sensation.

Harry is not permitted guilt about the other deaths: his daughter Rebecca in book one, or the girl-lover, Jill, in book two. "But the years have piled on, the surviving have patched things up, and so many more have joined the dead, undone by diseases for which only God is to blame, that it no longer seems so bad, it seems more as if Jill just moved to another town, where the population is growing" (p. 73). Harry was more afraid of death at a time when his fear of dying was a wrongheaded association with the guilt he thought had to accompany living as a powerful adult. Harry will die, but not of guilt.

Updike takes us a long way from those dusty-summer clichés of decline to this unfrightened midlife acknowledgment of death. He takes his time, in a long book with no great volume of plot. He doesn't feel he needs much more plot than that provided by the course of life with Harry and his family—the expectable domestic events of the 1970s in a three-generation household whose most agitated member is a not-quite-adult son. Apparently Updike loved writing it; he felt he had plenty of time and that the implied reader would too. After the shock of adulthood and its first wasteful hurry, the middle years can deal in time more expansively. (The book begins on June 21st, the longest day of the year, and ends on "Super Bowl Sunday"; forty-six turning forty-seven doesn't yet require the allegory of autumn.) "Lately he no longer ever feels he is late for somewhere, a strange sort of peace at his time of life like a thrown ball at the top of its arc is for a second still" (p. 227).

6. *Couples* (New York: Knopf, 1968), p. 343.

Like the new Harry, the book seems genial, open-eyed, embracing. With this book Updike has taken up all the middling people who never thought their midlives would make a book, to say nothing of a cultural revolution. Realism has never seemed so hospitable as in its vitalized mode of midlife kindness. It's as if it had wasted itself heretofore in young-adult "scrupulous meanness" (Joyce's phrase about *Dubliners*, written in his early twenties when *he* still anticipated the life course with dread) and sensationalism, not having discovered from experience how important are the things the middling are best at—staying alive, appreciating life, and, without even knowing it, growing. "Still, life is sweet. That's what old people used to say and when he was young he wondered how they could mean it" (p. 6). Midlife is the grateful age.

III. Moving Day

This is no model of development familiar to literature, this novel in which nothing particular happens but a character changes in major ways. In the plot, the clearest sign of his growth (there are many other indices, to be discussed in their turn) is that he can buy a house of his own. From the beginning of the novel, when Harry revives this long-contemplated and long-deferred purchase, the reader is alerted to judge his progress by whether he can make it. If he moves, it's a Bildungsroman! Tasteless as Harry's house may be, that's what he wants, and getting it is meant to feel like a triumph. Moving into their own house clusters together all his psychic changes: Harry accepts his wife, feels secure, and no longer believes his own life has to be static as a self-punishment. Finally together, they can live on their own without help. Moving, that modest domestic event, also epitomizes a host of other new circumstances: his feeling free for the first time in his life, having extra money, and dealing with his dislike of his son Nelson. Moving from 89 Joseph to 14½ Franklin Drive constitutes a midlife journey. In his mid-forties (I warned earlier about belatedness), Harry is ready to be an adult at last. Like the original Odysseus, this erstwhile wanderer can measure his midlife success by whether he can get into his own home.

Readers familiar with the nineteenth-century idea of Bildung will notice what a departure this is: Updike's sense of development doesn't involve Harry's consciously knowing anything new—unless those one-liners about his "treasure" and the "meaning of life" and life's sweetness are his wisdom.[7] The "journey" we experience with him feels motionless—the way life must feel to those unconscious of change, or resistant to the idea of progress. Yet Updike has built in those strands of potentiality. If anything, he has created a more trusting—and egalitarian—image of development than the Bildungsroman of youth provides, because his does not require a special plot of events, or (on the part of the central consciousness) a special sensibility or a particular effort to change.

Charlie Stavros, Janice's ex-lover and Harry's best friend, not Harry, thematizes the house-move as a mode of freedom, reminding him that he has "freedom you don't even use. How come you and Jan keep living in that shabby old barn with her mother?" (p. 272). Language levers him out of Ma Springer's house, through his own persuasive metaphors of dark confinement and light spaciousness, which refer, respectively, to being coffined underground or ascending freely toward the stars. The death/transcendence imagery his mind is stored with is a remnant of the Christian cosmology, with its freight of sin and its eschatological hierarchy, that had tormented him as a young man; now it gets worked out in earthly terms, on the horizontal level of real estate. (If Updike had handled this theme satirically, Harry's move would be blasphemous.) The purchase also results from his having too much money and needing someplace to put it. But this potentially satirical point also loses its edge because the house has been tied to metaphoric systems that represent his craving for freedom.

What finally ejects Harry is his need to escape from Nelson—or rather, from his reactions to Nelson. It is Nelson as a sexual being whom he resents: their open trouble began when Harry thought Nelson (at thirteen) was trying to "take" his girl, and it grew worse as Nelson expanded in assertiveness, critical power, and sexual need. By the time this rivalry is fully apparent, however, the novel is wedded to comic outcomes. Far from being satiric, this model of development coolly sees Harry's desire to move as a new, better way of handling interpersonal tensions. For him the move is an escape from the kind of anger he used

7. I believe they are intended to be wisdom, and a Blakean-Keatsian wisdom at that. The "meaning of life," according to Harry, "is not something you dig for but sits on the top of the table like an unopened dewy beer can" (p. 231). In lieu of that edgy unconvincing "quest" he was on at twenty-six, Updike has given him a sensuous experience of the world, mediated not by the language of Romantic poetry but by his own middle-American vocabulary. All our progress novelists give their favorite protagonists some updated version of Romantic access to beauty and truth.

to be helpless against. "The kid was no threat to him for now. Harry was king of the castle" (p. 456). Putting distance between father and son also protects Nelson against his own weak rage at his father, and the move protects Janice from growing old arguing with her mother. A deliberate, considerate, escape seems like a sensible solution to conflict in the middle years. It's a far cry from the unpremeditated, harmful running away that was Rabbit's young-adult mode of escape, as he scampered from woman to woman without knowing what he was looking for.

The scene where Harry and Janice tell her mother that they are moving is the midlife revision of the discomfiting, tension-denying scene at the end of *Of the Farm*, sixteen years earlier. In both narratives the middle generation refuses to live in the house the prior generation has provided: a couple is bonding together against the wish of an older woman. *Of the Farm* blurs this truth with equivocation, and yet magnifies the drama by placing the equivocation, and the scene, at the very end of the book. The old mother in *Rabbit Is Rich* is given her sorrow and her tears, where the mother in the earlier book was made to be stoic and cheerful about her deprivation. Now older, Updike admits this toughness in the situation. His male protagonist, given the last word in both versions, this time makes it a jokey but unequivocal statement of the couple's resolve to leave. To be sure, the so-called Oedipal element (which might better be referred to as the Phaedra complex) has vanished: the older woman is not the man's mother but his mother-in-law, who does not require his love for her to be his primary love. She will be lonely, but not bereft. Perhaps for related reasons, Updike can also accept the durability of the old lady—he can let her look vulnerable without needing to doom her. The mother in *Of the Farm* was "dying"; Bessie Stringer is simply old, which permits more margin of life ahead. The middle aged have learned that old age can last a long time (Updike knows this personally, since his mother, also a writer, is still alive at this writing). "Watching a parent grow is one of the most reassuring experiences anyone can have, a privilege that comes only to those whose parents live beyond their children's early adulthood," Margaret Mead has observed.[8] Watching a parent survive your departure is part of the reassurance. For Harry, Janice's mother—the sole survivor of their four parents—represents an old age he can like. Updike's newer treatment of this situation has lost nothing in emotional complexity, avoids muddle

8. Margaret Mead, *Blackberry Winter* (New York: Pocket Books, 1972), p. 45.

and duplicity, and gains a sense of openness—of people living in an un-clouded medium. The Oedipal fog has lifted; the contemporary midlife progress narrative leads us out into post-Oedipal light.

Given such intricacies, disposed at different levels of the narration, clustered around so simple a theme as "moving," we couldn't expect Harry to be the one to teach us what he has learned—except in those brief asides that don't seem to cohere—until we realize that they all hint at the edifice of midlife accomplishment put together through the life course. The idea Updike had of learning when he wrote the book—as mostly unconscious, slow, cumulative and multicausal, but fundamen-tally developmental and ultimately on the side of freedom—produces the serene, reassuring pace of this midlife Bildungsroman. In it there are no epiphanies. There are surprises but no catastrophes.

IV. Watch Harry Grow

Harry's development has taken "time"—a space called "ten years," when major life events occurred: when many died, when Nelson grew up and Harry became jealous of him, when Janice got a lot of her lessons, when Harry gave up adultery and became rich and big and calm. Ten years is intended to connote a lot of time, because change as drastic as Harry's requires, in this world view, a leap of time over the life course. Readers of *Redux* remember Harry then better than he does himself. That novel, the second in the series (Harry at thirty-six) now seems even more full of his dread and confusion than it seemed in 1971 when we had only *Rabbit, Run* to compare it to. Looking "pale and sour" to the world, Harry found the world looking more or less the same to him; there was nothing he wanted to see. "Without going much of anywhere in his life he has somehow seen everything too often."[9] Learning for him was not something that evolved from within, but such as it was battered him from without; it never quite took. Pas-sive almost to the point of moral imbecility, he was subject to outbursts of violence against the weak. The treatment suggests that Updike was then still partly complicit with his angers and fears, but conscious of this and ready to admit some of it at the time, as when he briefly said to

9. *Rabbit Redux* (New York: Knopf, 1971), p. 104.

an interviewer, "There is a lot of anger in my books, really. Their secret ingredient." [10] What makes *Redux* such an uncomfortable book to read is in part this Doppelgänger effect, as if Updike wielded Rabbit like a self-scourge. Then to compensate, Updike also gave him some of his own enthusiasms. Between author and creature, this mix of inhabitation and alienation (a combination familiar from the decline novel's earliest days, when Flaubert said, "I am Madame Bovary" and then demonstrated how much self-hatred that statement contained) does not make for kindness.

And the plot of *Redux* was not, to put it mildly, kind to Harry. More heavily plotted than the later novel, as if life were a succession of perilous surprises, *Redux* gave him a dying mother, an adulterous wife, a failing work situation, a burned-out house, a dead girl-lover, a frightened son. Life was dangerous; other people were vulnerable, "fragile and sad." Ten years have passed since the baby died, but (as is the way in decline fiction) time hasn't healed. During that time, sex with his wife "had become too dark, too *serious*—too kindred to death, to trust anything that might come out of it" (p. 36). It was still the period (which includes *Couples*), when Updike's (male) protagonists connected sex and death in rather a confused way. [11] The confusion of death with pregnancy and reproduction goes back, of course, to Genesis, as Edmund Leach has observed: "death becomes inevitable (iii, 3–8). But now for the first time pregnancy and reproduction become possible." [12] Guilt, in another confusion, was written across both of the Rabbit plots: he didn't commit the violence, but he felt as if he had. "He knows he is criminal, yet is never caught" (p. 329).

By *Rabbit Is Rich,* the old anger, fear, and guilt are gone, and as if by magic, Harry's world has lost its sinister plots: its disasters, betrayals, sequences of unmitigated loss, and violent deaths. The most striking difference for most readers may be that Harry no longer frightens himself with his sexual neediness and its consequences; indeed, he can even imagine "how men can die willingly, gladly, into eternal release from

10. "One Big Interview," in *Picked-Up Pieces*, p. 500. This part of the interview comes from 1969.

11. A number of critics have noticed connections between sex and death in Updike's novels. Joyce B. Markle argues both that "sex is an antedote [*sic*] for death," and that "sex *recalls* death." See *Fighters and Lovers: Themes in the Novels of John Updike* (New York: NYU Press, 1973), p. 116. Because Updike has gone on writing, we can see that this contradiction was a phase of confusion that can subside, if not vanish completely.

12. Edmund Leach, *Genesis as Myth and Other Essays* (London: Jonathan Cape, 1969), p. 15.

the hell of having to perform" (*Rich*, p. 91). The first Rabbit and the third bracket Updike's decades-long attempt to decide whether male sexuality does more harm or good in the world. By the end, it might have seemed a silly problem. *Couples* (1968) took an intermediate position: adultery was again punished with the death of the next generation, through abortion, but remarriage restored the torn psychic fabric and progenitive power. It was the first time Updike had imagined a happy ending, in his own terms—and he felt at doing it a joy and power similar to Drabble's with her first Bildungsroman.[13] It can't have hurt that in *Couples* and *Redux* the craving male gets the kind of sexuality he wants—"In *Rabbit, Run* what is demanded, in *Couples* is freely given,"[14] Updike observed when asked about the passive form of sex that Piet Hanema and the young Angstrom prefer. Piet Hanema, the minister in *A Month of Sundays*, and Rabbit Redux all learn in some way that women also like sex. As women are more forthcoming, a man feels less demanding and ugly. Where Rabbit at twenty-six is avid and guilty, Rabbit at forty-six could be considered by turns uninterested or timid. In the interval (by the end of *Redux*) Harry is tired of sex, as he complains to Janice (who already thinks he "hates" it). "It's what makes everything so hard to run. . . . There must be something else" (p. 398). Sexual experience as represented in the trilogy takes the form of a cure, making innocent—and thereby less important—what one analyst has called the "evil, sexual impulses which were at one time imagined as the main content of the unconscious system."[15]

As the narcissistic sexual side of Harry dwindled, Updike became kinder toward what was left of it. He was brutal to Rabbit's selfishness when he wanted to use Janice's body a few weeks after the birth of their baby to have his orgasm against: when Janice objects by asking, "Why can't you try to imagine how I *feel?*" Updike has him answer, "I can. I can but I don't want to, it's not the thing, the thing is how *I* feel."[16] In

13. "I understand that it is a romantic book, a book written by a boy who went to a lot of movies. It has a happy ending. It's about a guy meeting a girl and the guy getting the girl" (*Picked-Up Pieces*, p. 497). "*Couples* was in some ways an old-fashioned novel; I found the last thirty pages—the rounding up, the administering of fortunes—curiously satisfying, pleasant. Going from character to character, I had myself the sensation of flying, of conquering space" (Charles Thomas Samuels, "John Updike," in *Writers at Work, The* Paris Review *Interviews*, 4th ser., ed. George Plimpton [New York: Viking, 1976], p. 449). The interview was composed in 1967–68.

14. *Picked-Up Pieces*, p. 505.

15. Ian D. Suttie, *The Origins of Love and Hate* (New York: The Julian Press, [1935] 1952), p. 204.

16. *Rabbit, Run* (New York: Knopf, [1960] 1971), p. 249; emphasis in original.

Rabbit Is Rich (so full of curious parallelisms, as if Updike were using it to revise past scenes with new mercy), Harry's first orgasm in the book occurs inside his wife's sleeping body, an action treated as momentarily selfish but harmless; as she says later, she'll get her turn. Theirs is a marriage that has grown in spite of (because of?) their taking turns. In *Redux* Rabbit was nasty about Janice's sexual experience, and his sister Mim's, as if sex was still to him something people were inevitably ashamed of, so that it could be used as a weapon against them; later, he's shown to have become tolerant. When Ruth says to him, "There aren't whores any more. . . . I always felt I was very innocent, actually," Harry responds mildly, "We all are, Ruth" (*Rich,* p. 446). Janice's affair with Stavros raised her value for him—not least because it gave her the confidence in herself that he needed to mirror; and about Mim's former life as a hooker he is simply curious. By making him slightly less solipsistic sexually at forty-six (he's not mean to Thelma, as he was to Jill), Updike was able to see him as harmless, still childish, still confusing new sexual practices with adventures, but more diffident about his claims and more grateful for favors.

The rage against women that made the first Rabbit betray both his wife and his mistress has by 1981 been transformed into admiration for women—not just for Janice, but also for Melanie, Prudence, Mim, and Mrs. Springer. It's as if Updike here was for once able to reclaim what the Jungians would call his Anima, the female side of himself that in fact he had early recognized but somehow feared or despised. The pent-up minister, Thomas, identifies "the mini-skirted female who, having bitten a poisoned apple at the moment of my father's progenitive orgasm, lies suspended within me."[17] At least in *Rabbit Is Rich,* women have been defanged. They have become articulate, capable, and self-reliant— unflappable, superior women.

In the treatment of Rabbit's mentors, we can see another way in which women lost their fangs. In the first book, the mentor he initially chose was Tothero, his coach, the kind of misogynist who seems to be suppressing homosexual tendencies; in the second, it was Skeeter, the angry young black male outsider who used sexuality as a mode of revenge. In the third volume, the people he listens to most carefully are Janice and his mother-in-law and Thelma; Webb Murkett, the older man he thinks he admires, has nothing to say that's useful to him, except about money. Harry relies on women, though he doesn't know it.

17. *A Month of Sundays* (New York: Knopf, 1975), p. 11.

When he taunts Nelson, "What're you going to do when you run out of women to tell you what to do?" Nelson answers promptly, "Same thing you'll do. Drop dead" (p. 208). Nelson echoes the confidence her mother makes to Elizabeth in Anne Tyler's *The Clock Winder:* "'Don't tell your father . . . but it's a fact that from the day they're born until the day they die, men are being protected by women. Here at least. I don't know about other parts of the world. If you breathe a word of this,' she said, 'I'll deny it.'" [18]

These changes working their way made it possible to end *Redux,* despite its dreadful mid-course losses, as a sort of Bildungsroman, a comedy of "remarriage" [19] in which Janice and Rabbit come together again, in bed, not to have sex but, exhausted yet hopeful, to set the new terms. This form of reconciliation constitutes the work as a progress narrative with the modest shape of a return. At that time, it was the closest Updike could come to imagining a progress ending that he would not have to disparage. Viewed in retrospect, it now seems to point forward more positively than it did initially. "All sorts of winged presences exert themselves in the air above their covers" (p. 404); "he feels them drift along sideways deeper into being married" (p. 405): these could have been illusions of the moment, but turn out to be prophetic. The way they talk, with Rabbit trustingly asking for information and judgments and Janice supplying them, is the way Updike decided to have them relate in *Rabbit Is Rich.* And in this book ("afterwards"), Harry's sex with his wife, whatever its varying quality, has been separated from procreation, and procreation has finally been disengaged from death.

18. Anne Tyler, *The Clock Winder* (New York: Berkley Books, [1972] 1983), p. 142. In 1969, Updike was already aware of male dependence on women and had a theory about it. "Nevertheless, I suspect that the vitality of women now, the way many of us lean on them, is not an eternal phenomenon but a historical one, and fairly recent" (*Picked-Up Pieces,* p. 503).

19. *The War Between the Tates,* by Alison Lurie (1974), is an interesting example of a satiric novel that turns comic, in which the man and woman who get together at the end, to live less unhappily ever after, have been married to each other from the beginning. The novel of remarriage is rare. The earliest English one I know (it describes the problem period much more feelingly than the reconciliation) is Emily Eden's *The Semi-Attached Couple,* written around 1830, published in 1860, and recently reprinted in facsimile (New York: Dial Press, 1982).

Only novelists who believe in progress in the life course show marriage as a sequence of adjustments of this kind. Stanley Cavell reminds us that film directors who believe the same thing also produce "comedies of remarriage." See *Pursuits of Happiness: The Hollywood Comedy of Remarriage* (Cambridge, Mass.: Harvard Film Studies, 1981). *Peggy Sue Got Married* is a recent example of the genre.

V. Laius Redux

The weak, especially children, are no longer fragile and sad, frightening in their vulnerability. The critic Shaun O'Connell has pointed out in a talk given at Harvard that it is the first book of the Rabbit series in which a child-figure does not die. To be sure, a pregnant woman falls down a flight of stairs, but she doesn't lose the baby. The baby gets born, whole; the next generation is allowed to begin. The mother merely breaks her arm. There's forgiveness here toward women, children (especially female children), the men who have fathered them; and, wound into all of this, the life course.

Updike's early novels and stories describe better than anyone's how threatening children can feel to male parents. Children come between a man and his wife, capturing attention that should be his—"She loves them more than him," is the beginning of the end for the Maples in "Wife-wooing"; [20] and they threaten, by living longer than he does, to replace him. Thus, the more afraid of death he is, the greater his hostility to children. Rabbit in his twenties thinks something that would be incomprehensible to Harry in his late forties: "The fullness ends when we give Nature her ransom, when we make children for her. Then she is through with us, and we become, first inside, and then outside, junk" (p. 226). A father (in "Plumbing") moodily concludes his story of houses decaying and being repaired, and children growing, by saying, "All around us, we are outlasted." [21]

Not the Oedipal problem, but what analysts after Freud have called the Laius complex, can make early parenting horrible. "Freud's father-worship shows itself again in his overlooking the primal fact in the Oedipus legend itself, namely that the initial aggression came from Laios, the jealous father, himself." [22] In the myth, Laius plots (like so

20. "Wife-wooing," in *Too Far to Go* (New York: Fawcett Crest, 1979), p. 33.

21. "Plumbing," in *Museums and Women and Other Stories* (New York: Knopf, 1972), p. 154. Women may worry about this at a later age—when childrearing is ending—as Drabble's Kate Armstrong does in *The Middle Ground*. (But no midlife progress protagonist can believe "we become . . . junk.")

22. Suttie, *Love and Hate*, p. 224. J. C. Flügel early suggested many causes for the "Laius complex." "Thus the new position in which a father finds himself in competition with his son for the affection of his wife revives in the Unconscious a memory of the former situation in which as a child he competed with his father for the love of his mother" (p. 161). Or, "the child is identified with the parents' own parent. . . . The fact that such an individual [the father] is now possessed of superior strength and power . . . makes it tempting for him to use this opportunity for taking revenge for the real or sup-

many modern male American novelists, according to Shaun O'Connell) to put his newborn baby to death. "Are there not tendencies in our private psychologies" (Updike asked rhetorically as he was turning forty) "that would give these cosmic propositions [about evil] credence? . . . Who has seen a baby sleeping in a crib and not wanted, for an instant of wrath that rises in the throat like vomit, to puncture such innocence?"[23] Laius does not kill the baby himself (nor does the novelist, of course, who has his characters as surrogate murderers) but has it maimed and put out of his sight, out of his house and human care. The baby does not die, however: the myth implies that what young adults fear is not killing their children, but rather giving them life, because when they live (as they somehow, considering their fragility, impossibly do), they somehow endanger *us*.

In Updike's fiction, as he eventually noted, the pattern might better be called the Agamemnon complex. Killing the daughter-figures apparently came to feel like a crime to him, which had to be expiated in the only way fiction can expiate—that is, by the expansion of favorable discourse on the side of females and life. In *Rabbit Redux,* the transition novel, Janice rather magically helps her lover Stavros recover from a heart seizure by clinging lovingly to him. Updike intended that life-giving to be a compensation: "Certainly Janice bringing Stavros back to life is some kind of counterweight to the baby's death in the first book. She too had to make a passage—go through something to return."[24] But in male compensatory fictions it wouldn't be enough for women to give life; men have to change their relationship to daughters, have to

---

posed injuries he had suffered in his childhood." See his *The Psycho-analytic Study of the Family* (London: Hogarth Press, [1921] 1950) pp. 160, 162. Analysts dispute the invention of the Laius complex, one writer calling it "the Abraham complex," others considering it under the rather too limited heading of "father-son" hostility. (Flügel notes from the dreams of pregnant women that there is such a thing as mother-child hostility. The form it takes in this Updike story is a variant of father-daughter hostility.) Works on this subject are included in the excellent bibliography of Lowell Edmunds and Richard Ingber, "Psychoanalytic Writings on the Oedipus Legend: A Bibliography," *American Imago* 34, no. 4 (Winter 1977): 374–86.

The Laius complex has been stressed in ego-psychology; no doubt it will become better known as students of the midlife (and feminists) welcome it as another way of de-centering the fixation on the Oedipal complex.

Without reference to the Laius complex, Franco Ferrucci, in "The Dead Child" (paper delivered at Harvard University, March 1987), has documented the history of European writers' assaults on "children" from Goethe's *Wilhelm Meister* to Mann's *Doktor Faustus.*

23. "[Introduction to] *Soundings in Satanism,*" in *Picked-Up Pieces,* p. 89.
24. Ibid., p. 510.

want daughters. In *Rabbit Is Rich,* a daughter is actively imagined, wished into existence out of Harry's complex need for her. When her mother's all-powerful, undeniable denial removes his claim to paternity, it feels like a loss as well as what he calls it, a "relief." From the beginning, this possible daughter offers one of the forward "tilts" of suspense (Updike's coinage) that constitute plot. She's one of the few things that Harry dares to want. It may be the relationship he seeks most actively; other relationships came to him. And the main reason he gives for longing for a daughter seems to go beyond the relief of compensation for crime, indeed goes some way toward healing the split in Updike's work between man and the entire female part of creation: it images father-and-daughter genetic involvement as a transformation of the father into a woman. "Her eyes his blue: wonderful to think that he has been turned into cunt, a secret message carried by genes all that way through . . . the bloody tunnel of growing and living, of staying alive" (p. 34).

Harry's relationship with his actual son, Nelson, a fine-tuned portrayal of midlife grudgingness and teenaged resentment, parodies the Laius complex in the comic mode. The psychological situation has been brought to the surface: Harry feels "how threatened his position is, Nelson on his tail" (p. 221). "If only Nelson would get married and go away and come back rich twenty years from now" (p. 229) is Harry's detailed fantasy of the perfect solution, in which their two wills would not clash but coincide. The true Laius complex imagines the next generation's usurpation vaguely and tragically; when Nelson actually tries to muscle in on Harry's car lot and change what it sells, Harry's resistance may be petty and defensive, but it's feeble, and ultimately based on a (correct) intuition of what Nelson needs at his stage of life, which Nelson in his muddle-headed way finally realizes too.

We can be sure that Updike has himself grown out of identifying with the terrors of young adulthood because he treats Nelson (who duplicates Rabbit's problems at the same age) comically. The plot rushes Nelson into a shotgun wedding, and has him take Rabbit's old way out, by running away from the baby. Updike gives Nelson a put-upon whine, a Keystone cops' way with cars, and a far easier fate. When Nelson runs away from a pregnant woman, he doesn't run in an impossible circle but runs *home*. When he has an affair (with the pregnant woman's best friend), it's a meaningless incident for both. Melanie comes to the wedding, a piece of the *gamos*. Nelson even acts out the hostilities Rabbit kept inside—when he nudges his wife Pru down the stairs—and still little harm is done. When Nelson runs away for a second time, it's back to the college his father is paying for. The worst side effect of Nelson's Rabbity behavior is that Harry loses a chance to sleep with his fantasy. Updike refuses to make Nelson a dark figure.

Yet he sees the misery of young adults; sees that time hasn't released Nelson from the awful events of his childhood in the way that the same number of years since his daughter drowned have released Harry (Nelson clings to grief, or to a willingness to have his father grieve); and recognizes that whatever danger threatens comes from the recklessness of young adults. Harry and Janice no longer have problems with the ideas of infancy and responsibility; it's the next generation, Nelson and Pru, who have lived their way into the Laius phase, and run the risk of enacting its fatal drama. Pru wears high heels in advanced pregnancy, Nelson drives too fast and feels too trapped. Updike sees now, as he didn't years ago, that it's not the individual who makes danger, but the age—the age at which the adult decisions (marriage, work, children) get made under pressure and out of fear. And the gender—with a man (Nelson) shying away from the next stage that a woman (Pru) faces with some composure. Through Harry, who separates himself from all that, Updike distances the special psychic situation of young adults: their claustrophobia and their rush. "You want to make a mark. The world seems indestructible and won't let you out. Let 'em by" (p. 35). If Updike hadn't put the following thoughts into a more learned character's head in 1975, he could almost have given them to Harry: "Walking these streets, Ferguson saw how right Shakespeare was: life is a matter of stages. . . . These roles, thoroughly performed, need not be performed again. A paradox: though Ferguson in theory dreaded death, in practice he was glad, relieved, that he would never be asked to be young again."[25]

Updike's own development enables him to risk a new, slightly more forthright notion of desire now. All the things that Harry wants, he wants more actively. He is capable of working for something rather than letting things just happen to him. "Rabbit's feeling has been that if it doesn't happen by itself it's not worth making happen" (p. 406). Now his wants rather than his aversions, accidents, and self-punishments produce plot: encouraged by Thelma's loving advice, he goes to Ruth's farm to find out whether the girl he's been dreaming of is his daughter; feeling more able to take risks and try new experiences, he

25. "The Egg Race," in *Problems* (New York: Fawcett Crest, 1981), p. 260.

plans to use the trip to the islands as a way of getting Cindy into bed; and he makes his most passionate love to Janice when he's trying to persuade her to agree to move into their own house. He also wants Nelson to move out; and that wish too (although for Nelson's own reasons, on Nelson's initiative) comes true.

He gets half of what he wants. It's a realist percentage, in my opinion; a headier Bildungsroman would give him more than half. In true Bildungsroman fashion, however, the two wishes he doesn't get are not as important as the one wish he makes come true. (He feels some "relief" at not getting Cindy, just as he did about Ruth's daughter not being his: there are complications this simple man still can't imagine himself handling.) The midlife progress narrative gives its characters some practice in not getting everything they want, unlike the Bildungsroman of youth. Unlike the decline novel, on the other hand, it can tuck in some loss, even the death of loved ones, without losing heart.

Of course, he gets an additional possession, which doesn't feel like a burden or a complication, at the end of the novel. His grandchild has "happened by itself"—"pushed to be here, in his lap, in his hands" (p. 467)—his favorite way of having things happen, as if a higher power wanted them for him. His fatalism hasn't entirely disappeared, only taken on a rosier character. (Updike could have called the book, *Rabbit Is Lucky*.) Talking about the way endings work, Updike has written, "the *echt* ending is finer than analysis, an inner release, as Aristotle said, of tensions aroused. A narrative is like a room on whose walls a number of false doors have been painted; while within the narrative, we have many apparent choices of exit, but when the author leads us to one particular door, we know it is the right one *because it opens*." [26] When Pru hands Rabbit his granddaughter, and he accepts her with mixed ruefulness and pride—"Fortune's hostage, heart's desire, a granddaughter. His. Another nail in his coffin. His."—twenty years of narrative tensions in Updike's work dissolve. That it's a woman who gives him the gift, that the gift is female, that having a granddaughter is sexually uncomplicated in a way that no previous relationship with females has ever been—these connotations contribute to a reader's sense of having a door open here. With his acceptance of the next generation, the novel ends with its most concentrated sign yet that Harry has finally made peace with the life course.

26. John Updike, Introduction to *The Best American Short Stories, 1984* (Boston: Houghton Mifflin, 1984), xvii; emphasis in original.

VI. Personal History

Updike comes first in this book because his was the hardest case: he came most slowly to the Bildungsroman; his temperament was the one least likely to find a way of reconciling itself to aging or admitting that good could come of it. Many clustering, reinforcing tendencies from childhood and adolescence worked against his cure by heightening his sensitivity to decay. His curious "materialism," which admired the beautiful skin of the world as if mimesis could render it immortal, made him first think of himself as a painter, and as a writer led him to render imagery statically; description, as an expression of affect toward the world, is still fundamental to his style. His Lutheranism, which he quoted Tillich as "itemizing" as "a consciousness of the 'corruption' of existence, a repudiation of every kind of social Utopia (including the metaphysics of progressivism)"[27] set God over against poor mortal man with all his shame, guilt, and abasement. "Self-humiliation is one of the writer's most useful aids" (he wrote, circa 1971); "it puts him in touch with the basal humanity that dignity, honors, flattery, and prosperity would estrange him from. . . . any serious writer needs keep some access to shame and abasement."[28] Then, or perhaps first of all, he believed in the descent to him of the Freudian/family curse, "The trauma or message that I acquired in Olinger had to do with suppressed pain, with the amount of sacrifice, I suppose, that middle-class life demands, and by that I guess I mean civilized life. The father, whatever his name, is sacrificing freedom of motion, and the mother is sacrificing in a way—oh, sexual richness, I guess; they're all stuck."[29] And perhaps most basic of all was his grieved body image, which because of his skin condition, psoriasis, mirrored to him a self ruled by the impossibility of being "presentable."[30] He came to believe that the self that wants isn't nice; that's why his heroes had been so passive, because in this view good things could come only by being given—given by fate, or by women. "I think we would all like to be 'nice' but there is in us an animal or angelic some-

27. The Tillich quotation appears in *Picked-Up Pieces,* p. 123. Updike now calls himself a card-carrying Episcopalian.

28. Ibid., p. 139.

29. Ibid., p. 498.

30. "Personal History: At War With My Skin," *New Yorker,* September 2, 1985, p. 44.

thing that wants infinitely, has infinite demands in a way and isn't really nice at all."[31]

Thus for a long time he could not imagine writing fiction about "satisfied" people. Talking about the "happy ending" in which Piet Hanema gets his new wife and loses his guilt, Updike once said "he becomes insignificant. He becomes merely a name in the last paragraph: he becomes a satisfied person and in a sense dies."[32] Writing the kind of short stories he did also exacerbated his tendency (as in "Should Wizard Hit Mommy?") to wrench an ending downward, shockingly, into a degree more of cynicism or disillusion than the story necessarily prepared the reader for. His last lines even out of context often read bitterly, opening out the episodes that precede as allegories of loss. "'We'll both pay,' Joan said." is the last sentence of "Giving Blood."[33] That story was written in the early 1960s; its counterpart in *Rabbit Is Rich,* after Nelson's third auto accident, is Janice's reassuring way of concluding the discussion after Rabbit has whined, "Who do you think pays for the increase in our insurance rates?" "'We do,' she says. 'The two of us'" (p. 233).

All these beliefs and habits fed into his need to dread, and disparage, the passing of time. Temperament colors event. What would Updike's personal successes matter with powers of ruthless observation and scant expectation like these?

The Rabbit trilogy shows that none of these tendencies survived the life course in its original negative form. *Rabbit Is Rich* proves that big fiction can be made out of a relatively satisfied person (or several people)—a demonstration important for the future of midlife Bildungsroman (or the Bildungsroman of old age, for that matter). It provides a clearer demonstration than Joyce's in *Ulysses* (with which it has much in common), because Rabbit wants more, gets more, changes more, and is better satisfied than Bloom.

Updike's account comes first also because he is unique among our authors in having recently represented himself, personally, as in some ways a progress figure. His own understanding of his life's curve is that his gains were made gradually in adulthood over seventeen years, from twenty-five to forty-three, when he and his family left New

31. Robert Cromie, "Interview with John Updike," in *Bookbeat,* National Public Radio, November 1971; quoted by Albert H. Griffith, in *Modern Fiction Studies* 20, no. 1 (Spring 1974): 100 n. 9.

32. *Picked-Up Pieces,* p. 504.

33. "Giving Blood," in *The Music School* (New York: Knopf, 1966), p. 34.

York and moved to Ipswich, Massachusetts. "Ipswich is where I took possession of [my life], the place where in my own sense of myself I ceased to be a radically defective person."[34] He lost his self-contempt and its related "existential terrors." "The existential terrors . . . were eased aside by the cooperative nature, now, of growing older. . . . All misfortunes were compared, and confessed, and revealed as relative. Egotistic dread faded within the shared life."[35] His life became more precious to him when he took responsibility for it away from his rather cold-eyed God and into his own hands. Like the man in "The Egg Race," he found "all was nestled like a spoon beneath his life, his only life, his incredibly own, that he must not let drop."[36] His public version of the story links all these changes to improvements in his body image: he recovered from his severe psoriasis, and over time also lost his asthma, his stutter, his habit of choking. When the psoriasis went away, he felt as if God had forgiven. "To be forgiven, by God: this notion, so commonly mouthed in shadowy churches, was for me a tactile actuality."[37] The short story, "From the Journal of a Leper," telling a story of radical cure, breathes relief, claims a lessened interest in sex, prophesies a new, less self-conscious, "rougher" art. Updike's own difficulties in marriage, his divorce, and his remarriage go discreetly unmentioned in this version, perhaps because his relations with same-generation women (and by inevitable implication, mother-figures and daughter-figures as well) have been his more or less well-disguised subject in all his fiction. The inner curve has been described to some extent in the preceding chapter, as a story of his deconstructing through the Rabbit trilogy the confused animosities of adolescence and early manhood, and replacing the decline narrative they produced with belated, at first tentative, and then more assured progress narratives. (The real puzzle, for readers who have followed my arguments so far, might be why Updike has not been able to give this preponderance of good gifts to his better-educated midlife characters—his African revolutionary, his Jewish novelist, his professor of divinity. It's as if he thought that too many gifts ought not to coexist in the same person, or that a rise in intellectual/social class and ambition had to bring dissatisfaction in its wake.) Active desir-

34. Updike, "Personal History," p. 44.
35. Ibid., p. 48.
36. "The Egg Race," in *Problems,* p. 268.
37. Updike, "Personal History," p. 54.

ing more successful than Harry still scares him a little. In *S.* (1988), he shades it toward acquisitiveness and gives it to a woman. Whatever account we want to give of his other fictions, whatever happens in his own life, and whatever he produces in the future, the trilogy of novels that wound up telling about Harry's life-cure is our permanent possession.[38]

38. One particularly negative assessment of Updike's oeuvre by Frederick Crews, specifying his weaknesses as a writer and a person, omits *Rabbit Is Rich* entirely and ignores the trilogy. See "Mr. Updike's Planet," *New York Review of Books* 33, no. 19 (December 4, 1986): 7–12.

4

Ugly Ducklings and Swans: Margaret Drabble's Fable of Progress

I. The Fable

Margaret Drabble's favorite story has always been the myth of the ugly duckling who becomes a swan. Rising motion (as of birds, angels, and heroines of Bildungsromane) could be the emblem of her fiction. I am not talking about upward mobility—although she is certainly the teller of that good story too—but of an ascension more psychological and spiritual. In *Jerusalem the Golden* (1967), Clara Maugham discovers herself in flight, with solitary guilt and elation. In a tangled image that combines Calvinist uniqueness and urban congestion, Clara discovers that she flies:

It occurred to her to wonder why she should so suddenly feel herself to be peculiarly blessed, and a dreadful grief for all those without blessings took hold of her, and a terror at the singular nature of her escape. Out of so many thousands, one. Narrow was the gate, and the hillsides were crowded with the serried dwellings of the cramped and groaning multitudes, the ranks of the unelect, and she the one white soul flew dangerously forth into some glorious and exclusive shining heaven.[1]

1. *Jerusalem the Golden* (London: Weidenfeld and Nicolson, 1967), p. 67. The first bird image I have found occurs in *The Garrick Year* (London: Weidenfeld and Nicolson, 1964), pp. 117–18, when, after Emma has triumphantly accepted a daring dinner invitation, she discovers that her self had been "curled up and rotten with grief and patience

At the end of *The Middle Ground* (1980), Kate Armstrong is also shown in upward movement, but now—thirteen years later—the movement is guiltless and assured. She is elated but no longer awed, possessing a staccato energy that shows she is ready for anything. "Ripeness is all," as another late bloomer remarked. Kate's language is more brusque and abstract than Clara's—indeed, it is barely metaphorical—and is grounded in solid, busy domestic reality ("her house") to which she returns, rather than in rhetorical multitudes of the "unelect," from whom Clara escapes.

Anything is possible, it is all undecided. Everything or nothing. It is all in the future. Excitement fills her, excitement, joy, anticipation, apprehension. Something will happen. The water glints in the distance. It is unplanned, unpredicted. Nothing binds her, nothing holds her. It is the unknown, and there is no way of stopping it. It waits, unseen, and she will meet it, it will meet her. There is no way of knowing what it will be. It does not know itself. But it will come into being. . . . She hears her house living. She rises.[2]

Change is dangerous for Clara—"I risk condemning all that I have been," as Jane Gray says in *The Waterfall*[3]—but Kate needs no rhetoric of effortful alteration or risk. Like Viola in *Twelfth Night,* she could say,

> O Time, thou must untangle this, not I;
> It is too hard a knot for me t' untie.
> —*Twelfth Night* II.ii

Where Clara assumed the future would be "heaven," Kate knows it is unknown but looks trustingly forward anyway. For Clara her "exclusive" rise hurts the unelect, who would by implication try to prevent it; but nothing holds Kate back: anyone, by implication, can feel the way she feels. The direction is the same for both: up and on.

It is no surprise, but it is surely fortunate for Drabble, that the motion of the myth is also part of her dreams.

My favorite dreams are where I'm traveling through landscapes very rapidly, but by no known means of transport, not flying but going through it. I dream a

---

and pain. I walked quicker and quicker as myself stretched and put out damp bony wings." Fittingly for this point in her career, it's an image of a bird in the stage of preparing for flight.

2. *The Middle Ground* (New York: Knopf, 1980), p. 277.
3. *The Waterfall* (London: Weidenfeld and Nicolson, 1969), p. 56.

lot about . . . all sorts of beautiful landscapes. Those are my favorite dreams because they're spectacularly beautiful. And I'm quite conscious of the fact that I'm dreaming, and I try to prolong it. And there's a very strange moment . . . almost as though I turn to the next shot and make it happen, and there's a tremendous exhilaration as things get extremely beautiful.[4]

Drabble has often said that she is a lucky woman. Her powerful belief in private and continuous transformation has clearly been the secret of her psychological growth through young womanhood and the middle years, and of her ability to change as a writer. As her language about her dreams suggests, her creativity is intimately connected with her love of beautiful transfigurations. "I turn to the next shot and make it happen, and there's a tremendous exhilaration as things get extremely beautiful." The fable gave her an inner story to believe in, a way of reading her outer life, and the power to tell it all. The deep structure of the fable has engendered plots, her protagonists' character traits, and her philosophy of time.

Of course, the Bildungsroman was and is her literary form. Of our four novelists, she is the only one who has *never* written a decline narrative; her endings always pose the main characters overcoming adverse circumstances and/or adverse conditioning.[5] Her first novel, *A Summer Bird-Cage* (1963), was a typical Bildungsroman of youth, *Northanger Abbey* transported from swinging Regency Brighton to trendy London. From the beginning she had an instinct for what would help her. At twenty-one, even before she started writing, she was lucky enough to come upon and to love a midlife Bildungsroman about "the evolutionary destiny of man" (her own words): it was *Henderson the Rain King*.[6] She memorized its passages about the imagination being a force of nature, and about "surprising" life by breaking out of predetermined forms (the passage is quoted in Chapter Six).

The darker elements in her personal fable she has hinted at: the silences and submissions of childhood, her mother's depressions, resentment at the low level of cultural possibilities and expectations for women,

4. Dee Preussner, "Talking with Margaret Drabble," *Modern Fiction Studies* 25, no. 4 (Winter 1979–80):573.

5. On her endings, described as anticataclysmic, continuous, and survival oriented, Lorna Irvine makes some good points. See "No Sense of an Ending: Drabble's Continuous Fictions," in *Critical Essays on Margaret Drabble*, ed. Ellen Cronan Rose (Boston: G. K. Hall, 1985), pp. 73–85.

6. Margaret Drabble, "A Myth to Stump the Experts," *New Statesman*, March 26, 1971, p. 435.

a prolonged period of extrication from her first marriage, and the par-lous condition of contemporary Britain. Even her first novel, rather brittle and clever, could scarcely be called blithe. Her "determinism" was for a long time the doubt (also built into the myth) that ducks can truly change into swans. Even when they change appearance, the doubt for a long time remained: how much can they change, how perma-nently? And there were other doubts: does everyone change? Like our other novelists but perhaps more steadily, she has pictured the fate of those who do not (most recently, Liz Headleand's reclusive mother in *The Radiant Way,* 1987) and their effect on those who do.

The passing of time has not altered the structure of the fable—its necessary progress from a lesser to a better state. Only, as Drabble got older, the dangerous-age story of the self-describedly ugly duckling slowly emerging as a swan developed into her midlife story, in which the swan, knowing herself from the beginning to be a reasonably well situated midlife bird, still needs to move on. She has been extremely generous in giving gifts to some of her midlife protagonists (when she got a heroine to Africa, in *The Realms of Gold,* Frances had far more of a success there than Henderson did). Drabble's continuous urge to write about development, which the present chapter describes, has given her life-course fiction its shape and emotional resonances, and its place in this book. It has also given her an interesting problem, special to her alone: once the midlife has provided or revealed its great gains, how is one to continue constructing progress narratives?

II. The Practice of Transformation

The myth of "transformation" has many moments. The first moment, inevitably, is what it feels like to be an ugly duckling. Drabble readers are familiar with the almost obligatory crummy child-hood: the embarrassing parents, the awful neighborhood, the cruel peers, the unappreciated talents of the child. Although Rose Vassiliou, the heroine of *The Needle's Eye* (1972), is rich, her childhood too is sad. Clara, Kate, Rose, and Liz all look back on a terrible past, a past that should have prevented them from becoming beautiful and flying away.

The point of this past, of course, is precisely that they look back on it. Early Bildungsroman figures like Pip and Jane Eyre we see first as miserable children. We never see Clara or Kate or Rose or Liz as miserable children: we only see them thinking about how they once were. As adults, therefore, they gain—in their own minds—not by contrasting themselves with others but by contrasting their present with their past (childhood and young-adult) selves. They linger in exposition over the evils of the past, relishing the safety that comes of no longer being young.

This comparative safety once made possible Drabble's debates about determinism. How far Clara has escaped is the true subject of *Jerusalem the Golden*. The events of the story—a lonely girl's discovery of a whole admirable, worldly, welcoming family; her amazing capture of a kind, dreamy married man—are the felicities Clara is heaped with, only to bring out the more her astonishment and insecurity: "even after years of comparative security she was still prepared for, still half expecting the old gibes to be revived" (p. 7). Her apprehensive situation appears on the first page. Even after swans become graceful, they tend to go on believing they are ugly. Clara goes on believing that she will "never" recover from "the weight of those empty, rolling, joyless years, years without hope and without pleasure" (p. 188). The word *never* is the sign of her obstinate, irrelevant determinism. "She had no confidence that time would bring with it inevitable growth: she grew by will and by strain" (p. 29). To believe this, she has to ignore a lot of evidence, since, Drabble notes, "time had converted liabilities other than her name into assets, and things surely more integral to the nature of her progress" (p. 8).

In fact, Clara is rolling along away from her disabilities all the time, in a travel metaphor that is remarkably persistent and explicit: "she was aware that she had as yet much ground to cover, and that she had followed many a false trail" (p. 97). When Clara says to her friend, Clelia, "You think I'll go back," Clelia answers in Drabble's own high rhetoric, "You can't hold [*sic*] back. . . . Knowledge cannot be forgotten, no will power can forget knowledge" (p. 140). An implicit sign of Clara's continuous motion is that she is sometimes exhausted, "as though she had walked for too long" (p. 117).

By the end of the book she bears all the Bildungsroman signs of youthful success. This is the third and final moment of the myth, what it feels like to be a swan. She has taken literal voyages—to London and beyond, to Paris—these destinations symbolizing to Drabble (much more unambivalently than to early *Bildungsromanciers* like Dickens and Balzac) a rich, playful, interesting, and more freely chosen life. Clara has lost her early solemn anxiousness about her future: "some marvellous indestructible frivolity stirred in her again" (p. 221). *Now* what is "indestructible" and permanent in Clara is seen as "marvellous," not crippling. She loses her fear of error, her fear of effort. She begins to have enough confidence in the future to give advice to others; and when she does, she gives the advice that a comic writer gives all of us: "You have but to wait."[7]

If we define comedy now as a story of coming to rely on time, in Viola's confident words, then we have to say, after a list like this of Clara's successes, that Drabble's structure is already comic.[8] By the middle of the novel, she puts in Clara's mouth a meditation on time that in its crooning, elegiac excess suggests an experience she deeply identified with.

The childhood objects were not only lovely in themselves, they were a link with some past and pleasantly remembered time, a time not violently shrugged off and rejected, but a time to be lived with, in happy recollection, a time which could well bear remembering. (pp. 101–2)

The word *time,* repeated four times, each time becomes more coated with love. A sentence like this represents the slow progress, in Clara's mind, from rejecting "time" because it had meant her bleak past, to embracing "time" because it has now come to mean the happy present and the promising future. It also represents her desire to revise her own past so that it too can "bear remembering."

Thus we are not surprised when Clara eventually begins to reconcile herself to her past—a project that Kate Armstrong and Liz Headland are still involved in, although with less "violence" to overcome. Returning to her parents' house and looking over the ugly objects she has loathed, Clara learns that she has already escaped them completely and that her fear that she would not escape was an "immense folly."

It frightened her to think how much violence she had wasted upon such harmless things. What chance had there ever been, ever, that she would have been condemned to them for life? What immense folly had ever made her fear such a fate? (pp. 211–12)

Drabble gives her duckling one more boost up the ladder of mature being: she allows her a sympathetic identification with her awful mother.

---

7. Clara is talking to a man her own age who complains of his dull job: "but then, she gently reassured him, he had but to wait" (p. 196).

8. Lee R. Edwards has written on this novel as a "new [female] comic form" (p. 334) in "*Jerusalem the Golden:* A Fable for Our Times," *Women's Studies* 6 (1979): 321–34.

Looking at photos of her mother in an old album, Clara sees that she too was once a hopeful woman, craving intimacy, very much like Clara herself. As a girl, Clara had "recoiled" (p. 62) from knowing how her parents had evolved to be what they were. It is a piece of lucky timing that she finds the album after she has recognized her escape, and not sooner, before she possessed Gabriel and the other Denhams—just as it's lucky timing that Liz Headland's discoveries about her father come after she has recovered from her divorce, and not sooner. Drabble gives them sequences that make cure possible. (All of this—including Drabble's unstated beliefs about normal psychological development—records, with great complexity, the second moment of the myth: how the transformation is effected.)

"Luck" of this kind is compounded of particular qualities and social conditions: in Clara's case, intelligence, intense volition, free higher education, the discovery of a surrogate family, the capture of an ideal man, and of course her new trust in the future. "And Clara . . . wondered whether she should fall on her knees and thank Battersby Grammar School and the Welfare State and Gabriel Denham and the course of time, or whether she should reserve her gratitude until more safe and later days" (p. 214). But despite being overdetermined here, luck is really Drabble's norm. When Clara, crying over her mother's disappointments, declares, "It was possible, then, to go disastrously astray; tragedy was possible, survival was no certainty, there was no reason why anyone should escape" (p. 214), we do not take the possibility of "tragedy" as a truth higher than Clara's comic pattern, or as a premonition of her future. She believes now that the future holds safer days. Tragedy has become remote, someone else's experience which may touch us but cannot deny our own course.

Despite Drabble's relative maturity and her belief in maturation (more astonishing in 1967, when "Trust no one over thirty" was becoming a prominent slogan), she was young, and she still partly believed that a childhood like Clara's (that is to say, one remembered as miserable) had to be somehow crippling. So there are odd sentences in the book that are rigidly deterministic: Drabble says omnisciently that Clara's parents' isolation "was so deeply bred in her that all aberrations from it were for the rest of her life to seem to her perverse" (pp. 61–62). Only a young and rather melancholy person could write the adverbial phrase of that sentence: midlife teaches all but the most pessimistic that *nothing* lasts "for the rest of [one's] life."

Like Clara, Drabble suspected that "progress" inevitably harmed others. She made Clara ambitious because she believed then that success was somehow tied to struggling and straining away from the ugly youthful state. And ambition was punished in her mind by coldness, so she has Clara say that she is "too full of will to love" (p. 181), and she shows that Clara is mean to her mother when her mother is dying because she does not know the gestures of filial love. Even five years after the publication of the novel, Drabble seemed to think that Clara had a hard, "fearsome" character.[9] She did not remember that elements in Clara's character contradicted this: her ability to *give* a kiss, at last; her sensitivity to kindness; her impressionable youth, which admires and could eventually imitate the Denhams' family love. Later, she showed an even more ambitious and assertive woman—Frances Wingate in *The Realms of Gold*—accepting offered love. It had not occurred to her yet that a Clara Maugham might—fifteen years older, with a Gabriel Denham and a poor first marriage behind her—turn out to be a Frances Wingate. Liz Headleand has a past much like Clara's, but her mother didn't "conveniently" die. She's more unforgiving than Clara, persistently refusing to visit her aging mother, leaving the burden of care to her more docile sister. But her behavior is supposed to be a matter of choice; she has enough warmth to have "saved" one stepchild and kept the love of the rest after her divorce. She's tough, but not uniformly tough. Aging— Drabble's own life course and what she learned about swans by writing novels—diminished her determinism and gave her more complex ideas of what her heroines could survive and become.

III. Beyond the Deterministic Moment

Clara in *Jerusalem* is only twenty-three, actually five years younger than her author (born in 1939). Since then, with the married and postmarried ones, Drabble has given them less difference in age. Jane Gray in *The Waterfall* (1969) is twenty-eight; Rose Vassiliou in *The Needle's Eye* (1972) is in her early thirties; Frances Wingate in *The Realms of Gold* goes from her mid-thirties to forty; Anthony Keating in *The Ice Age* (1977) is thirty-eight; Kate Armstrong is in her early forties; Liz Headleand by the end nearly fifty. Separately and together they provide a remarkable opportunity to study Drabble's idea of progress as

9. Nancy S. Hardin, "An Interview with Margaret Drabble," *Contemporary Literature* 14, no. 3 (Summer 1973): 278.

it confronts adulthood and the middle years. Starting out with the protagonist of *The Waterfall,* she tried out her fable of hope on "older"
characters who feel somehow trapped. What she saw as the unhappy
side of young adulthood—the marital complication—was the hard test
for her fable. The miseries of childhood, for which others were to
blame, she saw in comic fashion as inevitably receding; but the marital
misery, self-created, she saw (particularly in *The Needle's Eye*) as going
on a long time, blurring into forever. Her older dangerous-age characters, like Jane Gray and Simon Camish, feel it's their nature to accept
unhappiness, they've lived so long with it. Drabble struggled hardest
against their determinism and her own in her two relatively dark books,
The Waterfall and *The Needle's Eye,* in which Jane and Simon seem to
answer her question ("Can ugly *ducks* turn into swans?") by default.[10]
But Drabble stacks the deck by giving these passive people a tiny will-
to-happiness, and the plot breaches the impasse of their lives by intro-
ducing them to their savior figures: for Jane, James; for Simon, Rose;
for Rose, Simon. (As in *Rabbit Is Rich* and *The Accidental Tourist,* a new
character embodies a protagonist's new desire.) No one but Tyler in
that novel has used mentors, or lovers, as positively and catalytically as
Drabble did in this stage.

The fable of transformation glimmers in the dark novels—and not to
make the darkness seem darker, but to suggest future light. At a sad
time in Rose Vassiliou's childhood, a practically unknown child who
turns out to be her lifetime friend asserts the power of aging.

"Shall I tell you something? It doesn't go on getting worse for ever, there comes
a point when it gets better and better. What about that? Eh? . . . I know," said
Emily, "because I've made my mind up. I'm not going to put up with it. You
wait and see. And you won't put up with it either."[11]

Even Simon Camish, "a habitually hopeless person" (p. 176), discovers,
"like the weak light of dawn," a "vision of felicity" when he thinks of
Rose (p. 175). His hopelessness is shown as a bad habit. Although it
has been fixed longer in him than in Clara Maugham, it weakens as he

10. See also Marion Vlastos Libby, "Fate and Feminism in the Novels of Margaret
Drabble," *Contemporary Literature* 16, no. 2 (Spring 1975): 175–92. Pamela S. Brom-
berg's essay, "The Development of Narrative Techniques in Margaret Drabble's Novels,"
Journal of Narrative Technique 16, no. 3 (Fall 1986): 179–91, is excellent on the way
Drabble simultaneously breaks from determinism and from older narrative patterns in
The Waterfall.
11. *The Needle's Eye* (New York: Knopf, 1972), p. 222.

becomes habituated instead to the mild, innocent pleasures of Rose's life. Another sign that his life improves is that he can admire physical aging: "Emily had grown so beautiful with the years that it was now almost unbearable, one could hardly bear to gaze at her, so moving were the marks of time and beauty" (p. 360). Drabble's rhetoric—the severe enthusiasm of run-on sentences—transfigures weary eyes, wrinkles, discolorations. (The "moving," time-touched Emily, older readers may note, can scarcely be more than thirty-five.)

Even the *idea* of joy or relief may carry one through. Drabble's idealism grew to the point where Frances Wingate finds a city because she has imagined it. Rose's imagination is more vague, but still a guide. Early on she thinks that "if one has an image, however dim and romantic, of a journey's end, one may, in the end, surely reach it, after no matter how many detours and deceptions and abandonings of hope" (p. 51); and we remember this quiet assertion at the end when Rose lets her husband come back, very wrongly, and thinks she has "sold . . . her own soul" (p. 365). The novel has taught us that for people with these innate qualities, misery cannot be permanent.

As Drabble has become a more secure and more philosophical novelist, she has paid more attention to the other possibility, innate unhappiness. She usually gives the decline mentality to young people who succumb to self-destruction. As early as *The Garrick Year* she gave suicide to a boy—who couldn't have killed himself, Emma implies, if he had had children. Stephen Ollerenshaw in *The Realms of Gold* has just had a child, and murders both her and himself. As he knows, his way of being is the opposite of the life-loving heroine's. He reads Freud—the wrong Freud.[12] Where she saves herself by action, he is afraid even to move parts of his body. He has the real fear of time, that only danger is ahead. In explanation of these signs, Drabble makes him male, trying to

12. "His last conversation with Frances, the epitome of innate vitality and resilience, concerns Freud's *Beyond the Pleasure Principle,* with its assertion that 'all living things strove for death.'" See John Updike, "Drabbling in the Mud," in *Hugging the Shore* (New York: Vintage, 1983), pp. 362–63. At some point in their careers, Bellow, Updike, and Drabble cast Freud as the patron of hopelessness, the Antithesis of Bildung who needed to be fought.

Drabble's use of allusion supports the idea that she became quite detached from determinism and the tradition of fiction that embodied it. As John Hannay comments: Kate, in *The Middle Ground,* "chooses the intertext of a hostile and inhuman fate, a Hardy-like fate, to express her sorrow and self-doubt. . . . The recognition helps her to be her more optimistic self, but that self was what helped her to manipulate the intertext in that way." See John Hannay, *The Intertextuality of Fate: A Study of Margaret Drabble* (Columbia: University of Missouri Press, 1986), p. 110.

be mother as well as father to his child. But most of all she makes him *young*. What Frances knows about making her life interesting to herself, about discovering the excitement of fecund life in ditches, he has not learned yet. He dies before survival into the middle years convinces him of his own resilience and the resilience of babies.

With the rare same-age figure who declines from an earlier capacity for survival, Drabble's touch is less sure. She turns away from Alison Murray, who has committed perhaps the one irredeemable crime in the Drabble canon—the maternal crime of giving her life to one daughter, the retarded Molly, and denying her other, savable daughter, Jane—and who, as a result, concocts an odd notion of nonsequential time. To Drabble, Alison's future is "beyond imagining."[13] This is not rhetoric, but a true blinking of her imagination away from a situation she had decided to present as static. The static is precisely what the myth cannot handle.

Believing in determinism—which Drabble came to connect with "weakness"[14]—in the long run is for her major midlife creations a sad moment in their lives, or at worst a side of their temperaments to be reckoned with and managed; but it is not a controlling truth of their being. In the terms of the fable, determinism is seen as part of the early, duckling moment. This is why Drabble tends to begin her novels with her protagonists at their lowest point, while she suspensefully casts doubt upon how long the lowness will last. Frances Wingate, Anthony Keating, and Kate Armstrong are depicted initially with signs of weakness, prognostications of decline. Frances is drinking and weeping alone in a hotel room and talking about things "going from bad to worse";[15] Anthony has had a premature heart attack, and the first object he sees in the book is a bird falling, dead in the air of a heart attack. Kate's signs are much more ambiguous, but she is apparently moving backward into believing that her former sense of freedom is the illusion. Liz Headland starts off fearful about the consequences of being divorced by her husband of twenty-one years.

The Ice Age, Drabble's most somber midlife book, contains more blows of fate and more exhausting choices or exhausting adjustments

13. *The Ice Age* (New York: Knopf, 1977), p. 295.
14. In 1972 she said of her protagonists that "they've alternated between strong and weak characters fairly consistently" (Hardin, "Interview," p. 294). She called Jane Gray, self-proclaimedly passive, "feeble." The metaphor of alternation is a way of asserting that she has been "consistently" free to decide which type would come next.
15. *The Realms of Gold* (New York: Knopf, 1975), p. 4.

than any of her other novels. It is the apparent exception that demonstrates just how firmly the fable can carry her over bad times in English
social and economic history (and perhaps in her own life). Again, she
gives more signs of failure to a male figure. The story Anthony Keating
creates about the shape of his life is a story of decline; it is deterministic
because the series of failures derives, he feels, from an early failure in
relation to his father; and it bores him to tell it: "his whole career had
consisted of careless gambles and apostasies, most of them springing,
no doubt, from the first—from the denial of his father and all his father
had expected of him. The usual story" (p. 14). Whenever the idea of
change has occurred to him, he has apparently repeated, to his detri-
ment, the saddest, most imprisoning formula connected with the middle
years: "it was too late. . . . It had always been too late" (p. 21). At first
sight, then, Keating has elements of Lambert Strether in James's *The
Ambassadors,* of Prufrock, of the Dubliners—all arising out of the literature of midlife decline, low-energy division.

In a decline novel Keating's heart attack might mean "middle age"
(the final downturn of one's luck), being linked as it is now semiologi-
cally to physiology (helpless genetic coding), and irreversible male ambition and stress. And Drabble darkens it in her own way by linking it
with boredom and by making Anthony a man who "preferred the action of death to the passivity of boredom" (p. 36). Like Bellow, she has
become an expert on midlife boredom; she can make boredom interesting. And this is another typical way for the midlife Bildungsroman to
part company with the novel of failure. Decline fiction conveys the ennui of static malaise or decline in desiccated sentences. *Something Happened* by Joseph Heller is so complete an example that it must have exhausted the vein of monotony. For the Bildungsromancier, boredom is
worth a good paragraph or so; it is another topic, not a shared condition. Indeed, the liveliness of Keating's meditations about his decline
should tip readers off that he is not going to be a despondent of the
Malcolm Lowry or Jean Rhys kind. Boredom is *placed* as a moment the
way, for Frances Wingate, her mental suffering is placed as a moment.
She knows in advance that it is episodic; she knows her own process.
"And yet . . . it doesn't matter, it doesn't matter, it will pass," she warns
herself beforehand, and by the end of the same paragraph she says
bravely, "It wasn't so bad, really, after all. More of a nuisance, really"
(*The Realms of Gold,* p. 8). She takes it well, as a person with experience
of her own nature, competent and unsurprised.

Like *The Realms of Gold*—like *Rabbit Is Rich,* for that matter—*The*

Ice Age shows, briskly enough, how misleading first impressions are. (Indeed, one major accomplishment of the midlife Bildungsroman from *Middlemarch* on is to show how misleading early patterns are, whether they are the patterns set early in novels or, by implication, those apparently fixed at any age, in life.) Not even a heart attack closes off the future.

What Drabble does with a long midlife experience of repetition and ennui, like Keating's, is to present it as a powerful impetus for change. She recognizes the power of inertia, as she shows in Jane Gray, but (like Saul Bellow) she believes in the power of reaction more. People tire even of what they have worked hard to achieve. In *The Needle's Eye* Simon Camish, who feels so fixed, can see a "natural progression, an inevitable progression" (pp. 45–46) of this kind. For people who, like Simon, have wished to avoid physical intimacy, and have succeeded in reaching "this clear, empty space," the next step would be to "wish once more to find touching, . . . intimacy and contact" (p. 46). Because Simon had "intimacy and contact" in his childhood, it might be more logical to call his motion a "reversion" rather than a "progression," but Drabble's fable reaches deep into her value system and diction. For her, it is not *in nature* for feelings to stay the same (the static is ontologically impossible); and a new wish implies the possibility of its fulfillment. Getting what you want may be the best assurance that you are ready to move on to another, better goal. Keating moves on to noble action, noble resignation. When he is imprisoned in an Iron Curtain country, he finds he can do without all the modern appurtenances he has lost. "I think, thought Anthony, I think I can really do without all this. I think I can manage on my own" (p. 216). He is not especially proud of this attitude, because he thinks of it not as an acquisition, but as an innate piece of him. "He knew that he had no reason, other than a congenital personal optimism, as arbitrary as [another person's] spleen, for his posture of faith" (pp. 221–22). Despite her story of transformation, Drabble still cannot entirely relinquish the language of essentialism. She will not explicitly declare that optimism, although it is a great gift, can also be *learned*.

Trust the tale. In *The Realms of Gold* the story of Janet Bird tells us, very briefly, that it *can* be learned—via mentorship, fun, and patience. Janet is Frances Wingate's cousin, the young foil whom Frances meets for the first time when their elderly aunt dies of starvation in her solitary cottage. Janet is the one shut up with a baby all day, with no faculty for enjoying domesticity, and an edgy, snobbish, belittling husband. Her dull predicament is familiar to many as "housewives' disease"; we recognize it as a female version of the dangerous age, viewed from beyond. Trapped by motherhood, Janet starts off by believing that "it would take a cataclysm to release her, and a cataclysm, even via the gas main, was not likely to come her way" (*The Realms of Gold*, p. 129). But despite this exaggerated sense of her own debility, which draws her toward disasters as a mode of change, she has her tiny powers, her real joys (her baby, the beauty of nature). Frances briefly regards her with aversion, but that quickly turns to sympathy: she recognizes the stage, and unable to take it *en tragique*, responds by inviting her cousin out for the evening. Eventually, they come to know each other well. And by the end of the novel Janet too has learned to think of time as a process that can, without cataclysm, bring about change. Disregarding Frances's talents and fame (and ignorant of her erstwhile depressiveness), Janet focuses on the lessons of her life course.

Gradually, Janet came to believe that instead of confronting a life of boredom, she was merely biding her time. There was Frances at forty, as lively as anything . . . so how could her own life be over, when she wasn't even thirty? Even if the gas mains didn't blow up under Aragon Court, something else might happen, after all. (p. 353)

However vague and undifferentiated, Janet too is a Bird who will fly.

IV. Swans

The Realms of Gold, The Middle Ground, and *The Radiant Way* (so far) constitute a three-part series about the middle years of women. In them Drabble's heroines increasingly *begin* as swans. Each one can say of herself what Kate Armstrong says, "In those days she took this weakness for granted, but now . . ." (*The Middle Ground,* p. 20). This is the duckling-to-swan retrospection encompassed in a single sentence: "In *those* days . . . but *now*. . . ." These women possess characteristics that her earlier heroines envied. They have become what Clara Maugham wanted to be: "intense, smart, well-connected, impulsive, communicative, insatiably interested in the affairs of others" (*Jerusalem the Golden,* p. 104). Now *they* are the admired ones. On the public, social side, their lives have ease: being perturbed in a social situation is rare for them, a sign now of special emotion. Other people find them charming, and they know it. They take attention gracefully: "for many things that Kate did were little performances, requiring applause, enquiry or comment" (*The Middle Ground*, p. 3). They take the envy of others gracefully. They talk, unlike the earliest figures. Drabble says humorously of Peter Harronson and Clara that "they would both have liked to continue talking, but they could think of nothing to say. They were too young" (*Jerusalem the Golden*, p. 92). In midlife, moreover, the heroines have qualities her young women did not have sense enough to envy. Their conversation, for example, has progressed beyond cleverness. They can risk banality (as Drabble does too) to represent sincerity. Their domestic disorder and unconcern about clothing represent eclecticism, diversity, comfort, a rich life—as these things do for some of Anne Tyler's heroines too. The most recent disregard makeup—they're all Emilies. Partly because of their gregariousness, partly because of the thickening of life around them (professional acquaintances, friends, children, the friends' children), they no longer need to fear solitude.

With age, her protagonists have become kinder to themselves. They no longer see themselves as "dangerous" women, in whom sexuality is likely to go out of control. Far from it. Having gained freedom to choose their love objects in a modern, male way, they eschew the next male step, promiscuity. Discovering their own sexuality (as opposed to culture's female body) ranks as one of the best self-taught lessons in their adult educations. Liz Headleand takes full advantage of the new adult/divorced/female options. "Since she had given up sex and contraception, her bodily existence had been of an exemplary calm and regularity. . . . Odd to think of, almost impossible to remember, the tormenting anxieties of those earlier decades. Tempestuous times. So much anxiety, about one's reproductive system." [16]

Always quick at self-judgment, Drabble's heroines have moved, over time, from self-deprecation to self-appreciation. Emma Evans in *The Garrick Year* asserts, mistakenly, "My tastes are shallow, my life is shallow" (p. 90) before she knows herself to be a dedicated mother and a loving pro-tem wife. Frances Wingate, on the other hand, listening to herself be introduced before a lecture, "sat there neatly, happily, listening to the long list of her achievements. . . . I did all that, she thought to herself. . . . I am a vain, self-satisfied woman, she said to herself, with

16. *The Radiant Way* (London: Weidenfeld and Nicolson, 1987), p. 258.

satisfaction" (p. 24). To be sure, Drabble has given them impressive achievements; but the most impressive may be that they are shown to be free of irrational anxiety. Like some of their midlife peers—Harry, Charlie Citrine—they even *worry* calmly. Their security may make dull material, but for Drabble it is one accomplishment of the middle years.[17]

More important than their objective successes, but no doubt intimately related to them, is the fact that the older heroines have tremendous personal power and know it. Emma Evans has to wait until the end of the book before she recognizes that she has a strong life force.

During those weeks in bed . . . I became increasingly aware of my own strength and of what a mistake I had made in trying to relapse into self-pity. . . . The truth was that I could survive anything, that I was made of cast iron, and that I would have to spend my life not in protecting myself but in protecting others from myself. . . . I was never going to have a nervous breakdown: the most they could do to me would be to squash me up against a wall with a big car. (*The Garrick Year*, p. 220)

Frances Wingate *begins* knowing this: not that she can possibly resist big cars, but that she is a positive force, like a tornado.

She had occasionally felt . . . that herself, suddenly put down in transit, was so powerful that it might burst through the frail partition walls and send all the things swirling. Towels, fittings, coathangers, things like that. (*The Realms of Gold*, p. 3)

Frances is given the most comprehensive success of all. She does much more than survive: she thrives. She is given a permanent reunion with her lover, Karel, proper taxing of her energies in work and family, and even a vision of God's plan: "God had done it all for fun, for joy, for excitement in creation, for variety, for delight. Why seek to justify? There it all was" (p. 103). This is really her own attitude to life, projected onto God. Death, which had not until now been one of the tribulations to be overcome, cannot modify this optimism much. She manages to take suicide and infanticide in stride, too. "In the end, Frances got over it. One gets used to anything" (p. 348). Drabble's tone is often

17. Elizabeth Fox-Genovese doesn't see such characteristics as achievements, and takes a much harder line than I do: for example, Drabble "superficially acknowledges difficulty and struggle . . . but refuses the reality of female, and indeed human, life." See "The Ambiguities of Female Identity: A Reading of the Novels of Margaret Drabble," *Partisan Review* 46, no. 2 (1979): 247.

matter-of-fact; astonishment at the healing power of time is many years behind her.

In the last four novels, we begin to feel, Drabble has been giving her characters deprivations and troubles, not to investigate determinism or fate, but to show how they will survive, to show off their flexibility. Given the kind of inner strength that her heroines (and the odd hero, Keating) possess, the events that will test their mettle usually come from outside them, like the deaths of Frances's aunt and nephew. In *The Ice Age*, Max Friedmann is killed by a bomb, and his wife Kitty loses her foot at the same time. Kate is forced to have an abortion because the infant would be born with spina bifida. The deformity and Keating's heart attack only prove this rule, since the body is as much outside the control of the self as the IRA and violent Rastafarians. In *The Radiant Way*, Liz's father turns out to have been a pedophile and a suicide. All these events are incursions from without, and those who suffer them are innocent of blame: "subject to the blows of circumstance" (*The Ice Age*, p. 247), they can only react, and they continue to do that well. They are all adaptable people. Briefly, it occurs to Drabble to wonder whether the ability to cope may, at the extreme, have its own psychological cost. Alison "thought about Kitty: was it unnatural, to adapt so well to such a double loss?" (p. 160). But this kind of wondering is brief, and limited to a character like Alison, who loses her own power to adapt. Drabble, like most of us, has too great a stake in contentment to question its achievement very hard.

Very little happens to Kate in *The Middle Ground*, although the book is full of incident. Although almost too much happens to Liz and her friends in *The Radiant Way*, their fast recuperations minimize the plot overload, keep the emotional level down. No one who has followed the history of Drabble's fable this far should be too surprised that her fiction changed when it hit the middle years, or that it changed in such ways. The story of a swan who becomes only more swanlike is bound to be low in contrast: it will have smaller successes to record; it will have less suspense. It will not be ironic, because the writer has not transcended her protagonists. In the middle years it is hard to move fast enough to be wiser than one's best characters. Some of the powerful emotions of the earlier novels are impossible: heroines are no longer surprised to have turned out swans, so they do not have the thrill of discovery. They no longer have guilty feelings about the vast distances they have traversed from their roots: they compare themselves now (if at all) with their peers, not with their parents. Longing—that continuous intense craving that arises out of a state of neediness—also disappears. Readers who mildly expect that something will come of Kate's affectionate relationship with Hugo find, in an unconventional scene, that Drabble disappoints their expectation. Kate's view about falling in love is that "I've done all that. Once or twice too often, in fact" (p. 259). Readers of Liz's story don't expect her to have an affair with her male friend. Discoveries about their sexuality, as about other inner facts, barely count as discoveries, because by now they have no recesses of soul that are entirely mysterious to them.

Life as anticlimax has its own interest, of an intellectual kind. Nothing happens to Kate when she goes back to her home ground "to find out something really interesting about myself. But I didn't. It wasn't there, after all. Or if it was, I couldn't see it. I shall stop looking. The past is the past" (p. 257). Strangeness of all kinds has gone out of Kate's life (although she has still a lively curiosity about others, which provides, as it always has, the sociological side of Drabble's novels). Clara Maugham, after meeting a family of wonderful people, went home and got "suddenly and violently sick. She could not assimilate, however hard she willed to do so, such strange food" (*Jerusalem the Golden*, p. 125). No food so strange is left in this midlife world. Drabble anticipated this situation as long ago as *Jerusalem*, when Clara looked at her swan, Clelia, and said reflectively, "It always seems to me that it must be hard for you, coming from this house, to know where else to go" (p. 152). Certainly the sudden midlife discovery of one's childhood secrets might count as strange food, but Drabble has Liz Headleand make out of her father's despair little more than a theory of knowledge. Lying in bed, recovering rapidly from the discovery of his secrets, Liz "studied the unsatisfactory nature of knowledge. The anti-climactic nature of knowledge. So this was it. A night of bad dreams, a day of sweat, then a desire for omelette and chips. Already she was losing interest in the riddle that had teased her for decades" (p. 388).

Far from losing interest, Drabble let herself get high on the middle years—even more in *The Middle Ground* than in *The Realms of Gold*. Perhaps it was a special relief to write out in Kate's plot her sense that women did not need to devalue themselves because their childbearing and childrearing years were ended (although freedom in the postfamily years could not loom large as a problem to one who had written so bitterly about family constrictions, and who was then writing so sanguinely about the development of children into young adults). Whatever the reason, Drabble invented a new tense to commemorate Kate's accomplished serenity, the memorializing present. The early chapters are written as if she had been interviewing a celebrity. "Kate has by now knocked around so much that she says she finds it hard to remember" (p. 28); she "still enjoys cooking adafina" (p. 33); she "was heard to say only the other day in mock despair" (p. 35). There is a flavor of the authorized biography about this style.

On the whole, however, Drabble is less sentimental about her midlife heroines. The tone she has them think in is far dryer than it was in the lyrical, self-pitying novels of the dangerous age. Increasingly, she has let them share the stage with other characters, to the point where *The Radiant Way* can boast two centers of consciousness aside from Liz. (Readers don't all agree that Liz is the center, in fact.)

All our novelists are practicing some version of this midlife tolerance. It's as if narcissistic projection had been satisfied by the writing of young-adult narratives, and was withering. Updike paternally allows Harry's son Nelson to think in his own terms. Tyler, in *Dinner at the Homesick Restaurant,* acts like a remarkably fair-minded mother of all, giving three adult children in a family equal time with their mother. Even Bellow, it could be argued, is trying for split consciousness in *More Die of Heartbreak,* giving his Marlow, Kenneth Trachtenberg, a continuing situation (if not a life) of his own, aside from his superior vantage point as his uncle's confidant.

Another characteristic figure, this time a supporting player, arises from the dispersion of consciousness: the same-age friend who is shown to be a better person than the protagonist, without being felt as a threat because of it. The friend can be more sensitive, better attuned to ethical issues, or more self-sacrificing. In *The Middle Ground,* it's Kate's social-work friend, Evelyn. In *The Realms of Gold,* it is Karel, In *Rabbit Is Rich,* if it isn't Janice, it's Charlie Stavros. The novelists' stance has become that of a mother who realizes that her adult child doesn't need her undivided attention any more.

V.

For nearly twenty-five years, Drabble has been celebrating the triumph of time in her own way. Whatever reservations readers may have about her work, her way has enabled her to produce not only several classics about young-adult and midlife women, but also something remarkable in the history of fiction: an extended and still unrolling progress narrative of the life course. Apparently she has no regrets about retiring her early, thrilling, high-contrast duckling-transformation plots, any more than she misses the juvenile leads whose weaknesses produced them. She's not even ambivalent. She celebrates psychological resilience and equanimity in the middle years without bemoaning the features in them that make them unsuitable for a Bildungsroman of her old fabulous kind. Already she has given us a credible, earnest, trusting view of more than half of an adult lifetime. Through all its changes, the fable has remained coherent, unflagging, seductive. Unsated, we want to know what will happen to the swans next.

5

Anne Tyler:
The Tears (and Joys)
Are in the Things

I. The Thickening of Life

Anne Tyler's narratives of adulthood are packed with *things*—well packed, with each item in a fictionally useful place, crammed with meaning. Over the years she has given us funny, troubled, complex versions of what it's like to be involved with things. They are mostly items of daily domestic use, or familiar artifacts: the three-story house with the children's rooms on the top floor, where a single family has lived forever; Jeremy's collages in *Celestial Navigation* (1974); Justine's Breton hat and family bureaus and her single set of sheets in *Searching for Caleb* (1976); Morgan Gower's eclectic wardrobe and Emily's leotard in *Morgan's Passing* (1980). These are ordinary things, yet they have extraordinary *presence*. Take the dollhouse furniture Charlotte Ames Emory's brother-in-law makes for her living room, in *Earthly Possessions* (1977). "Now on every tabletop there were other tables, two inches high. Also breakfronts, cupboards, and bureaus, as well as couches upholstered in velvet and dining room chairs with needlepoint seats. And each tiny surface bore its own accessories: lamps with toothpaste-cap shades, books made from snippets of magazine bindings, and single wooden beads containing arrangements of dried baby's breath."[1]

1. *Earthly Possessions* (New York: Knopf, 1977), p. 134.

This fantastically exact image of miniaturized duplication tells us nothing that realism would want us to know—it does not imply wealth or poverty, taste or talent. Until Charlotte decides to pack away the doll furniture, along with all her rugs and her curtains and her doilies ("What I was aiming for was a house with the bare, polished look of a bleached skull" [p. 172]), we couldn't guess that the category of significance is *amount*—wanting more or less. Charlotte thinks she wants less; she's always had a dream of less. To get away from these things, and of course the life they represent, she decides to run away. It's as she's leaving that she is kidnapped. She gets the trip she has been longing for, but under the gun.

Already we are in a peculiar world, in which material things loom so large, but the most important attribute of a set of objects is their quantity. The reason, in this most tangible of fictional worlds, is that her characters have to decide whether accumulation is a good thing for them or not. It's a momentous question, as it turns out, because early on in life whether you can become an adult seems to hinge on it, and later, how you want your adulthood to be—whether you want it to be stationary (with a family, house, and furniture), or whether you need it to be mobile and sparse. Through *Dinner at the Homesick Restaurant* (1982) and *The Accidental Tourist* (1985), these remain central issues for Tyler's characters.

Hers is a wavery, unfixed sign system—unlike Drabble's birds and flight, so conventional in Romantic imagery. To understand the way Tyler uses "things," we need to work away from the *Odyssey*. Its original—male—pattern of adulthood is one we keep in the back of our heads: it postulates a hero who spends the dangerous age warring and then roaming around rather promiscuously, without any baggage (so to speak) of family, impervious to losing goods—a man who finds it hard to get home but finally manages (Odysseus at about forty) to settle down with his family, in his fixed abode, with the property he has fought for and familiar objects about him. Restlessness is a sign of early days. Accumulations matter later. Odysseus's marriage bed, we recall, is immovable, literally rooted in the ground. In this schema, in midlife "things" mean responsibility, fidelity, and fixity. One implication of this story is that these values become more appropriate later on in life; another is that you need to age enough to appreciate them properly. This life-course plot continues to be enormously influential. Updike's *Rabbit Is Rich* takes it for granted. It dominates the young man who postpones marriage to go to Europe—the one who as an older man grumbles a bit in his den but relishes his armchair and TV set. Youth gets backpacks, midlife sixpacks.

Both men and women can now react against this traditional life-course plot, with its rigid conjunction of a particular life stage and particular values. But Tyler has been writing her novels as if she couldn't decide what the plot demanded. All the signs of it abound in her work, as I have said. But her plots assign the things and the trips to different parts of the life course. In her version, which stands the male pattern on its head, "things" come first, impatience with them later. This is or was a female pattern in our culture, but she has given it to men too: Morgan fits it and, to some extent, Macon Leary. She started using furniture and moving as signs of adulthood as early as her third novel, *A Slipping-Down Life* (1970). Gradually, her use of these signs became more intentional, extravagant, and (to those familiar with the tradition she's remaking) unexpected and delightful. She has expanded the simple category of "possession" until it gives the illusion of containing the whole adult condition (Samuel Beckett, with his bicycles and stubs of pencil, has contracted the category to the same end).

Readers soon notice that *how* her people relate to things is important—whether they inherit them or collect them, whether they fix them or merely own them, whether they yearn for them or reject them or simply forget them. Whether they like travel or can't bear it matters; and how they travel too—whether it's little trips from a fixed center, constant relocations, or a real departure; whether they are after somebody or escaping somebody; whether they are taking anyone with them or not when they go. One (Justine) is always in motion, a speedy driver whose husband tries to keep up in the second car; another (Charlotte) doesn't even know how to drive.

Tyler has been teaching us how to read the signs of adulthood her way, but she has been making up her mind, and changing it too, as she goes along. The value of the signs has flicked up and down. In one novel, nest building turns out to be the "right" behavior; but in another, for another kind of character, it is shedding the goods and moving on. Sometimes—the most radical departure from convention— possessing and journeying are not antithetical. After Charlotte walks away from her kidnapper and returns to her Ithaca, her husband from time to time asks her whether she wouldn't like to take a trip. No, says this female Odysseus, this American philosopher with a southern accent: "I don't see the need. . . . We have been traveling for years, traveled all our lives, we are traveling still. We couldn't stay in one place if we tried. Go to sleep, I say" (p. 185).

II. Menders and Mothers

"I mean, if you catalogue grudges, anything looks bad. . . . But after all, I told him, we made it, didn't we? We did grow up. Why, the three of us turned out fine, just fine!"

—Tyler, *Dinner at the Homesick Restaurant*

Tyler has told us that as far as her own life course was concerned, adulthood was all that mattered—not childhood, not adolescence: "I hated childhood, and spent it sitting behind a book waiting for adulthood to arrive."[2] Perhaps she anticipated that it was going to be her true subject. Her project has been to discover what adulthood consists in, or perhaps, requires, and whether its requirements are compatible with what individuals instinctively and idiosyncratically want. This is not so different from Updike's project, except that he started, resentfully, from the chafe adulthood brings after the triumphs of being a successful boy, and she started, sadly, from the internal difficulties people experience in becoming adults, even though they want to leap away from childhood and adolescence. Of course it's better to be older . . . , but every novel tackles a set of difficulties being older entails.

On the whole, she's shown that people do get what they want, or want what they get, without doing violence, making up their compatibility as they go along. Most turn into responsible adults. In short, although Tyler has no *theory* of progress (and has said she doesn't believe in it), she has been telling development stories all along, about the imperceptible and implausible ways people manage to grow up.

Hers is a quirky, unromantic view of young adulthood, in which the typical fictional signs of crossing the threshold—courtship, love, marriage, the intimate marital relationship—don't have much importance. Even more drastically for her than for Drabble, life becomes real when the children come. Adulthood is marked, first of all, by the things that come along with having a child. And because pregnancy can happen

2. Anne Tyler, "Still Just Writing," in *The Writer on Her Work*, ed. Janet Sternburg (New York: W. W. Norton, 1980), p. 13.

immediately and recurrently, life begins to thicken around her heroines while they're still young.

This pattern is plainly established in the peripeteias of *A Slipping-Down Life*. Evie Decker, one of the least attractive teenage girls ever to heave her bulk and insecurities onto the twentieth-century page, first claims our interest by cutting into her forehead, in the ladies' room of a bar, the last name of a local rock singer who strikes her fancy. She begins to seem like a human being one might know only after she marries him and they are about to have a baby, when she begins to worry about "finding the money for a tip-proof high chair with a snap-on tray and safety traps" and wonder which other baby equipment is "essential."[3] Evie comes out of her exhibitionistic adolescent infatuation—a stage of self-absorbed impulse—propelled by the baby.

For most of Tyler's women, the baby, not the husband, is the true sign of entry into responsible adulthood. "Gina was the whole point; even what Emily felt for Leon seemed pallid by comparison," Emily thinks to herself in *Morgan's Passing*.[4] In *Celestial Navigation*, the first husband whom Mary leaves (taking their little girl with her) writes to her bitterly, "Oh I don't count I'm just a man."[5] When later on Mary's additional children interrupt her conversation with their father, Jeremy, her face "took on that change that always happened when her children spoke. She bent her head, her eyes grew instantly opaque with concentration, and every muscle seemed tensed to listen" (p. 155). Tyler's male characters don't feel so intensely about the young. This is a picture of adulthood in which women star. Tyler, who has two children—and a husband she has great consideration for—has said straight out what she thinks are the most binding ties. "It seems to me that since I've had children, I've grown richer and deeper. They may have slowed my writing for a while, but when I did write, I had more of a self to speak from. After all, who else in the world do you *have* to love, no matter what? Who else can you absolutely not give up on?"[6] At some deep level, children signify the life course, like change and aging. They must be accepted, and yet they can be hard to accept.

Thus her terms here recognize a distinction, a possible tension, between family obligations and personal expansion ("more self"). This tension furnishes much of the conflict of her plots.

3. *A Slipping-Down Life* (New York: Berkley Books, [1970] 1983), p. 192.
4. *Morgan's Passing* (New York: Knopf, 1980), p. 90.
5. *Celestial Navigation* (New York: Knopf, 1974), p. 79.
6. Sternburg, *The Writer*, p. 9; emphasis in original.

The tension arises because children trail along behind them all the paraphernalia of the grown-up world—not just high chairs but "income tax and license renewals . . . bank statements and dental appointments and erroneous bills" as the heroine says in the aptly titled *Earthly Possessions* (pp. 133–34). It's not the fault of the children (Tyler is particularly careful to locate the problem elsewhere), but it turns out that once you have one (or six or seven), earthly possessions turn out to be weighty. They can include other people as well as things: not just a father of the children, but (depending on which novel) brothers, a grandfather, mothers, in-laws, an old lady boarder, an old man from the mourner's bench, dogs. A whole extended family descends on her heroines: what in Yiddish is called the whole mishpocheh. "Are you keeping track?" asks one of her exasperated female heads-of-household, one of those who doesn't think she can bear it: "There were seven of us now, not counting those just passing through" (*Earthly Possessions*, p. 103). Once you get started taking care, those who need care seem to proliferate demandingly. Her numerous three-generation novels are a sign of this situation, in which the heroine finds herself willy-nilly pressed in the middle.

Sometimes they bear the wild rumpus stoically: in for a penny, in for a pound. Other times they glumly or angrily yearn to escape into simplicity. In the 1970s, Tyler invented this new binary test for adulthood—whether you love to have this plenitude, or can only just barely bear it. Motherhood is either absurdly easy or desperately tense: either a woman slings a baby on her hip, like Mary in *Celestial Navigation*, or, like Emily in *Morgan's Passing*, she leans out the window to test the temperature before she takes the baby out for an airing. Tyler saw that motherhood was not in every case a happy instinct, a gift of the life course. For some it comes as a curse. She has a series of reluctant, hard-pressed, unloved and grudging mothers, all from the previous generation: the two who are sure they've been given the wrong child at the hospital, and the angry Pearl Tull of *Dinner at the Homesick Restaurant,* who slapped her kids around when they were small and once yelled that she wished they were dead.

The mothers she has liked best are the relaxed and detached ones (often they are the daughters of the grudging, unloved ones, just to show how crookedly determinism works). She loves to make up little scenes that show their endless patience, their calm under stress: Mary, unflappable in a cold shack bursting with kids and wet diapers; Charlotte at the height of her frustration, kissing "the small nook" that is the bridge of her son's nose. Her kidnapper pleads with her at the end of the story to stay with him and his pregnant girlfriend: "Charlotte, it ain't so bad if you're *with* us, you see. You act . . . like this is the way life really does tend to turn out. You mostly wear this little smile" (p. 182). Jenny Tull, Pearl's daughter in *Homesick Restaurant,* talking to her stepson (whose mother had left him) about the father who left her and her brothers: "'You're overreacting,' Jenny told him. 'I can't even remember the man, if you want to know. Wouldn't know him if I saw him. And my mother managed fine. It all worked out.'"[7]

One of Tyler's favorite plots shows how the unready or impatient women turn into (or recognize themselves as) good mums.[8] Jenny Tull (Dr. Jenny Marie Tull Baines Wiley St. Ambrose) had started off in her own lonely mothering as a medical student with thirty-six-hour days, slamming her daughter's face into her Peter Rabbit plate, before she became a pediatrician (what else?) and the reassuring mother of seven just quoted. A person can *learn* to be the most responsible kind of adult. Jenny did it by going around watching people who did it better: "you could almost say she took notes. . . . She was trying to lose her intensity" (p. 212). Two of the 1970s' novels, *The Clock Winder* and *Earthly Possessions,* are about the apprenticeship necessary before a woman is ready to accept family life. Elizabeth Abbott of *The Clock Winder* serves an actual apprenticeship to the Emerson family's possessions—by becoming their handyman—before she marries into the clan and becomes the caretaker of them all. (Inevitably, people who can fix things have privileged positions in Tyler's world. The world needs constant mending, and constant menders. And because it is a comic world, deep down, there are plenty of true adults: the needs get met.) Elizabeth was clumsy in her own family of origin, but at the Emersons she finds she has a magic touch for things. Fixing things prepares her to learn that she can get involved in the real world, risking real disaster. It's a tri-

7. *Dinner at the Homesick Restaurant* (New York: Knopf, 1982), pp. 202–3.

8. "Like adulthood, parenthood is a relatively neglected topic in psychology. . . . we do not, as a rule, study the effects of parenthood on *parents* themselves. Thus, we study the routes whereby an infant may come to develop basic trust in the good intentions and continuity of the parent; but we do not study the equally crucial process whereby a new mother, a primipara, comes to trust her own capacity to keep an infant alive, after it has been turned over to her care." See David Gutmann, "Parenthood: A Key to the Comparative Study of the Life Cycle," in *Life-Span Developmental Psychology: Normative Life Crises,* ed. Nancy Datan and Leon H. Ginsberg (New York: Academic Press, 1975), p. 168; emphasis in original. Drabble's equivalent novels would be *The Garrick Year* and *The Millstone.* Updike and Bellow don't have equivalent novels about learning to trust oneself as a parent, unless the late novels where men try to take care of children count as such. *Rabbit, Run* is probably the starkest novel about *mistrusting* oneself in that phase of life.

umph for her to realize, at the end of the book, that she can be a minimally competent caretaker, the kind of babytender whose constancy she admires. The electrical cords, smooth-sliding windows, dripless faucets and toilet tanks have provided the discipline she needed to enter the world where things are simply adjuncts of the busy, forward rush of midlife. Macon Leary, moving in with his unlikely new love, Muriel, and teaching her son how to fix a faucet, unites mending and tending. He learns to be a better father than he was with his own son: less anxious and fussy, readier to be delighted.

For Tyler, artistic creation too depends on appreciating things, and (after Elizabeth Abbott) on having an accumulation of them. Her artists are collectors, whose objects come to them in a haphazard, unintended way, over time. Their art evolves incidentally and naturally, like the prose of a writing spider. They're taking photos or gluing things together, without the self-consciousness that comes from knowing that these are job categories carrying some prestige in the post-Romantic world. Jeremy, the magpie agoraphobe of *Celestial Navigation,* is probably her best-known character and certainly her most archetypal artist (he is, as an artist, what his Mary is as a mother, a person with a developing instinct for plenitude). As his talent grows, his collages become thicker and then larger, and (of course) more full of domestic artifacts: a shred of a child's stocking cap, wrapping paper, "a bicycle bell, a square of flowered wallpaper, and a wooden button" (p. 211), a plastic banana, a baby's feeding spoon. When Mary leaves him because he missed their wedding day, he finds he wants to incorporate it all, the whole world of famiily he had formerly thought of as so much *clutter.* In his collage-box, he enshrines Mary, the tender, represented in his art (as in Tyler's) by the things she has swept into her care.

In describing his collage, Tyler justified—apotheosized—motherhood's minute, blinkered attention to the things of this world, justifying it not only because it nurtures the species, and proves one is an adult, but because it can be the subject matter of art. For a few wonderful unambivalent pages she inscribed her gratitude, as an artist, for the accumulation of things that comes with motherhood.

III. Surviving the Family

In fact, *Celestial Navigation* is an allegory of ambivalence about adulthood: if Mary represents family obligation, Jeremy represents privacy and the freedom to create. The one novel in which the two sides of self are embodied separately in a man and a woman is the only one that doesn't end with some image of family happiness: their requirements are too different. They can't be married.

Tyler is double-minded, like so many people. (Unlike Drabble, though—from *The Needle's Eye* on, all Drabble's midlife heroines like a full house. They may not want to live in it all the time, but enjoying it is an article of faith with them. And unlike Bellow on the other side— all his midlife men want to slough off possessions.) In most of Tyler's characters, plenitude is *not* an instinct; instead, a genuinely austere self crouches beneath the burden of adult requirements. This self regards having things as a painful discipline, the proliferation of family as a mistake to be undone; even getting a spouse seems to be a kind of accident. Tyler, now in her mid forties, has written herself well beyond this transitional stage, but she has never lost the sense that some people get on the threshold, of how singular human beings are, and how odd it is that anyone should ever let her life be joined to a stranger's.

Taking up adult responsibility—children and things—seems initially to cause a lot of loose panic, as well as real anxiety. What Tyler expressed most strongly at the time of *The Clock Winder,* was how risky it would be to get involved in a family of predilection, and at the time of *Celestial Navigation,* how threatening living in that big overwhelming family was to the private self. Charlotte fears the furniture, because it became the symbol of being trapped. Apparently, Tyler was afraid that the bonding within a family, precisely at its strongest (when the children are young), was derived from weakness, repetition-compulsion. She had noticed obsessive, reluctant returns to scenes of past family bitterness. She expelled these fears mainly through *The Clock Winder* and *Celestial Navigation,* written in her early thirties. Contrast *The Clock Winder,* written just before *Celestial Navigation,* with *Earthly Possessions,* written soon after: the later novel, a first-person account with a much sassier narrative voice, revises the earlier in every way. Both describe the oppressiveness of family life, and, in both, objects are envisioned as heaping up. Close to the end, both Elizabeth and Charlotte are shown surrounded by people, taking in strays, making meals for untidy groups of eight and ten. Elizabeth is supposed to be in her element, while Charlotte does little but complain. But when Charlotte comes back and settles down after being kidnapped, the return seems appropriate—this is the life she has deliberately chosen. Tyler doesn't convince us that the Emerson family can be a desirable place for Elizabeth to dwell. *The Clock Winder* denied Tyler's fears at the level of structure but revealed them in its violent atmosphere and details of plot; *Celestial Navigation* admitted, compartmentalized, and exaggerated these fears in the mild, withdrawn person of Jeremy; and *Earthly Possessions* brought them in as Charlotte's obstinately held but mistaken opinions about her character.

After *The Clock Winder,* Tyler immediately created her most genuinely loving and contented mother, Mary, who innately needs all those children and takes in boarders and waifs as well. And after *Celestial Navigation,* she never again created a plot to demonstrate the impasses of adulthood. Even her slowest midlife protagonists—like Morgan and Macon—are relatively resourceful people who succeed in making different kinds of lives that they can inhabit with genuine willingness. Over time, her women became braver about assuming responsibility; Tyler stopped regarding it as "interference." Elizabeth Abbott tried her best not to intervene in people's lives, and still somebody shot himself on account of her. Justine, the slapdash fortune-teller, is the first one daring enough to give advice: "Take the change," she advises her clients over the cards, "Always change."[9]

After *Celestial Navigation,* with both fear and apotheosis of motherhood behind her, Tyler could change her presentation of the crowded maternal world of things—ease her way away from it. She has a series of rather careless and yet harmless mothers: Justine in *Searching for Caleb,* or the rather marginal Bonny of *Morgan's Passing,* with seven grown-up offspring, who "had let the children slip through her fingers in some sort of sloppy, casual, cheerful style that was uniquely hers" (p. 102). (And then, at last, a few men who manage to lead nourishing lives that don't center on children: Ezra, who designs the Homesick Restaurant; Morgan, who wants to leave behind the debris of family life that Jeremy has made art out of.)

Justine, with only one well-behaved, methodical child, leads a footloose rambling life in which she gradually sheds the family furniture and travels light—the kind of life Charlotte only thought she wanted. Justine and Duncan have escaped from family riches and sweetness and constraint. She maintains her serenity in their drifter's life, inventing a mobile career (fortune-telling) that uses the close observation she developed as a silent, watchful child. The suspense of the book is based on our bourgeois/bohemian query: Will they finally get tired of having only one pair of sheets and go back to the solid formal standstill life that their Roland Park families represent? It's a feminist query too: is Justine

9. *Searching for Caleb* (New York: Knopf, 1976), p. 29.

bending her will to her husband's need, without noticing her own? Tyler's answer is to have it be Justine's idea that they join a traveling circus, where he can be a mender of things and she can read the cards and advise people to go ahead with what they want.

Because Tyler came to understand how natural it was to want to get out from under the burdens of a houseful of dependents, she could become more compassionate toward the awful Mom of the previous generation. Pearl Tull mellows as her children become independent adults: her fierce resentments fade; she worries about how the children have turned out, and blames herself. Tyler does question her own long-term optimism (Pearl is eighty-one when she's having these thoughts) and the hardest questions come up in *Dinner at the Homesick Restaurant,* particularly in the son Cody's chapter, "This Really Happened," which is told from the point of view of *his* son, Luke, exasperated by the way his father hangs on to his catalog of childhood grievances. But she comes down on the side of her early view, from *The Clock Winder,* that even minimal maternal competence is something to admire, when you consider the alternative. . . . Elizabeth Abbott has a revelation at the end of the book about what species continuity requires:

For every grownup you see, you know there must have been at least one person who had the patience to lug them around, and feed them, and walk them nights and keep them out of danger for years and years without a break. Teaching them how to fit into civilization and how to talk back and forth with other people, taking them to zoos and parades and educational events, telling them all those nursery rhymes and word-of-mouth fairy tales. Isn't that surprising? People you wouldn't trust your purse with five minutes, maybe, but still they put in years and years of time tending their children along and they don't even make a fuss about it.[10]

Even Beck Tull, who did not put in his time, can be shown as no worse than a negligible guest when he returns belatedly, a man adequately punished by his self-made exclusion from his children's lives.

Tyler likes to show little kids getting sturdier despite their parents: Luke running away from Cody and then being so relieved that his father loves him and knows Luke is his son; Muriel's son getting more independent despite being overprotected. *Homesick Restaurant* asks the standard questions about environmental determinism again, but at novel-length, and long after, when the children are in their middle years and the evidence is in. "Was this what it came to—that you could never

10. *The Clock Winder* (New York: Berkley Books, [1972] 1983), p. 247.

escape? That certain things were doomed to continue, generation after generation?" (p. 209). Taking this long generational view, Tyler's judicious representation shows that Pearl's three abandoned and mistreated children grow up diversely. Only Jenny embraces life as if unscathed; Ezra never marries and never seems able to focus on a single individual other than his mother despite his generic kindness and desire for the forms of family "unity"; and Cody, although married and a parent, sounds at times bitterly neurotic: he catalogs the grudges. Yet even while doing a neurotic voice, Tyler let us hear antidecline notes, like the prideful reverberation of Cody's self-identifications. We're meant to see that all of Pearl's children have survived to shape some life that works well enough for them, and even Cody, who has lived in competition with his absent father, begins to understand how distorted his memory has been, and to find that the members of families are bound by more than the bitter need for revenge. This is a modest view of midlife recovery, more modest even than Updike's, and much more modest than Drabble's in her comparable book, *The Middle Ground*. But it too represents healing, achieved over time and by that token guaranteed. Healing is what now has to be accepted as the irreversible process.

IV. Knowing What You Want

It's a literary feat, and a psychological one too, after having written two novels about your fears of adulthood, to use several to argue that family and things (the more the better) are your highest value, and also write a book or two in which you show that people just as likable prefer to travel light.

What Tyler discovered is that neither the old male life-course pattern of wandering followed by stability, nor her new female pattern of maternal plenitude followed by restlessness, would stand up as a universal idea for the middle years. Instead, what she has been developing in this series of interargumentative texts is a discourse about true and false desire.

They are slow learners, these characters of emphatic naturalness, who talk as if they didn't know we were eavesdropping on them. They have so little self-consciousness that what they finally learn, in unastonished surprise, about their need for plenitude or simplicity, carries immense conviction. Justine goes on believing she wants to carry her uncle Caleb

Peck along on her rapid voyage through life, not realizing that she has as much Peckness as she needs in her husband and her Breton hat. Jeremy thinks he wants only the claustration of artistic production, without guessing that he really needs to marry Mary's world of things. Charlotte, likewise, goes on mistakenly planning to depart, when her life in one place has been "blessed with eventfulness" (p. 58), the condition she has always truly admired. "Oh, I've never had the knack of knowing I was happy right while the happiness was going on" (p. 176), she complains retrospectively.

These protagonists in the marriage novels of 1974 to 1977 already have what they want, if they only knew it. But since then Tyler has written more about characters who decide they want something new—who leave everything and start over. Unlike Evie and Mary (who move away from their men out of anger, in reaction to their behavior), these older characters move toward new people, new self-conceptions, new roles. And Tyler makes the move seem easier. These changes in her fiction arose out of and consolidated a considerable development in her own attitude toward desire. After she showed Evie Decker cutting her forehead, Tyler shied away from describing a strong will, because she saw it as disruptive. This is an odd reluctance for a Bildungsromancier, an association that (as in Updike's case too) has to be overcome. Tyler has managed this task gradually. In *Searching for Caleb* Duncan and Justine inadvertently harm her parents by going after each other so resolutely, but they themselves don't suffer long-term harm. Recent midlife characters like Morgan and Macon struggle and hurt someone to get what they want, but the harm is ephemeral, the will benign. Perhaps it was easier for Tyler to make this change because she has attributed willfulness mainly to (older) men who don't have child-care responsibilities. And ambition, ruthlessness—attributes that Drabble has given to some of her strong-minded women—have appeared in Tyler marginally, in characters like Cody. Morgan disarranges lives momentarily in order to make people see what they really want: Emily's ex gets the kind of life that requires three-piece suits, and Morgan's gets a new man she doesn't find as tiresome as Morgan. Macon has to leave his wife too, but only after she left him, and then with a hint that some relationship between them will continue. There's no ferocity in desire, and very little evil in Tyler's private worlds (Vietnam happened, but offstage, while Jenny Tull was in medical school). It's not *getting* what you want that Tyler posits as the problem of adulthood: it's knowing what you want.

Each time it takes a whole plot for the main character to discover what is personally right, moving rather unconsciously through the long span of years. Progress brought about this way may take a long time: *Morgan's Passing* begins in 1967 with Gina's birth and ends in 1979 (when she has gone to live with her father); *Dinner at the Homesick Restaurant* starts with Pearl's recollection of 1931, and ends on the day of her funeral in the fall of 1979. Aging (fictional time passing) settles many questions. Earlier, in *Searching for Caleb* (which looks back over all of Justine's life) or even *Morgan's Passing,* length of reported time was a sort of apology to unseen adverse powers—first parents, and later the child Gina—for having been persistent enough to make things come out right in the end. It provided a way of dealing with guilt without mentioning guilt, a plausible reason for needing to write long progress narratives as well as progress narratives that cover long spans of time. The second time Tyler handles the divorce-with-a-happy-ending story, in *The Accidental Tourist,* it doesn't take as long to get the man into the arms of his new love; but then, *she* pursues *him.*

In general, starting with *Earthly Possessions* in 1977, Tyler has been unapologetically treating the midlife Bildungsroman as a wonderful patient form. Hers don't have Jenny Tull's bravado—"We turned out . . . just fine!"—yet somehow, life as inscribed therein leaves people in a better state by the end. It's not clear *how:* some luck, some slow cure, some reinterpretation, some shrouded aims, some deserving, and then, a moment of choice. "'Isn't happiness expecting something time is going to bring you?'" Cody asks in *Homesick Restaurant* (p. 256), in a long disquisition about progress and decline attitudes toward time. He, who stole his brother's girlfriend by assiduous wooing, expresses the view that happiness is merely a waiting game. In general, in this gentle world, we're asked to focus on the period of preparation for knowing and choosing. Then the moment itself is muted—only the outcome of what has gone before. Tyler's characters mostly go along intent on their daily ordinary necessary lives, too preoccupied to expect anything special and usually too ego-less to grab for it; they're edging toward their true desire. The midlife novel itself, sure of its genre, doesn't mind how long it takes them to get there.

V.

Tyler's people need to be a little eccentric in the external things (as every reader notices they are), to defamiliarize what they're about, which is so homey and familiar, and yet at the same time so serious and crucial—growing up though the psychosocial stages, answering philosophical questions in their plain concrete language and modern literalized ways: getting on an Amtrak car, lugging around their family bureaus. The solitary self that Tyler usually posits has a grand pedigree, from Pascal to Thoreau to Sesame Street's "Love of Chair," all arguing that a person's best chance of happiness could come from learning how to live in a room alone with a single piece of furniture. Tyler's innovation was to mesh this authentic urge with another equally urgent need: to learn how to live in the much-peopled, overfurnished room of adult responsibility. At bottom, Tyler presents the ideal pattern not so much as one chosen for us by our gender, or even determined by our stage in the life course, but as one each of us is bound to disclose in the course of our own peculiar journey.

6

Saul Bellow:
Inward and Upward,
Past Distraction

I. Crises of Aging

Bellow didn't start out by writing progress novels: he didn't like aging past the kingdom of boyhood, as his two downers about young adulthood, *Dangling Man* and *The Victim,* testify. His history as a writer of progress novels is a curious interrupted one, but in fact it's a wonder, given his beginning, that he came to write progress novels at all, and all the more remarkable that most of these should have been set in the middle years. Of all the midlife Bildungsromane considered here, *Humboldt's Gift* (1975), his fast-moving midlife pendant to *The Adventures of Augie March* (1953), is the most venturesome—indeed, risky—in its ebullience. It gives its hero ample energy for a philosophical quest as well as a couple of psychological cures.

Bellow's life-course fiction implies that he endured almost all the crises of aging a person can have in our culture. He pulled himself out of the first, the young-adult crisis, by going back to his childhood and writing *Augie March,* the first half of which is possibly the most exhilarating boy-Bildungsroman of all time. Losing interest or nerve after Augie's marriage, the end deposits him just the far side of the threshold. Only three years later, however, forty-one years old and feeling "forty"[1]—he was born in 1915—Bellow slid into another decline novel

1. Forty "came to represent middle age and symbolized a kind of last chance at personal transformation," according to Stanley Brandes, *Forty: The Age and the Symbol*

filled with young-adult themes, but set in the middle years, *Seize the Day* (1956). It was a fictional throwback to his earliest books, darker than either. But then came a more durable recovery. His next book, *Henderson the Rain King* (1959), claimed Bildung for the middle years, and over the next twenty years—interrupted by another life-course crisis, the anticipation of old age—he produced two more progress novels of the middle years (*Herzog* and *Humboldt's Gift*) and a theory of the novel as a genre that deals in progress. The present chapter concentrates on the big midlife group: Henderson at fifty-five, Herzog at forty-seven, Charlie Citrine in the mid-fifties again.

Reading Bellow's oeuvre with age in mind (watching his protagonists age, so often in chronological sequence along with him [2]), we can't help but feel that he has had a preternaturally heightened sensitivity to the cultural constructions of age and stage. Having this sensitivity has not proved, for consciousness in our time, an unmitigated blessing. On the contrary: it has made the life course seem discontinuous, it has sharpened the metaphors of loss and failure, it has made aging seem a falling away—and that not once in a lifetime, but many times. Through Bellow's life-course narratives, these problems of age-consciousness in our time are magnified; (fortunately) so are his solutions. As each stage has come along (or rather, whenever he has identified a new stage as a critical one), it has taken him a book, or two or three, to come to grips with his trepidation about it, to work out the life tasks that the crisis appears to urge forward, to recognize that aging per se is not the problem, and finally to recover or invent well-being. In each stage he begins by writing a rather depressed and chaotic account of an awful situation—a "realist" fiction, which if not precisely a decline story in its conclusion has the tone of one, and includes as much pessimism about time-present and time-future that it might as well end in hopeless stasis. Age does not figure prominently in *Dangling Man,* the first of the young-adult set. But in each first novel of the next sets (*Seize the Day*

(Knoxville: University of Tennessee Press, 1985), p. 126. Earlier in the century, thirty or thirty-five was the marker. In the 1980s, fifty may have become the crucial age. The "crisis" creeps upward.

2. Joseph in his first novel was twenty-seven when Bellow at the time of publication was twenty-nine; Charlie was mid-fiftyish when Bellow was sixty. Like our other novelists, he has usually donated his own age to his (male) protagonists—an apparently neutral and yet intimate connection with himself. The major exceptions have been Henderson and Sammler and (in *More Die of Heartbreak*) both Kenneth Trachtenberg and Benn Crader.

and *Mr. Sammler's Planet*), age is mentioned immediately and not forgotten, but anxiously alluded to thereafter. Clusters of bitter ideas gradually come to be associated with the character's age—confusedly, as might be expected, so that it isn't clear whether age is cause or sign. (This confusion is typical of decline narrative.) Tommy Wilhelm is made to be forty and a failure. Sammler is "seventy-plus" and would just as soon see the world end. That Bellow jumps sequence in assigning Sammler that age is a sign of some disturbance: at seventy Sammler is not only fifteen years older than Bellow was in 1970, and much older than the next after him, Charlie Citrine, but also pointedly "old" where Charlie is assertively a youthful middle-aged type.[3] It's as if "forty" and "seventy" were to Bellow symbolic clocks, striking times of self-appointed reflection and dissatisfied self-judgment. He had to recover from his own symbolic chimes.

As Bellow continues to write his way through, he finds a way of transcending this original apprehensive and discouraged version: he discovers simultaneously a more positive way of being and a genre that allows him to represent this new mood. Wilhelm is followed shortly after by increasingly autonomous, sane, goal-creating figures, with *Humboldt's Gift* the final upbeat of his midlife series. *The Dean's December* (1982) replaces Sammler's bitter anticipation of being "old . . . old . . ." with Albert Corde's account of what it's like to be "not quite elderly but getting there."[4] Bellow has not gone on to invent a progress plot for a truly elderly man. Instead, Benn Crader, in *More Die of Heartbreak* (1987), allows Bellow to avoid writing about old age now that he's actually over seventy. Crader dwells in the late fifties, the golden (Henderson/Citrine) age, when a man can still suffer interestingly from love-nonsense but is able, when he wants, to snap out of suffering. We might say of Bellow that he feels safe at least in the middle years.[5]

3. Bellow told Ruth Miller, his friend and biographer, that he wanted to "look back" in *Mr. Sammler's Planet;* but no one can look back from seventy when he is only fifty-five (private communication with Ruth Miller, who has been extremely generous in answering my questions and offering me information from her manuscript, *The Quest for Transcendence*).

4. *The Dean's December* (New York: Harper and Row, 1982), p. 2.

5. Bellow's critics can be divided into those who think his oeuvre is affirmative, those who think it's pessimistic, and the hedgers: "enigmatic laughter," "desperate affirmation," "desperate faith," and so forth. This static division seems to recur regularly in literary criticism. One of my aims in every case is to disaggregate the "oeuvre" by asking, "When?" For a brief bibliography of the affirmers, see Jonathan Wilson, *On Bellow's Planet: Readings from the Dark Side* (London: Associated University Presses, 1985), p. 172, n. 4.

II. "That Elementary Confidence"

This speculative theory has the advantage of explaining the blips in genre that have puzzled Bellow's readers all these years, and seem to have puzzled him as well. The first of these came when *Augie March* appeared, to everyone's surprise, after the two pared-down Flaubertian stories of young-adult misery. Sometimes Bellow explains the radical release into progress narrative with a semiautobiographical explanation, sometimes with a purely formal one. He has described his first two (highly praised) novels as dutiful mistakes, "formal requirements" for a novelist of the time.[6] After the war, out of the Merchant Marine, and living in Paris, he apparently started writing a third and a fourth novel of the same sort and was sinking "into a depression by trying to do the wrong things."[7] Suddenly he found his own voice. His later diagnosis was that he had first tried, mistakenly, to be an American of the "nihilistic" school, in which he includes Hemingway, Fitzgerald, and Faulkner.[8] Augie's was a different American voice: "It genuinely corresponded to a kind of Americanism of the 'thirties—naive, easygoing, tolerant, all-accepting, youthfully affectionate."[9] Not everyone experienced the Depression era this way, but this unexpected description charmingly and obliquely conveys the mood of the thirtyish Saul bellow, living in Paris (where good Americans go when they die, in the legend of the era) on his Guggenheim award. Life had surprised him, not disagreeably.

Augie March enabled him to lay in a store of fictive groceries—character traits, defensive strategies, tones of voice—that he could use to nourish later progress novels about midlife figures. His own adult suc-

6. Gordon Lloyd Harper, "Saul Bellow," in *Writers at Work, The* Paris Review *Interviews*, 3rd ser., introd. Alfred Kazin (New York: Viking, 1967), p. 182.

7. Michiko Kakutani, "A Talk with Saul Bellow: On His Work and Himself," *New York Times Book Review*, December 13, 1981, p. 28. Some of the same material appears in Harvey Breit's interview with him, "Talk with Saul Bellow," reprinted from the *New York Times*, September 20, 1953, in Breit's *The Writer Observed* (Cleveland: World Publishing, 1956).

8. "Funny they should all be considered so American when they were so nihilistic. But they gave Americans an image they wanted to be known by": see William Kennedy, "If Saul Bellow Doesn't Have a True Word to Say, He Keeps His Mouth Shut," *Esquire*, February 1982, p. 52.

9. Matthew C. Roudané, "An Interview with Saul Bellow," *Contemporary Literature* 25, no. 3 (Fall 1984): 279.

cesses (he had outdistanced Augie in finding a career rather than a set of opportunistic jobs) helped him to develop that other American voice. It came with a longer pedigree, derived from the excited, life-struck transcendentalism of Emerson, Whitman, and Thoreau.

Bellow's alter egos before Augie, we recall, had been anxious people, filled with vague guilt and vague anger. To change genre and style so completely, Bellow had to start the new book by reaching back to his adored childhood, where he could draw affectionately on the sense of growth that he (like Wordsworth) associated with children and adolescents. Augie allowed him to create his first lovable, unselfconscious, steadily developing character.

The other inhabitants of his world could not be more different from him. Bellow redefined otherness here (in Grandma Lausch, Einhorn, Mrs. Renling) as self-centered and needy and therefore manipulative, but only incidentally hostile. He let the supernumeraries fascinate him, and he let them fascinate Augie. For Augie himself, he gracefully developed an attitude that could cope with their attempted "Machiavellianism" (the first title of the novel was *Life Among the Machiavellians,* but that had to change when Bellow realized how powerless they were)— an attitude that is unresentful, respectful but independent. Augie starts off as a listener. Toward his would-be mentors he at first displays a big bump of veneration; then he learns to be devastatingly critical, as when he comments on Mrs. Renling's dreadful tongue: "You needed a strong constitution to stick to your splendor of morning in the face of these damnation chats." [10] Bellow thus revised his own problematical relationship with detestable otherness: he presented it not as an endless, chaotic enmity, but as a crisp set of stages—awe followed by loss of faith and withdrawal—coming fairly early in life. When Augie needs a voice, he gets one. "I don't know how it all at once came to me to talk a lot, tell jokes, kick up, and suddenly have views. When it was time to have them, there was no telling how I picked them up from the air" (p. 125).

Because Augie has these powers, Bellow could drop anger as an attribute. Fighting is given only to a reluctant seasick boxer; Augie hits only to defend his life. The mood is so pacific in this novel that even the eagle doesn't like to strike game. Augie is made to be lovable because he tries to understand and not blame what he doesn't like in the people he loves, like his sweetheart Thea when she's ferocious and his brother Simon who betrays him twice. Anger came out elsewhere, in a novel

10. *The Adventures of Augie March* (New York: Viking, 1953), p. 128.

called *The Crab and the Butterfly,* possibly one of the two novels Bellow threw away before *Augie* because they were "too sad." [11] Weyl, the protagonist of a chapter ("The Trip to Galena") that Bellow did publish in the *Partisan Review,* twice tells an anecdote against himself, about hitting a complete stranger on the head with a whiskey bottle. [12] Bellow used Weyl/(Vile) as a depository for what would otherwise have been Augie's toughness. Originally he intended Augie to be a more belligerent type: the first published version of the opening of the novel, the famous passage about knocking on the door of life, was defensive and slangy. "I'm curious myself to know what knocks will come when I set up a bid. . . . so it's a daring decision to say, 'Okay, slam away, I'm ready.' But that elementary confidence. Man! it isn't too much to ask of myself at the age of forty, or near it." [13] In the writing, Bellow came to want him to be milder, more genuinely confident, more easygoing.

Most progress narratives let the decline view enter in somehow, as a test of reality and a foil: often, minor characters (Freddy the dentist, for instance) embody it. In Drabble, they are sad, wistful people, personally hopeless but rather quiet about it. In Bellow, they're "reality instructors": [14] they don't bottle up their bad outlook; from *Augie March* on, they're sure they're right. If you look closely, the novel is packed with damnation chats. Most of Augie's interlocutors, even Thea, show by their argumentative rhetoric that "That's the struggle of humanity, to recruit others to your version of what's real" (p. 402), and all the weighty talkers around him propound basically one version, "the trustful, loving and simple surrounded by the cunning-hearted and tough, a fighting nature of birds and worms, and a desperate mankind without feelings" (p. 10). Only the mother, a "worm" in the fight, has no rhetoric of recruitment, only helpless affection. To Bellow, the decline view is not a neutral idea; there is malice and envy in the would-be mentors, as when one of Augie's comforters admonishes him, "You've got to find out about this and not be so larky" (p. 400).

The book is set up as a series of conflicts in which the Party of Hope turns out to be a minority of one. If Augie were not strong in hope and obstinate denial, and if he did not have authority over the ruling version

11. Breit, "Talk with Saul Bellow," p. 272.
12. "The Trip to Galena," *Partisan Review* 17, no. 8 (November–December 1950): 787.
13. "From the Life of Augie March," *Partisan Review* 16, no. 11 (November 1949): 1077.
14. *Herzog* (New York: Viking, 1964), p. 125.

by dint of being first-person narrator, this would be a Nathanael West world. Although Augie starts off as a child with "all the influences . . . lined up waiting for me" (p. 43), he finds internal strength: he has opposition in him. (In the Bildungsroman of youth, opposition can be the first weapon that children discover, as we see in *Jane Eyre* and *Portrait of the Artist as a Young Man*. Bellow has kept it as a major midlife weapon.) Opposition is more detached than rage, and so less inclined to succumb to the influences; its resource is withdrawal (physical or mental), operating unconsciously, like an instinct.

But opposition can't lessen one central vulnerability, this otherwise confident novel confesses. Augie is shown to be undermined from within—three times, and worse each time—and every time from unhappiness with women. Women never lose their power over him; rather, their power grows as he ages. (This pattern contains a potent unrecognized source of decline material.) In youth, Esther Fenchel turns down his offer of a date; in young manhood, Thea Fenchel refuses to take him back; and in early married life, his wife turns out to be psychologically in thrall to an earlier lover. Women don't argue "us" down, in this particular male view; they just let us down. *Augie March*, that "ingénu" book, as Bellow came to call it, is the place to begin in order to explain Bellow's later misogyny and recurrent misanthropy. What sources of hurt feeling underlie the misogyny we can guess at, knowing that Bellow's mother died young, leaving him when he was in his teens, and that three of his marriages have ended in divorce. When bitter, his protagonists are victims of both fears, but the progress plots untie them and try to cure each.

Augie nevertheless gets stronger to deal with the ascending evils of life (as a progress hero must). By the time Bellow finished writing the novel, he had made him a master of accommodation and resilience. He had also made him younger. The tough-knuckled young man in the first version was near forty. Augie has no exact age in the final version: he's simply an ageless type of person whose future is perennially open.

III. "Victim Literature"

If we read chronologically, *Seize the Day* (1956) comes as a shock after the expansiveness and generosity of *Augie March*. Now Bellow readily agrees with an interviewer that "*Seize the Day* is victim literature, very much like *The Victim* itself. . . . Wilhelm belongs to the victim-group. However, I have long since done with that."[15] In midlife, he talked about Wilhelm as if he were a real person but an alien one. "I can sympathize with Wilhelm but I can't respect him. He's a sufferer by vocation. I'm a resister by vocation."[16] Bellow's own answer to the anomalous placement of the novel in his oeuvre is to point to the "two sides of my psyche," "the brooding side and the exuberant,"[17] but this simplistic answer (so much like Drabble's evasive answer to similar questions) can't explain why the resister released the brooding side only at certain critical times of his life.[18]

As we have seen, the self that had identified with Joseph and Leventhal did not wither away entirely in the writing of *Augie March*. Some of it went underground into other fiction that Bellow decided to keep buried in the back issues of *Partisan Review* or in the collection of the Regenstein Library in Chicago. Wilhelm's situation allowed or required the introduction of the material that *Augie March* (and even the earlier novels) had repressed: specifically, the two figures of the hostile (male) parent and the alienated spouse. Augie ostentatiously lacked a father (Bellow said he was "saving" him for another book), and he was slow to feel apart from his wife. *Seize the Day* represents both parent and spouse as more hostile and destructive than their counterparts in *Earthly Possessions, Rabbit, Run,* or *The Needle's Eye,* all of which contain variations on this basic young-adult combination.

Tommy Wilhelm is Bellow's worst loser. (Mr. Sammler, with all his terrible and truly permanent losses, does not despair of himself in the same self-absorbed way.) Wilhelm is a man with dangerous-age problems who feels old enough at forty to judge himself as if his story were concluded, and discouraged enough to interpret his story as a series of failures mostly of his own making or, at any rate, out of his power to change. The determinism that Augie overcame is Wilhelm's private disillusioned credo: "there's really very little that a man can change at

15. Chirantan Kulshrestha, *Saul Bellow: The Problem of Affirmation* (New Delhi: Arnold-Heinemann, 1978), p. 23. Kulshrestha hypothesizes that *Seize the Day* was written before *Augie March,* but when he interviewed Bellow, Bellow said he had forgotten when he began it.

16. *Roudané,* "Interview with Saul Bellow," p. 279.

17. Kakutani, "Saul Bellow," p. 23.

18. For example, when he was writing *Seize the Day.* At that time, he was in Nevada getting a divorce from his first wife; he was living with Arthur Miller, also getting a divorce in order to remarry. The details of this story will be found in Ruth Miller's biography, *The Quest for Transcendence.*

will."[19] "In middle age you no longer thought such thoughts about free choice" (p. 25). "I'm too old, I'm too old and too unlucky," Wilhelm says bitterly to his father, echoing his father's view. He holds a typical decline view of time and aging: "The hint about his age had hurt him. No, you can't admit it's as good as ever, he conceded. Things do give out" (p. 38). Everything weighs down this aging pretty boy, crushed under "the peculiar burden of his existence" (p. 39). He's the "worm" now, but he can't be gently fatalistic, like Augie's mother; he's squirming. Unlike Augie, he talks too much, revealing weaknesses and then berating himself; and he's vulnerable to fast talkers, except that he can't adopt Tamkin's shallow optimism. Herzog too resists voices that praise and hope almost as much as voices that denigrate. Everything must be evolved from within in this slow working-out of an approvable identity.[20]

By way of overdetermining Wilhelm's misery, Bellow added, to problems from "middle age," the consciousness of how inappropriate and burdensome it is to be dragging old psychic material around with him. (This is the reason Seize the Day could earlier be discussed as a dangerous-age novel.) "And here he was still struggling with his old dad, filled with ancient grievances" (p. 29). Old as he is, despite years of paternal irritation, he clings to his father and expects to be protected. His unemployment and estrangement from his wife cause upheavals in what he thinks ought to be settled and satisfactory arrangements. Bellow crams his life with disorder in areas where an adult might expect security, and refuses him Augie's protective weapons. How can opposition be useful or blitheness obtainable when you feel you can't do without the love you're not getting? Family affection (that untidy emotion that Bellow's best-loved heroes—Augie and Charlie Citrine—overflow with) turns back against him. It seems crazy to cling to it.

In the wife, scarcely more present here than in the earlier decline novels (as if one phone conversation were all one could bear of her), Bellow has for the first time created the familiar figure of the estranged and vengeful woman, who reappears like a commedia dell'arte character with standard characteristics of injury, self-righteousness, and fluent

19. Seize the Day, "with three short stories and a one-act play" (New York: Viking, 1956), p. 24.

20. Tony Tanner puts this in a poststructuralist way when he implies that Bellow affirms the self "as an entity constituted outside the discourses into which he is born" (and, I would add, those to which he is exposed in later life). See "Saul Bellow: An Introductory Note," Salmagundi, Special Saul Bellow Issue, no. 30 (Summer 1975): 5. Wilhelm was not yet such an entity.

verbal aggression. This figure is Bellow's tic; each time she reappears, she is given less justification for her resentment or manipulativeness. Like the wife in *Henderson* who laughs at his idea of becoming a doctor, Wilhelm's wife reminds him of what he says to himself, that it's too late to have a different future. "Every other day you want to make a new start. But in eighteen years you'll be eligible for retirement" (p. 112). Because *he* left *her,* it seems unreasonable for him to expect compassion, but he does. Bellow's hedged antipathy and pity for this boy-man are extra punishments. Having loaded him with neurotic indecisiveness and helplessness, Bellow barely avoids the father's exasperation for this zhlub—worse than a schlemiehl, because he's a smart man who is nevertheless a real mess. If Wilhelm wants tears, and that's finally all he dares to want, he has to shed them himself, alone.

Yet when we see how Bellow developed progress characters in the novels to come, we can pick out in the representation of Wilhelm fragments where rescue might lie: in his occasional self-control and humor, in some meditations on the meaning of life, and once in a vision of brotherhood. Most of all in his prayer for change ("Oh, God. . . . Let me out of this clutch and into a different life" [p. 26]), a prayer that links him, weakly, to Herzog, who writes emphatically, "Each to change his life. To change!" (p. 165). Decline narratives always include fewer signs of the alternative mood than vice versa (they are a less comprehensive form altogether), but these moments momentarily wobble the mood of the novella; we can see that more of them might make possible a change in genre.

IV. The Three-Volume Cure

Seize the Day laid out all the problems that Bellow anticipated for the middle years that he couldn't anticipate resolving. Yet it was the last midlife decline narrative he wrote. It was crucial for him in dissolving psychic knots. In their different ways, the next midlife novels —*Henderson the Rain King, Herzog,* and *Humboldt's Gift*—follow the rising pattern that Bellow had Herzog wistfully identify as *"steady progress from disorder to harmony"* (p. 182). About 1957 he made a fictional principle out of this personal idea of the way progress occurs: "Novels are floated upon distraction. They begin in the midst of it. . . . A novelist begins with disorder and disharmony, and he goes toward order by an unknown process of the imagination."[21] One might say that, after he recovered from the spirit in which *Seize the Day* was written, Bellow's new idea of writing a novel was to go on until his hero attains something like holy readiness for order. *Henderson* begins with "a disorderly rush"—a rush to escape his accumulated burdens (but we note how tidily these burdens have been cataloged): "my parents, my wives, my girls, my farm, my animals, my habits, my money, my music lessons, my drunkenness, my prejudices, my brutality, my face, my soul!"[22] *Humboldt's Gift* ends with Charlie Citrine, at least for the moment, free of all contingent complications, ready to acknowledge springlike rebirth coming up through "some of last autumn's leaves." Menasha (one of the likable old men whom midlife progress narratives have room for) says to Charlie, his benefactor,

> "What's this, Charlie, a spring flower?"
> "It is. I guess it's going to happen after all. On a warm day like this
>   everything looks ten times deader."
> ". . . Here's another, but what do you suppose they're called, Charlie?"
> "Search me," I said. "I'm a city boy myself. They must be crocuses."[23]

The midlife Bildungsromane decide that the best way to treat the problems of life is as if they were primarily *internal*—and thus changeable. *Seize the Day* was crucial because it wrote out the decline version of a life story so much more plainly than Bellow's first two novels. "This was typical of Wilhelm. After much thought and hesitation and debate he invariably took the course he had rejected innumerable times. Ten such decisions made up the history of his life" (p. 23). Writing such a passage might have led Bellow to wonder whether the *character's* repetition was indeed the problem, rather than writing sad sentences like those summarizing "the history of his life." Couldn't it be said of *Augie March* that it described the world's invariable temptations and Augie's invariable evasions? Yet those patterns were not repetitions but "adventures." Bellow must have noticed that for him writing victim novels was not much fun. All of his are brief, as if he was afraid of boring his read-

---

21. "Distractions of a Fiction Writer," in *Herzog,* ed. Irving Howe (New York: Viking Critical Library, 1976), pp. 372–73. It may be observed that this content-oriented theory describes *only* progress narratives, not fiction in general.

22. *Henderson the Rain King* (New York: Viking, 1958), p. 1.

23. *Humboldt's Gift* (New York: Viking, 1975), p. 487.

ers, or had reduced energy for the restatement of unhappy feelings. Or perhaps control of form was supposed to keep down disorder.

In decline narratives often only symptoms or punishments—drunkenness, loneliness, exile—appear in the text, not the "causes" of developmental failure. On the way to progress narrative, however, it seems necessary to "discover" a cause: our writers have a moment in which they connect their adult protagonists' failures (in most cases, in marriage) with problematic relations to their parents. For Bellow too, writing the story in this overt way seems to have been a wise and lucky decision. At the most general level, the tight domestic focus forced him to treat Wilhelm's problems as at least partly his own. *Dangling Man* blamed history, as if it took World War II to shake up that shaky psyche. *The Victim* blamed anti-Semitism and the death of children. *Seize the Day* villainizes Wilhelm's father and his wife, but in a muddled (or call it subtle) way it also fingers *his* relationship to them as the source of his troubles: his panting needs, his self-undermining ego.

The next novel developed Henderson as a version of Wilhelm who is older and yet more capable of effort. Henderson's character is grounded in a psychic reality similar to Wilhelm's, but his attitude toward his own ample history of failure supplies the crucial difference: it is soberly sanguine. He knows he blunders, but after he has blown up the only water supply of the African tribe he worked so hard to assist, he contemplates without despair this additional proof of how hard it is to succeed.

And remembering the frogs and many things besides I sat beside the fire and glowered at the coals, thinking of my shame and ruin, but a man goes on living, and living, things are either better or worse to a fellow. This will never stop, and all survivors know it. And when you don't die of a trouble somehow you begin to convert it—make use of it, I mean. (p. 114)

The Henderson that Drabble kept in her heart was this "evolutionary" man, a combination of transcendental hope and humble pie. He knows that "most of the fighting is against myself" (p. 124).

Bellow shows him teaching himself not to be Tommy Wilhelm. He must also stop assuming that he is always to blame. When he sees an unknown girl weeping, "What I thought immediately was, 'What have I done?'" (p. 44). Bellow had noticed the narcissism of the decline tendency to refer every wrong to the self, and had transcended it enough to make soft fun of it. But Henderson is no fool; the worst you can say of him is that he's teaching himself to be wise slowly. Inevitably, he is working on his verbal defenses. "Don't ask for information with such despair," he admonishes himself (p. 150). He doesn't need to blurt out his sorrows into the face of indifference; indeed, he is slow to unburden himself even before faces of loving-kindness.

Having brought the problems inside and named some of them, each novel of the midlife series can then view these midlife obstacles with cautious optimism. Each man is given mistakes easier to identify, disown, and shed—Bellow's version of being less tormented, healthier. In sum, they constitute a three-novel cure, of a graduated kind whose stages (as far as I know) can be seen so clearly nowhere else in midlife Bildung. In all of them contrasts are implied between the strengths of the present protagonist and the weaknesses of the previous ones. In the way that Henderson says "I'm no longer Wilhelm," Citrine continues, "I'm neither Wilhelm nor Henderson nor Herzog." They're all chronological contrast-gainers. Bellow doesn't need to say in print that he grew in strength between 1956 and 1975.

As the self strengthens, most of the "outside" threats, objectified in secondary characters, weaken in power. If Bellow never forgave the "ex-wife" (or did so only during his fourth marriage), he did forgive the "father"[24]—that is, he slowly weakened the hold over himself of the adverse self-evaluation that he had named "the father" in *Seize the Day* and *Herzog*. The novels that follow *Seize the Day* have buried the fathers, of natural causes, thus giving the living child a midlife chance to think more suitably filial thoughts: he survives to identify himself (without risk of contradiction) as a loving, nostalgic adult child. This "child" is rewarded by having (like Augie) richer brothers from whom, unlike touchy Augie, he doesn't mind borrowing. Both the once-treacherous brother Simon and the ungiving father are replaced by this generous, affectionate, if rather obtuse middle-aged male remnant of the original nuclear family. Predictably, Citrine, the one most full of years, is the one most capable of rapturous, unalloyed reminiscences of childhood (mostly of his mother, to be sure) and these in turn are his greatest bond to one of his own (female) children.

Because same-age or younger ex-spouses survive and collect alimony and bitterness, Bellow's midlife novels set themselves the task of show-

---

24. For two psychoanalytic readings, see John Clayton, "*Humboldt's Gift:* Transcendence and the Flight from Death," in *Saul Bellow and His Work,* ed. Edmond Schraepen (Brussels: Vrije Universiteit Brussel, 1978), pp. 31–48, esp. 38–40; also, Daniel Weiss, "Caliban on Prospero: A Psychoanalytic Study on the Novel *Seize the Day,* by Saul Bellow," in *Saul Bellow and the Critics,* ed. Irving Malin (New York: NYU Press, 1967), pp. 114–41. Clayton notes that after "the Father" disappeared from Bellow's work, other

ing how reducing dependence on the opposite sex can be achieved, and relating the achievement as a form of progress. The typical situation is one where the hero's ex-wife or ex-wives and his current woman or women are treated as part of the demanding, messy, confusing world beyond the self, bothersome "phenomena" that get in the way of true life goals. They are on a par (*primae inter pares*) with the gangsters, in-laws, would-be comforters, and gonifs who muddle his life. At the opposite end of the male spectrum from Updike in *Rabbit Is Rich,* Bellow has used his novels (except for *The Dean's December*) to make separation from women seem first an emotional necessity and then a kind of philosophical virtue and a precondition for the good life.

V. Phenomenal Woman

Henderson, the midlife celibacy novel and (no coincidence) fantasy saga, makes this separation from women (delusively) seem easy. Henderson leaves his wife behind in Connecticut when he buys his one-way ticket to Africa. There's nothing clinging about this resolute seeker; he's not bitter, and how she feels is unexpressed. "Lily, my after-all-dear wife, and she is the irreplaceable woman, wanted us to end each other's solitude. Now she was no longer alone, but I still was, and how did that figure? Next step: help may come either from other human beings—or from a different quarter" (p. 80). So he's out looking in a different quarter. When Mtalba, a large exotic lovely, chases him with the idea that he may be husband material, he's polite but impervious, not an aggressive rejecter. Age is said to be responsible for his imperturbable immunity (we note that Bellow advanced his age eleven safe years beyond Bellow's own).

As for Mtalba, time was when I would have felt differently about the love she offered me. It would have seemed much more serious a matter. But, ah! The deep creases have begun to set in beside my ears and once in a while when I raise my head in front of the mirror a white hair appears in my nose, and therefore I told myself it was an imaginary Henderson, a Henderson of her mind she had fallen in love with. (p. 104)

---

grotesque and imposing father-figures replace him: he concludes that "the fictions can never permanently end the struggle" (p. 39). This is another static view of Bellow's psyche and literary production.

In *Henderson* (as in the *Odyssey*), the man finally plans to return to his wife—not out of sexual passion but out of some more comprehensive and discursive need. He feels sure that he can count on their long acquaintance to procure him loving attention. In narrative this feeling is represented, naturally, by the man having a tale to tell the woman: "Lily will have to sit up with me if it takes all night, I was thinking, while I tell her all about this" (p. 339), Henderson predicts. Because his African education has not touched on his problems with women, whether he or she will be less alone after the reunion remains open.

Many midlife progress plots take for granted that some degree of detachment is natural after the young-adult wave of sex-passion. Loosening the bonds of passion (or giving up sexuality completely) can permit freedom, or learning-in-the-world, sometimes true male-female friendship. In our time celibacy may be more readily treated as part of a progress plot by women than by men: I'm thinking not just of *The Radiant Way* but of *Mrs. Dalloway*, or Colette's *La Naissance du jour*. The question is how fraught is the idea of "detachment." When autonomy is viewed as essential but immensely difficult, then any degree of dependency may seem excessive, inappropriate. Requiring it of one's character could produce a decline scenario, or an extremely troubled progress plot. For Bellow, these issues have been not just central but looming since Augie. His younger men start out wanting close to total identification with a woman they love. Augie found this "scary" and discovered that it did not occur, and Wilhelm's similarly peculiar attempt went completely sour: "She was one way and I was another. She wouldn't be like me, so I tried to be like her, and I couldn't do it" (*Seize the Day*, p. 51). For Wilhelm and for Herzog, divorce shows, direly, how dependent a man can be. Herzog starts off in even worse shape than Henderson because his *second* marriage has failed.

Bellow continues (in *More Die of Heartbreak*) to repeat the plot in which women stop being sources of comfort and men must learn how to continue living afterward: in a kind of parody-plot of the detachment theme, Benn Crader flees to the North Pole to escape his wife's shoulders. To go deeper, the plot Bellow repeats in *Herzog* and *Humboldt's Gift* is one where a man learns, first with more and then with less pain, to disaggregate the two ideas, "life" and "sex." He wrote a one-act play, produced in 1965 just after *Herzog* had become a best seller, that shows how loath he was even after writing *Herzog* to do this. "A Wen" is about an "eminent scientist," a "middle-aged" Nobel Prize winner, who voyages from Detroit to Miami in the face of an oncoming hurricane to meet his first childhood sweetheart, unseen since then, with a curious request, that she let him see once again a little rosy mark that he remembers noting beside her "personal object." [25] When she finally accedes, he has an erection and a jubilant reaffirmation of the continuity of life under the sign of heterosexuality. The storm breaks and the lights go out and the building begins to collapse. Ithimar's spiritual life began (he tells us)—and his life as a whole appears to end—with the discovery, and rediscovery, of sexuality.

Only in a jeu d'esprit like "A Wen" could a person make a complicated confession of this kind. Bellow doubts that sex is life (a silly idea, sure to be ridiculed, and certainly unsuitable for an eminent man), but the play can't imagine life going on after the moment when the "illusion" of the power of sex is at its height: intercourse and death follow their mutual seeing of one another's genitalia as middle-aged people. Saying this publicly in a farcical, grotesque, melodramatic form may have proved liberating. From the opposite direction, it was also liberating to mock the obsessive sex impulse directly, as Herzog does: "And, as almost always, he heard the deep, the cosmic, the idiotic masculine response—*quack*. The progenitive, the lustful quacking in the depths. *Quack. Quack*" (p. 337). Citrine, a man lured by other phenomena more than by women, also jokes about himself as a "goofy old chaser" before he finds out how easy it is to live womanless. In between these two, Bellow tried out a last resort short of death, an obvious but not long-satisfying step: to imagine oneself elderly, celibate, puritanical, and disgusted with sexuality (an attitude to which contemporary *moeurs* contributed generously, as Bellow himself might say), all recorded in *Mr. Sammler's Planet* (1970). There was the headiness of unexpected progress in a plot about learning to want to give up sex, Citrine's case; there had been neither energy nor learning in Sammler's situation of having long ago renounced.

Since suffering accompanies the discovery of dependence in the divorce plot, *Herzog* mounts a full-length attack on suffering. In fact, its claim to being a Bildungsroman depends on the hero making an initial wish to end his suffering, and achieving his wish. We know on the first page that he succeeds: "But now, though he still behaved oddly, he felt confident, cheerful, clairvoyant, and strong." So the entire suspense of the novel is psychological: how did he do it? The answer is in part tauto-

25. "A Wen," in *Traverse Plays*, ed. Jim Haynes (Harmondsworth: Penguin, 1966), p. 20.

logical: he became strong because he was strong, confident because confident. At his worst (always early on in a progress novel), the narrator can already write in the metaphors of cure, "*Not that long disease my life, but that long convalescence, my life*" (p. 4). In this metaphor, the "crisis" came before. But there is plenty of suffering (humiliation, frustration, anger, fantasies of revenge) during the convalescence we observe.

Already in the first few pages, Herzog is not-Henderson. Far from being a self-acknowledged "bum," a drunken rich man, he is a respected self-made intellectual, endowed with "great gifts" (pp. 184–85). He stands comparison with Frances in *The Realms of Gold*, both rich natures and high achievers living through depressive circumstances. In this book, Bellow openly discards the extremes of self-irony, as all midlife Bildungsromanciers have to do: "and Herzog momentarily joined the objective world in looking down on himself. He too could smile at Herzog and despise him. But there still remained the fact. *I* am Herzog. I have to *be* that man. There is no one else to do it. After smiling, he must return to his own Self and see the thing through" (p. 67). We learn he is handsome the way we learned Augie was, from the admiration of others. Although he says he lives in the grip of his "eccentricities," these amount mostly to letter writing rather than performing rash deeds without considering the consequences. Even carrying a gun with murder in his heart, he does less harm than Henderson with explosives trying to do good.

The episode with the gun—his father's gun—shows Herzog freeing himself from parental determinism. It looks at first as if he's willing to repeat his father's impotent, threatening manner; and because the father's original threat was against Herzog himself (as we're told in a flashback), the repetition seems sinister. The episode makes a connection between the worst moment of his young adulthood and the worst moment of the present, and (because both stories are about asking a father for help when he refuses to give it) it implies a connection between *Seize the Day,* already an anachronistic story of father-son hostility in 1956, and 1964. But over the nine years, Bellow has changed the telling. Having survived the financial need of the moment, and learned more about death, Herzog, unlike Wilhelm, blames himself ("his monstrous egotism" [pp. 249–50]), and exculpates his father because his "despair [of death] was keen and continual" (p. 248). It's a sign that he forgives his father *and* himself, that when he can't kill the former friend who has hurt him, he thinks "with inexpressible relish" that it is because father and son are too much alike (p. 258). The long alternation that Bellow had constructed between rage and wimpishness has been superseded for good.

Herzog belongs to the modern and adult world where people already know, like Milton's Satan, that they can't solve the problems of their own character by changing locale. Herzog is better off than Henderson or Wilhelm, even though he has more tsuris objectively than either. He knows that his obtuse, obstinate suffering (not his enemies, or his letter writing) is his sickness, and he teaches himself how to slough off the grieved self. He recovers from being a cuckold and a betrayed man by interpreting these "identities" not as essential but as contingent and past. Lest this degree of insight seem like a low-level goal, Bellow's rhetoric asserts that it is the major life task of the moment. *Herzog* demystifies suffering. It blows it up, it makes suffering a vast, worthy antagonist; then it snuffs it out. In 1964, in a decade in which existential anguish had enormous prestige, this task was a greater feat than it might be today, but the process of self-cure that Bellow invents is still intrinsically interesting. When Herzog tells his upbeat lover Ramona that "suffering is another bad habit," her typically contemporary response is, "Are you joking?" (p. 195). Bellow structures the novel so that the intention to stop suffering comes first, then the mental efforts. "I'm not even greatly impressed with my own tortured heart. It begins to seem another waste of time" (p. 17). By doing it overmuch, he learns that he has to stop telling everyone the *story* of his shame, which with him means no longer harping on the way Augie-like innocence harmed him. "Against his will, like an addict struggling to kick the habit, he would tell again how he was swindled, conned, manipulated, his savings taken, driven into debt, his trust betrayed by wife, friend, physician" (p. 156). Misfortune (which Freud once defined as "renunciations externally imposed"[26]) should not be exacerbated by self-punishing denunciations—leading to interior renunciations—of one's good qualities.

Before the end, he has moved out of the learner stage (which Henderson never did); with wisdom to share, he's adopted a mentor role toward his friend Luke Asphalter, and is giving him the same sort of advice he has been trying to take himself. "Don't abuse yourself too much, Luke, and cook up these fantastic plots against your feelings" (p. 272). His friend Nachman had told him he was positively good (as

26. "Civilization and its Discontents," in *Standard Edition* (London: Hogarth Press, [1961] 1975), 21:128.

good as his *mother* is the form this opinion took); now Herzog tells Asphalter that *he* is a good soul. Giving up suffering is not such a low goal, it turns out; in Emerson's vocabulary (used by Moses Herzog young), it involves "the upbuilding of a man" (p. 160). In this novel, it requires giving up the project of causing others to suffer. Having post-humously forgiven his father, Herzog soon after renounces revenge on his ex-wife and her lover.

Bellow lets Herzog use his much-attacked intellect helpfully, to argue against the *idea* of suffering as part of his project to control his own. He learns to denounce the "preachers of dread" who warn you "to stay away from consolation if you value your intellectual honor. On this theory truth is punishment and you must take it like a man" (p. 272). He takes on the historical decline theorists: Nietzsche "seeing the present moment always as some crisis, some fall from classical greatness" (p. 54); Spengler (*"No, the analogy of the decline and fall of the classical world will not hold for us"* [p. 75]); Eliot and company, *"the commonplaces of the Wasteland outlook"* (p. 75). Bellow observed people making a connection (which twentieth-century psychotherapy also notices) between theories of history and life-course theories, and he wants to snap it. He has Herzog also resist in these historians the guilt injected into a decline theory of the individual life: If we all go down, then how can *I* dare to progress?

VI. Phenomenal Man

There's a gun in *Humboldt's Gift,* eleven light-years beyond *Herzog,* but its handle is not in the hero's hand. The Magnum belongs to Rinaldo Cantabile, a petty offended gangster from a minor crooked family. Passing guns on from one generation to another has been trans-ferred lock stock and barrel to this alien clan. "It must run in the Can-tabile family to be silly with guns. . . . No effing class at all" (p. 268). Cantabile answering a call of nature uses the gun to herd Citrine into a toilet with him. In its enforced intimacy, the scene echoes the intimida-tion scene in *Mr. Sammler's Planet,* where the pickpocket corners the defenseless old man and exhibits himself. The hostile intention fells the old man, who has survived much worse. But Citrine—a youthful man in his mid fifties, brilliant talker and digressor, Pulitzer prize-winner, chevalier of the Legion of Honor, a man "fertile of wishes" (p. 338)—is also a hero of imperturbability. "In a situation like this I can always switch out and think about the human condition over-all. . . . In this way, thinking improving thoughts, I waited with good poise while he crouched there with his hardened dagger brows" (pp. 79–80). A self-made Nick Carraway, feeling that life has given him extra privileges, he has to warn himself against feelings of superiority: he has reached the stage where modesty begins to come easy. He stands as much beyond Herzog in mental control and emotional security as Herzog was beyond the clumsy Henderson. No longer so self-centered, he has controlled 'fifties egghead display (notice the restraint with which he answers when Naomi Lutz asks him to think out loud for her!). He provides an answer to the charge of passivity leveled at Bellow's characters, victims and heroes alike. "What I thought was perfectly clear to me. Absorbed in determining what a human being is, I went along with him. Cantabile may have believed he was abusing a passive man. Not at all. I was a man active elsewhere" (p. 85). This is an idealist definition of activity. "All I asked was a small mental profit" (p. 83). Citrine has detachment and levity, a peak combination. More comfortable with himself, he can also be more generous to would-be friends, less bogged down by bitter memories, more at home in the wide world. As Augie was Bellow's best definition of youth, Citrine is his best definition of maturity. He even has a friend who is a woman (that role has not been filled since Augie's Mimi, for whose sake he lost a rich wife): Kathleen Tigler, whom he's known for thirty years, the first Bellow woman whose wrinkles are praised. And *Humboldt's Gift*, with this controlling intelligence in charge of the tone, is his liveliest, funniest, richest, most coherent book—an energetic, four-adjective kind of book.

Detachment lends Charlie immunity from suffering on most sides. The vampire ex-wife from *Herzog*, still out for blood money, is reprised to show how little power she has over him. What she doesn't get, he gives away. Indifference to money is the last stage of the trajectory that started with Joseph's single pair of shoes in *Dangling Man*. Ramona, the faith-in-sex healer, is brought back too, as the selfish, raffish Renata, to show that his need for a woman is now little more than vanity, superficial enjoyment of "the veil of Maya" (p. 339). His last-minute attempt to marry Renata displays two advances over Herzog's relationship with Ramona: it makes the hero look like a man who has overcome his fear of commitment, and (since *she* leaves *him*) it doesn't succeed in committing him. Recovering from Renata's marriage to the undertaker (Herzog would have called it a "betrayal") takes scarcely any time at all.

Cantabile, however, takes up more room in this novel than Dahfu and the lion in *Henderson*, more than Madeleine the despised wife in *Herzog*, more room than the father in *Seize the Day*, and arguably more than the complex figure of Humboldt. That Bellow moved to make one of the Cantabiles of the world a problem to overcome is peculiar enough to require a peculiar explanation. (Cantabile is not an important social fact, either, as the pickpocket was supposed to be in 1970.) Like Humboldt, the gangster is a sign that the Bellow hero is no longer absorbed by the old sad family dyads. Cantabile, like Kate's new job or her Iraqi student in *The Middle Ground*, is a new "interest" in the postfamily, postspouse phase of life. But the way Charlie deals with him corresponds to a cure for misanthropy as well.

Representing otherness that is neither family nor female, Cantabile brings out and puts in high resolution the old ambivalence that all of Bellow's men, including Augie, have with otherness. "You love 'em and you want them dead," another front man said during Bellow's (and the nation's) dreadful Freudian-clarity period.[27] In Augie's time, the others included both well-intentioned mentors and egocentric influencers; it took Augie a long time to get wise to their designs on him because his own identity, still being shaped, was willing to try out patterns. Charlie may be allured, but he isn't malleable and he has outlived his last mentor. The novel doesn't explicitly notice, but there's no one around to teach him anything anymore, except himself. His way of dealing with Cantabile's importunities is to yield until a point of honor is reached or, ultimately, a point of satiety. Then it's easy to get rid of him.

In the middle years, as Bellow sees it, the power any of the phenomena has over a man is precisely the amount of power he confers on them by his attention. Although Charlie is slow to notice, Cantabile is a projection of long-established parts of himself. On the one hand, he represents Charlie's love of sensation, his Chicago state.

How should I describe this phenomenon? In a Chicago state I infinitely lack something, my heart swells, I feel a tearing eagerness. . . . There are some of the symptoms of an overdose of caffeine. At the same time I have a sense of

27. "Scenes from Humanitis: A Farce," *Partisan Review* 29, no. 3 (Summer 1962): 340. The speech from which this comes was softened for *The Last Analysis*, and this line was dropped.

being the instrument of external powers. They are using me either as an example of human error or as the mere shadow of desirable things to come. (p. 66)

Devoted replication of the old known world—with its Hispano-Suizas, "step-ins," Russian Bath on Division Street—seems to accompany this state: the phenomena become luscious, lustrous, exciting, and a bit of a joke. Charlie resembles Harry Angstrom or Frances Wingate or Justine Peck in loving the exterior world and making vivid prose out of it, but Bellow mocks some of his desire to do this, while the other writers treat it (as writers usually must) as a high value. Charlie concentrates on such things as Cantabile's nostrils: "People so distinctly seen have power over me" (p. 62). His response represents his (writerly and philosophical) ability to transmute the leaden stuff of the world into gold, knowing what he's doing. "I too am sentimental about urban ugliness. In the modern spirit of ransoming the commonplace, all this junk and wretchedness, through art and poetry, by the superior power of the soul" (p. 72). Cantabile is Bellow's way of asserting, after the sideshow freaks he put into motion around Herzog and Sammler, that human otherness isn't dross, but material he is grateful for. In your fifties you don't move beyond the phenomena by despising them; you can love them and leave them.

VII. The Comic Surprise

As many readers have noticed, Bellow's more recent (mid-life) characters are exceptionally concerned about "the higher life," and how one starts to achieve it. A theory of aging is involved in this development. From Henderson on, they regretfully look back on their pasts as adults as lost periods; Henderson and Herzog don't find much to salvage from what they denominate periods of brutishness and illusion, while Charlie more kindly conceives of his adulthood as a period of dormancy. But all of them produce a progress theory of the life course out of their desire to scrap the past and redeem it. If we compare Bellow's progress theory with those of our other writers, we can see its uniqueness. It's the only one constructed out of a need not to see the main portion of adulthood as a waste. Any of the others, with the grim days of the dangerous age behind them, might have invented it. But Bellow's need to see midlife as a contrast-gainer was more imperious than theirs; perhaps it is this that has made him increasingly ambitious in imagining the good. Henderson is a puzzled needy person, wanting to want the good if he can only find out what it is; even prone, Citrine has his eye on the philosopher's stone.

While these midlife males seek whatever they seek—an enlargement of spirit, awakening, truth—the novels show in sharper focus what gets in their way. *Humboldt's Gift* finally lands and lingers on distraction. As an opponent in the big quest, distraction is certainly preferable to the earlier evils. It sets you (Bellow said in 1957, laying out a program for his protagonists that it took him almost twenty years to deliver) in some lofty place where even "false hope and error and fear of death" constitute "noise" in the system.[28] As Bellow continued to write midlife novels, the comedy inherent in this kind of detachment has come to the fore, as have the philosophical implications. Unpleasantness, a situation with comic possibilities, replaces suffering, an apparently tragic condition. Charlie offers us a jaunty account in which "so many cantankerous erroneous silly and delusive objects actions and phenomena are in the foreground" (p. 177). Divorce proceedings are about as obstructive as Cantabile's shenanigans. In Humboldt's life *his* obstruction was his tragic obsession with America's idea of the artist. Humboldt represents the noblest distractions, but in Charlie's long mellow view paranoia and fritter and passionate desire and the male-female debacle (everything but children, who take up so little space) get viewed as a set of life-long distractions. When all the other claims are removed or lessened, then the hero can clearly see what in his own nature he has had to contend with all along, now calmly labeled as its penchant for disorder and distraction. Bellow has been making vigorous worldly fiction out of an increasingly interior drama.

Bellow has shown in his midlife Bildungsromane how he believes the proportions of life are related: years of embeddedness in confusion to minutes of comprehension, or anticipated comprehension. As soon as he accepted this ratio as a norm, which I think he did in *Henderson,* his attitude toward those who live a long time in confusion became much more genial, because he redefined them as seekers rather than failures. "Hah! Life may think it has got me written off its records. But life may find itself surprised, for after all, we are men. I am Man. I myself, sin-

---

28. "Distractions of a Fiction Writer," p. 372.

gular as it may look. Man. And man has many times tricked life, when life thought it had him taped" (p. 95). (This is another of the passages that Drabble quoted admiringly.) As Bellow aged, his characters become less bitter about their wasted past and more optimistic about being able to change in the future. Nobody has given beginning a better press. "Any Bildungsroman . . . concludes with the first step. The first *real* step. Any man who has rid himself of superfluous ideas in order to take that first step has done something significant."[29] It all begins to come easier, as Augie liked it. Henderson still believes hard blows are required for truth to come, Herzog feels he only needs to recover from past blows, while good-luck Charlie has an idea that finding may come before seeking.

VIII. Late Starters, Slow Learners, Eager Happy Beginners

Bellow's midlife Bildungsromane go on so much longer than his decline novels partly because he likes being with the characters better (as he liked being with Augie) and partly because these progress narratives need to be the equivalent of the hero's reluctant disengagement from false idols and mentors. In different ways it's hard for Henderson and Herzog—and even Citrine—to free themselves from inappropriate models. Charmed by Dahfu's beauty and physical grace, the obverse of his own felt lacks, Henderson keeps descending into the lion's den and heavily trying to imitate the lioness. If he were roaring like a lion in an apartment on Central Park West, this would be a satire; but in the sign system of fantasy Africa, his admiration of Dahfu is so poignant that it never becomes clear quite how wrong it is for him. There is no alternative mode of being noble lying around in the text, except possibly his servant Romilayu's stoic loyalty, which is a quieter version of what Henderson is doing noisily in the foreground with his chosen master. Herzog's mentors—like Valentine Gersbach, his wife's lover, who markets self-serving advice as life-wisdom—painfully deconstruct the idea of mentorship. Despite Humboldt's paranoia, Charlie finds it hard to wean himself from this erstwhile father-figure, Virgil to his Dante. And one of the successes of this book in contrast to

29. Harper, "Saul Bellow," p. 194.

Herzog is that he can work through deidealization and remorse toward a father-figure without deprecating the shade of his guide, in fact in a grateful and pious spirit.

The structure of these novels could be said to "deprive" the hero of people or objects that had originally been suffused with descriptive beauty or power or influence or seductiveness, but the rhetoric makes those deprivations seem a spiritual gain. For Charlie, no longer having the midlife accumulations (a wife, a girlfriend, money, a home) is more appropriate and desirable than having them. Like some of Tyler's heroines, he has shed burdens—but he has shed far more than the furniture. Updike has expounded the "principle" in *The Witches of Eastwick*. "A natural principle was being demonstrated, that of divestment. We must lighten ourselves to survive. We must not cling. Safety lies in lessening, in becoming random and thin enough for the new to enter. Only folly dares those leaps that give life." [30] "Divestment" as a piece of the life course may have curious consequences for novelists who live long enough to want to make fiction out of it. In the meantime, complaining that characters who take these new routes are not in "dialogue" with the world, or that they've lost connection even with private life (as responsible critics from time to time have done) seems beside the point. Charlie brings us news—hints of what detachments are possible—from a point in the life course beyond that which most novels have envisioned. And it's not sour grapes: he has had a full life, and he'll go on having it.

The last pages of Bellow's midlife Bildungsromane are unusual in that the situation in which the hero finds himself is ostentatiously transitional. Henderson is running in circles with a strange child in his arms, Herzog is lying down, and Charlie is leaving a funeral: none of these moments can be prolonged indefinitely, and the actual future each protagonist will have is only sketched out. All are shown open-endedly looking forward to the *next* stage in their lives as to the time of fulfillment of their desire to lead a new kind of life. In the texts themselves, we never see this desire satisfied—which may appear to be a curious structure for a progress narrative but in fact is quite common in a genre that distrusts doubt. The salient fact about the state of desire is the certainty with which the protagonist—who is really the narrator, even in *Herzog*—feels that it is *about* to be satisfied. "When I've taken care of these necessary items and tied up a few loose ends I'm coming back to

---

30. *The Witches of Eastwick* (New York: Knopf, 1984), pp. 97–98. This approbation of divestment comes (as it were, inevitably) in a passage in praise of autumn.

Europe. To take up a different kind of life," Charlie asserts without much fear of readerly contradiction (p. 483). Perhaps his record is not good: this is a man who up to that very minute has always found loose ends to tie. But Bellow gives him a disarming tone of soberly enlightened self-scrutiny—a relief after the frenzied energy of the Chicago state. "Although I have only my own authority for saying so, my mind appeared to become more stable" (p. 441), Bellow has him say about the effects of his reading to the dead. We don't have to believe in Steinerism to accept Bellow's belief that tones like these represent trustworthy postlapsarian convictions. In this definition of maturity, not the contents of mind, but the attitude of mind, is what counts.

How do these novels know when to end? Bellow once complained that he has trouble with endings, meaning the endings of the big-bodied, phenomena-charmed Bildungsromane. His solution is to end them all at the same point in terms of fictional conventions: to wit, before the complications of living through the proposed solution begin. In essence, they end much like the old Bildungsroman of youth, on the threshold of consummating the "marriage" rather than within the married state itself. Having gently given up on otherness, the Bellow hero marries, so to speak, his future reformed and rehabilitated self. To avoid the anticlimax of describing the contents of the new utopian life, and the technical problem of differentiating it more than tonally from the old way of being, the novels end in expectation. We shouldn't complain. Like our other Bildungsromanciers, Bellow has found a way to rescue the state of happy anticipation from its literary connections with youth-on-the-threshold-of-life and restore it to the middle years. The midlife progress narrative, a deeply referential form, makes a good wish for its readers: that people of all ages might live so.

7

In Defense of Midlife
Progress Narratives

I. The Powers of Pessimism

It says quite a lot about our culture that any defense needs to be written. The value of the midlife Bildungsroman as a genre should be obvious, if only because it helps us reconstruct our ideas of the reality and potentiality of the maligned middle years of life. Any countercultural vision shakes us up invigoratingly; but this positive new vision of aging, to the degree we are able to use it in our own lives, promises more benign self-judgments, better interpretations of the world, braver resolutions, more confident desiring—pieces of what we might want to call an education "into gladness."[1] In the homely ways in which some fiction enacts its vision (with likable circumscribed characters, slow plausible plots, and motley props), the progress narrative of the middle years domesticates images of what Keats famously called "soul-making." What may be most daring about the genre is its implication that there is no necessary contradiction between gladness and the self as it lives in time.

This should be good news. Nevertheless, the genre needs defense, even now, because "optimism"—which is taken to be the narrative message of the midlife Bildungsroman—has had such a bad reputation.

1. The words are Elizabeth Barrett Browning's, in Italy: "our poor English . . . want educating into gladness." Quoted by Virginia Woolf in *Flush* (New York: Harcourt, Brace, 1933), p. 123.

The consensus since ancient times has stacked the cultural cards in favor of grim assessments and prognostications. "We must call no one happy who is of mortal race, until he hath crossed life's border, free from pain."[2] This totalizing, romantically stern, sententious pronouncement from the ending of *Oedipus Rex* has impressed many as the last word in agreement on what kind of life-course story should not be told. How can anyone refute this level of fear of the future?

A superstitiousness properly called primitive still prevents some of us from uttering the forbidden vaunt of happiness. Saying you are "safe" is perilous, while philosophical pessimism on the Sophoclean scale is safe, or would be *if* there were gods and *if* they were jealous of human good fortune and *if* they had the power to withdraw it. And the totalizing utterances of pessimism have grandeur, as if we spoke with the gods, on their side rather than on our own. (We have a modern way of interpreting this superstitious ventriloquism, which I will come back to later.) The curiously disproportionate upshot of the pessimistic tradition, at any rate, as one of its scholars concludes, is that "every age has associated pessimism with wisdom, so much so that Nietzsche, in derision, could call this sentiment the *consensus sapientium:* 'In every age the wisest have passed the identical judgment on life: it is worthless.'"[3] Pessimism may locate this worthlessness in either the world or the self. Nineteenth-century thinkers especially arrogated to themselves the superior power of denigrating the self. "The names that have gained respect" among those positing "the nil and vacuum of the self," in the miscellaneous list of one cultural recordkeeper, "are those of Carlyle, Schopenhauer, Dostoyevsky, Kierkegaard, Melville, Baudelaire, Nietzsche, Henry Adams—to weave a dour trans-Atlantic fraternity of soothsayers."[4] The list could be considerably extended without giving offense. Try labeling a thinker an optimist; from the supporters of most you can expect not qualifications but denials. Privileged utterances of the recent past reiterate the old harsh conclusions. Some of the high-culture literary pessimists like Beckett and E. M. Cioran sport an alarming rhetoric, which doesn't *argue* but takes for granted that we would

2. Sophocles, *Oedipus Rex,* trans. R. C. Jebb, the last lines of the play. Dudley Fitts and Robert Fitzgerald's translation emphasizes not what we say, but what we are supposed to think: "and let none / Presume on his good fortune until he find / Life, at his death, a memory without pain."

3. Steven J. Rosen, *Samuel Beckett and the Pessimistic Tradition* (New Brunswick, N.J.: Rutgers University Press, 1976), p. 19.

4. John O. Lyons, *The Invention of the Self: The Hinge of Consciousness in the Eighteenth Century* (Carbondale: Southern Illinois University Press, 1978), p. 3.

all be in a kind of ironic agreement that life is a decline story, if we the readers would only tell the truth. In Cioran's Pandora's box of aphoristic gripes about "the catastrophe of birth" and what follows, he states that, "As a general rule, men *expect* disappointment: they know they must not be impatient, that it will come sooner or later."[5] This is the contemporary statement of the Sophoclean rebuke.

Despite the prestige of its position, pessimism takes a fists-up combative position. It rhetorically degrades what it defines as its opposite, "optimism." The complete story of the way pessimism has belittled optimism is too complicated to tell here. But en gros, pessimism has claimed the high ground of wisdom and experience, and has appropriated a related vocabulary of values. "Truth," "reality," "profundity," it takes to itself. In its binary divisions, it captures all and optimism is left with nothing: false versus true, appearance versus reality, illusion versus truth, superficiality versus profundity. Age should be wise, wisdom should be disillusioned, the disillusioned must be pessimistic. Bellow picked up this discourse (sarcastically) in a draft of *Herzog:* "And truth is true only as it brings down more disgrace and dreariness upon human beings, so that if it shows anything except evil it is illusion, and not truth."[6] Pessimism utilizes a body of metaphors that implies the same unequal divisions, based on the dichotomy between blindness and insight. As in Thomas Hardy's prescription for acting optimistic: "Blind the eye to the real malady, and use empirical panaceas to embrace the symptoms."[7] Nineteenth-century guardians of intelligence like Flaubert and Schopenhauer mocked optimism for its stupidity.[8] An even-handed man like William James, whose own life history should have taught him better, managed to make a then-prevailing form of optimism look foolish by the terms of his praise.

Pessimism claims to have on its side disciplines beyond philosophy— history, for example, seen as the record of evil that people have done to one another, and psychoanalysis, insofar as it is the record of internalized harms that cannot be undone. Pessimists have not literally had

5. E. M. Cioran, *The Trouble with Being Born,* trans. Richard Howard (New York: Viking, 1976), pp. 4, 6.

6. Quoted by Daniel Fuchs, "*Herzog,* the Making of a Novel," in *Critical Essays on Saul Bellow,* ed. Stanley Trachtenberg (Boston: G. K. Hall, 1979), p. 106.

7. Michael Millgate, *The Life and Work of Thomas Hardy* (Athens: University of Georgia Press, 1985), p. 413.

8. On the other hand, Flaubert immensely admired George Sand, who represented meliorism to him; and Schopenhauer believed that happiness became possible, if at all, only later on in life. See the second half of "The Ages of Life," in *Complete Essays of Schopenhauer,* trans. T. Bailey Saunders (New York: Wiley, 1942), Book II, pp. 132–146, esp. 140.

to say, "This is the worst of all possible worlds" (the most extreme definition of their position), because they can simply point to its evils and leave the extended finger up. As John Dewey noticed in an entry in the *Dictionary of Philosophy and Psychology,* "empirical pessimists" dwell on "the actual bulk of pain and evil in the world."[9] The twentieth century has been profligate in producing evidence for empirical pessimists to point to. And the world was never short of such material, as Voltaire demonstrated with a kind of wicked persistence in *Candide.*

Retreating into the self somewhat limits the amount of pain and evil that needs to be taken into account but seems to fix an intense amount permanently, which partially explains why empirical pessimists who want to make a hard case against the world are probably now outnumbered by literary pessimists, whose most common genre, the decline narrative, dwells on the accumulating misery of the self (to which the misery of the world is contributory). In contemporary fiction, the cosmic dissatisfaction that used to emphasize the vanity of human wishes now lingers on a particular character's inability to stop drinking, make a living, keep a girlfriend, marry a rich man, "find" meaning. Or, at the level of high failure, to withstand revolutions and keep one's children alive and well. But however self-centered its utterance, it can always ally itself verbally with the grander tropes of pessimistic discourse. And the core of that utterance has not changed in the thousands of years since Genesis encoded humanity as a Fall. That core has always been a self-curse, projected as if it came from outside.

"Optimism," however, altered its understanding of the world and the self in the nineteenth century (when it was attacked more contemptuously, perhaps, than ever in its history); more exactly, it changed its name to consort with a new identity, repudiating charges of naiveté or willful blindness. In fact, the main charge—that optimists believe ours to be "the best possible world," or even a "thoroughly good" world—has long been patently ridiculous; only one figure since Leibniz had expressed this view, and he was imaginary (Pangloss). Leibniz himself was making what he thought of as a logical, religious argument, not describing the world as he personally saw it. It was George Eliot— as far as lay in her power, an enemy to binary thinking—who employed a new term "to express a view which she put forward as a *via media* between these two extremes."[10] "To a friend who once playfully called

---

9. John Dewey, "Optimism and Pessimism," in *Dictionary of Philosophy and Psychology,* ed. James Mark Baldwin (New York: Macmillan, 1902), 2: 211.

10. Andrew Seth Pringle-Pattison, "Meliorism," in Baldwin, *Philosophy and Psychology,* p. 62.

her an optimist she responded, 'I will not answer to the name of optimist, but if you like to invent Meliorist, I will not say you call me out of my name.'"[11] What "meliorism" did, under the influence of the new historicizing consciousness, was to reject the essentialist view that pessimism has stuck with (the world is always the same and therefore describable in final terms) and that had been foisted on it by the discourse of pessimism needing to construct a counterpart. It allied itself with the idea of progress and the idea of education. Often with a tremendous wrenching, it transferred the idea of progress from the social world to the subjective realm. Idealist philosophers like A. C. Bradley gave a psychological content to the project of soul-making. William James after his Renouvier-led renovation did important work at the intersection of belief and health. G. E. Moore gave a more delightful content to the idea of the good.[12] In short, meliorism became dynamic, individualistic, process oriented—a philosophy in these ways ideally suited for fiction.

Cultural history is full of contradictions, and some forms of fiction expose them. Although essentialism has been widely discredited wherever it can be discovered, forms of literary pessimism that rely on it have not thereby lost ground. For narration, which needs the illusion of change, pessimism invented the plot of decline—simple, formulaic, an exercise in subtraction. Its proliferation has been astounding—in novels, film noir, the detective story, and slice-of-life and minimalist fiction. It has even invaded the Bildungsroman of youth. All of them rely on an alleged "truth": that the passing of time always, and inevitably, involves irreversible decay. Where personal time is concerned, aging is the enemy.

Meliorism firmly and forever renounced the grandeur of final (or essential or totalizing) terms. It married the humbler and more tentative discourses of possibility and process.

II. Meliorism and Midlife Fiction

If we speak precisely, then, not optimism but meliorism is the narrative message of midlife Bildungsromane. They do not therefore necessarily praise the "world"; they assert (in the ways assertions are indirectly framed in narratives) only that one important individual's

11. Edith Simcox, "George Eliot," *Nineteenth Century* 9, no. 51 (May 1881): 787. Pringle-Pattison cites the Simcox article in his entry on "Meliorism."

12. The midlife Bildungsroman's intellectual pedigree will be treated in Part II of *Midlife Fictions*.

life is capable of improving over time despite age. They recognize the possibility that something positive may increase. They don't ignore evil: it gets incorporated in the fictional vision, but not as the last word. In the protagonists, too, belief in meliorism need not be "congenital" (they are not necessarily born on the opening page possessing it) but comes, if it comes to consciousness, as a victory plucked from adversity. As we have seen over and over, for the writers concerned, the meliorist vision has come hard-won and not without setbacks over the life course.

All the issues ought to change when what is being represented in fiction is not taken to be the will of the gods or the nature of the world but is instead the isolated, precious self, vulnerable to misinterpretation, liable to be made captive to superstition; its own most intimate processes (among them aging) describable in hostile terms; its inner resilience, or capacity for growth, endangered by circumstance. Indeed, some of the midlife progress narrative's bad press comes from its focus on the individual's private life, and the publicity it flashes—and by its nature, must flash—on all the intimate secrets of adult longing. Of course, the decline narrative also deals with the intimate psychology of self, even more exclusively than does the progress narrative, but decline has encoded this publicity as "revelation," the exposure of what people want to keep hidden, truth prised from beneath appearance. The Bildungsroman's "fault" and its main problem is that it openly sponsors the good wishes we are able to make for ourselves.

In fiction the issues of pessimism and optimism are still live—buried, but no less fervent and bitter for that. Philosophy stopped arguing about them early in the century, to the point where a recent *Dictionary of Philosophy* devoted to terminology has no entry on any of these once deeply engaging terms.[13] In clinical psychology, on the other hand, a consensus going the other way is developing: optimism, under many names, is looked upon favorably as an antidepressant, and pessimism is counterindicated as a toxin. (Some contradiction persists between analytic superciliousness about "wish fullfillment" and the clinical approval of optimism, suggesting yet again how perplexed our culture is about all these issues.)

13. A. R. Lacey, *A Dictionary of Philosophy* (London: Routledge and Kegan Paul, 1976). *The Encyclopedia of Philosophy* does have an article, "Pessimism and Optimism," whose author, L. E. Loemker, makes explicit what the absence of discourses elsewhere implies: "widespread doubt whether the terms 'optimism' and 'pessimism' are sufficiently precise for philosophical purposes and also whether optimistic and pessimistic beliefs are philosophically justifiable" (New York: Macmillan, 1967), 6:114. New interest in the subject (like my own) aims to historicize and theorize the controversy.

Pessimism's sway in literature is as yet almost unchallenged in the high culture. One obvious proof of this is that there are only a few exceptional genres that are permitted fortunate outcomes and the utterance of optimistic sentences. In some ways these genres—such as comedy, pastoral, romance, and the Bildungsroman of youth—have the standing of licensed fools, permitted to utter "nonsense" or qualified and partial sense. The mere existence of such forms is no counterargument to the dominance of literary pessimism, as long as literature's hierarchies undermine their value. Millennia after Aristotle, comedy is still a lower form, unless it takes the Beckettian view of "all that fall." Twentieth-century film, where these permitted genres can be seen to flourish, actually invented the good-guy loser (for example, Woody Allen, so often until midlife: *Zelig, Hannah and Her Sisters*) who through no fault of his own doesn't get the girl and isn't better off at the end. The rejoicing forms that used to mark adult achievement—epithalamia, birth poems, celebrations of military or literary or institutional triumphs—scarcely exist in the twentieth century or have been transformed by our irony.[14]

Two other exceptional genres accept inevitable loss but refuse to devalue the loser or the world on that account: elegy and tragedy. Elegy has readily been taken up into the midlife Bildungsroman. For three hundred years—from about the time the novel began to replace the tragic value system with its own—"tragedy" has become harder to write, or to recognize. Within the novel, many critics would now agree, since about the mid-nineteenth century the canon has privileged stories of failure, what I have been calling decline narratives. This is Saul Bellow's view. "Oh, I think that realistic literature from the first has been a victim literature. . . . Everything that people believed in the nineteenth century about determinism, about man's place in nature, about the power of productive forces in society, made it inevitable that the hero of the realistic novel should not be a hero but a sufferer who is eventually overcome."[15] The problem was that the decline narrative wouldn't side with the adult sufferer. It had a hard time seeing his or her suffering as meaningful because (with rare, sympathetic exceptions) it remorselessly

14. See, for example, on the epithalamium, Celeste M. Schenck, "Songs [From] the Bride: Feminism, Psychoanalysis, Genre," *Literature and Psychology* 33, no. 3–4 (Fall 1987): 109–19.

15. Gordon Lloyd Harper, "Saul Bellow," in *Writers at Work. The* Paris Review *Interviews,* introd. Alfred Kazin, 3rd ser. (New York: Viking, 1967), p. 187. Bellow composed this "interview" in 1965.

allied adult longing with vice, (bourgeois) greed, selfishness, or inappropriateness. It is time to ask why the Victorian prestige of these associations should infect our contemporary beliefs.

In our own day, fiction is most often praised for being "intrinsically painful." According to Anatole Broyard, "If fiction doesn't accuse us, it lacks authenticity, the scale on which seriousness is weighed. It's a curious time in American culture." "Novels are regularly praised for being searing, scouring, excoriating, cruel, alarming, devastating, merciless, remorseless, unrelenting, chilling, bleak, lacerating and unflinching"—a conclusion we can confirm by reading advertisements for new novels. Novels that end happily run the risk of being called "ladies' magazine fiction." Broyard concludes that the state of consensus about the qualities of "serious" fiction inhibits writers. "Only a few serious novelists seem to find the courage to go against the current."[16]

Most of the reasons for the present sway of literary pessimism are obscure, and even those that seem obvious become obscure the closer one looks at them. To discover the overt content of the attacks, we can look more closely at reviews of midlife Bildungsromane. Sometimes the praise is made possible by reading one of their novels as more pessimistic than it is. And some part of the criticism they receive derives from a critic's (unconscious) perception that the tone of one of their works is too sanguine.

Even Updike, the most cautious and belated Bildungsromancier of them all, has not been exempt from criticism on such grounds. All Updike's strategies of realism—ordinariness, apparent irony—have not disguised his unembarrassed liking for his new-rich Rabbit, who doesn't fear the gods simply because fortune has been good to him. (Perhaps being grateful drives out superstition.) Annie Dillard in China, asked which of our best novels should be translated, although she admires Updike immensely, struck *Rabbit Is Rich* from her mental list, recalling the scene where "a Toyota dealer and his wife make love on a bed of gold coins. A major American novel, out of the question."[17] Presumably puritanism, sexism, and poverty would make this scene seem trebly decadent in China. But it is our own puritanism, discomfort with the details of a case of long-married uxuriousness, and guilt about dispro-

16. Anatole Broyard, "Is Fiction A Pain?" *New York Times Book Review,* June 21, 1981, p. 39.

17. Annie Dillard, *Encounters with Chinese Writers* (Middletown, Conn.: Wesleyan University Press, 1984), p. 24. The group of writers she was with finally recommended European and Latin American writers for translation.

portionate American wealth that make some readers uneasily flash on this scene (of a married couple privately rejoicing at an unexpected access in their worldly fortunes) rather than on Harry's run in the Poconos, or the gift of the grandchild. Those who want to can still inscribe it close to scenes of pornography and greed. But doing so reveals a penchant for searching out contexts—cross-cultural contexts seem to work best for the purpose—that distort and embarrass and humiliate fictional efforts at portraying gladness. How can a fictional character in America publicly (that is, in print) rejoice while the Third and Fourth Worlds continue to suffer? Or, where their conventions frown on our conventions? Perhaps Bellow was trying to address this problem when he sent Henderson to Africa to learn from Africans that people want to be happy and that what a person is able to imagine can be converted into actuality thereby.

Tyler and Drabble (who actually do occasionally write for ladies' magazines—usually their darkest work) can be challenged with smaller arms than the distant heavy guns of comparative social misery. Drabble has been vulnerable at least since *The Realms of Gold,* because Frances is a successful professional woman whose life has many objectively glamorous aspects: foreign travel, country houses, undemanding children, male admiration of her sexuality, and, eventually, love in marriage. Margaret Homans attacked *Realms of Gold* for its "fantastic female account of career, love and motherhood." To her, "the novel's appropriation of dominant discourse exacts its price not from the heroine herself but from the story of Aunt Con" (the elderly recluse who dies of starvation); Aunt Con is to her "an eruption of the feminine." By the logic of this rhetoric, Homans would have been better satisfied if the pessimistic female story had been the central one and the progress narrative had been given to an unimportant female character or only to men.[18]

Elizabeth Fox-Genovese in criticizing Drabble took the same tack, that Drabble endorsed "the superwoman image—you can do it all, sister, if you only mobilize enough will, determination, courage and grace"—and that this endorsement suggests "the same willfully innocent denial of complexity, complicity and struggle with respect to female being and potential achievement as does her blandly optimistic picture of British society."[19] She too fails to see that the novel is a cure

18. Margaret Homans, "'Her Very Own Howl': The Ambiguities of Representation in Recent Women's Fiction," *Signs* 9, no. 2 (Winter 1983): 202, 202, 201.

19. Elizabeth Fox-Genovese, "The Ambiguities of Female Identity: A Reading of the Novels of Margaret Drabble," *Partisan Review* 46, no. 2 (1979): 235. Her highly critical essay is in general provocative and illuminating.

story, which invites us to consider what "mobilizing" forces means when a woman is forty, alcoholic, lonely, and afraid of inheriting her family's pessimism. What is also striking is that both critics refuse to permit us to identify with a successful woman, as if a successful woman cannot be a representative woman, or a vicariously useful alter ego for women and men too. This particular downgrading of female reality in the middle years is a subcategory of empiric pessimism that has gained some moody success by describing itself as feminism.

When Tyler published *The Accidental Tourist*, Diane Johnson's review fell into the most expectable formulas of naive pessimism: novels are mimetic and pessimistic readers decide what the truth is that novels are supposed to mimic. Tyler might have known in advance that if she wrote a novel about a man who survives the death of his son and marital separation, and goes on to fall in love, someone would reprove the novel for "a whole agenda of comforting, consoling ideas." "All these ideas are powerfully attractive," Johnson concluded, after listing what she thought they were. "It's just that they are not true."[20]

Of all four writers, Bellow has been treated as the most egregious spokesman for "affirmation," a situation that might not have arisen if he had not, outside his novels, positioned himself as a polemicist in the postwar Western debate about fiction and reality.[21] He had to, to protect his own fragile developments. But he broadened the debate beyond his own novels. A better sociologist of knowledge than his critics, he saw that the debate centered, as it had in the nineteenth century, on interpreting or labeling "reality."

It may be, however, that truth is not always so punitive. I've tried to suggest this in my books. There may be truths on the side of life. I am quite prepared to admit that being habitual liars and self-deluders, we have good cause to fear the truth, but I'm not at all ready to stop hoping. There may be some truths which are, after all, our friends in the universe.[22]

Bellow usually phrases his position cautiously enough, but taking the position at all has inevitably troubled some of his critics. Tony Tanner, a brilliant, early, and sympathetic critic, worried about his "unearned gladness" at a time when Bellow's gladdest midlife book was either

20. Diane Johnson, "Southern Comfort," *New York Review of Books* 32, no. 17 (November 7, 1985): 16–17.

21. Inevitably, some critics say that Bellow pays lip service to optimism, but that in his fiction the joyful parts are unconvincing.

22. Harper, "Saul Bellow," p. 196.

Henderson or *Herzog,* and in 1975 threw up his hands: "Perhaps only world events will decide whether such a brave optimism in the teeth of all negations is an anachronism or an essential constituent of our will to survive."[23] After the wars and genocides of this century, what "world events" would still be lying in wait for us that would help us decide on the value of meliorism, or the reality or usefulness of any particular Bildungsroman?

The argument can be rotated slightly to imply that fiction is *best* for us when it describes the lives of those who succumb rather than overcome. As readers, we are taken to be hopelessly, sentimentally optimistic, victims of *The Pollyanna Principle* who want language and the world to be as "pleasant" as possible.[24] "Pessimism is good for them," would be the unspoken judgment. The assumptions behind that judgment, as far as I can make them out, seem to be that evading "harsh reality" is possible, morally ignoble, and curable through a fiction course. The sanctity attached to suffering (in itself rarely questioned, except perhaps by people who have suffered greatly) is transferred in this judgment to the experience of *reading about suffering.* Although educating the insensitive should be somehow possible, it might actually be made more difficult by a theory that giving suffering characters "happy endings" would be a lie amounting to a cruel irony. *Ironweed* (1983), William Kennedy's Pulitzer-Prize-winning novel of homeless people in Albany during the Depression, allows a man who has been on the bum for twenty-two years (after accidentally killing his baby son) to redeem himself, at the age of fifty-eight. Novels like *Ironweed* resist the dominating conventions of the institution that decline narrative has become. Kennedy's drunk at first appears to live in the company of Gervaise in *L'Assommoir,* Hurstwood in *Sister Carrie,* the Consul in *Under the Volcano,* Graham Greene's priest in *The Power and the Glory.* Bellow came before Kennedy here. When both of the victims in *The Victim* wound

23. Tanner worried about "unearned gladness" in *Saul Bellow* (Edinburgh and London: Oliver and Boyd, 1965), p. 116. The "world events" quotation comes from "Saul Bellow: An Introductory Note," *Salmagundi* 30 (Summer 1975):5.

24. Margaret W. Matlin and David J. Stang, *The Pollyanna Principle: Selectivity in Language, Memory and Thought* (Cambridge, Mass.: Schenkman, 1978). The writers declare that even under the worst circumstances, when polled, Americans report themselves as being happy. This includes the poor, the old, the deformed, the underprivileged, and even (in one case) someone terminally ill. Their most interesting material is based on studies of linguistic usage, showing that "normal is considered to be moderately pleasant" (p. 49); "pleasant words are used more frequently than unpleasant words" (p. 57); in pairs of words, positive and negative, the basic or unmarked form is the positive, pleasant member (pp. 73–74); in the *Oxford English Dictionary* on average "the positive member was recorded 151 years before the negative member" (p. 79).

up better off at the end, Bellow had managed to describe the mentality of a victim without sacrificing the possibility of a meliorist ending. Like other midlife progress narratives mentioned in the Introduction, *Ironweed* is a small good sign that meliorism need not be linked in fiction only with more or less middle-class (white, male, heterosexual, well-to-do) characters. Perhaps we're in the process of rooting out the prejudice that only the privileged can experience normal development, survive the dangerous age, benefit from living longer, and know enough about their inner life to be grateful for aging. If some people have more to overcome to arrive at safe-at-last stories, their stories should be all the more worth telling.

But let's make the best case, that the decline narrative can at times be founded on intuitive sympathy for the sufferer. It would follow that although pessimism could not be *required*, it may be justified. This we cannot doubt. We don't demand, as the ground of "truth" in decline narrative, that writers have themselves been homeless, or have lost everything, or have been hopelessly addicted, or grindingly poor, or have tried suicide. Outside of testimonial writing, a separate case altogether, we don't demand first-hand "mimesis" (although we may become impatient at what look like standard decline conventions: too many dead children, too many female suicides, too many endings featuring death or alcohol, too many losses heaped up in any one plot). Most of us can intuitively understand a writer's desire, or need, to write decline fiction, either by thinking of this need as occasioned by a terrible event (to be expressed as so often in a short story) or as required by a relatively settled disposition, such as afflicted Thomas Hardy, Jean Rhys, Malcolm Lowry, or William Faulkner. Those who feel they have been maimed by life have the same desire to represent their condition as others. By introspection, we may understand their situation well. Idealist philosophy originally argued and much of contemporary thought assumes that each of us reads and represents the world independent of the "nature" of the world, whatever that is. Our reading is dependent on ourselves, our private experience, our mental configurations. One hundred years ago Nietzsche made this point and drew the conclusion: "After all, judgments and valuations of life, whether for or against, cannot be true: their only value lies in the fact that they are symptoms; . . . *per se* such judgments are nonsense. You must therefore endeavor by all means to reach out and try to grasp this astonishingly subtle axiom, *that the value of life cannot be estimated.*"[25] Like anyone else, he ignored his own axiom. Nor do people wait for the

25. Friedrich Nietzsche, *The Twilight of the Idols,* trans. Anthony M. Ludovici (New York: Russell and Russell, 1964), p. 10; emphasis in original.

hypothetical stage of the elderly "life review" to start estimating the value of life; after a point that I would put in adolescence, we do it all the time. Dangerous-age narratives show that quite young writers have already made some determination about what aging will bring.

The core of self on which all constructions are built is now believed to be psychological. As Unamuno put it, "It is not usually our ideas that make us optimists or pessimists, but our optimism or our pessimism . . . that makes our ideas."[26] As the result of midlife self-examination, Freud gained an insight into the phenomenon we are specifically interested in: that form of pessimism that is linked with reluctance to believe in one's own success. He explained this disbelief as "the expression of a pessimism of which a large portion seems to find a home in many of us," and derived it from "a sense of guilt or inferiority, which can be translated: 'I'm not worthy of such happiness, I don't deserve it.'"[27] Even if Freud's is not the whole answer, it seems plausible that many readers, especially as they grow older, have deeply held models of life that make decline narratives seem true to them a priori. I have sometimes called them "decline readers," with the reservation that I imagine most people as moving amidst admixtures of pessimism and personal meliorism. But this book has tried to show that a predominantly pessimistic orientation need not be permanent.

The first pages of midlife narratives will be read very closely indeed by decline readers looking for signs that their time view will be respected and confirmed. Indeed, the existence of the implied decline reader, who cannot be forgotten even though few writers may want to reify such a persona, is another reason why midlife progress narratives often begin so "low": Herzog talking about having been crazy, Frances Wingate weeping and moaning, Macon quoted as having said he had *never* thought there was all that much point to life. The implied meliorist reader, who will be looking for equivalent clues, will also be addressed in those opening pages and will be expected to note that these are not deeply endangered people: Herzog talks in the past tense; Frances recovers rather quickly from the first bout of depression; Macon is stolid, systematic, reticent, but capable of affection.

The aim of my reasoning to this point has been to place decline fic-

26. Miguel de Unamuno, *The Tragic Sense of Life in Men and in Peoples,* trans. J. E. Crawford Flitch (London: Macmillan, 1921; rpt. New York: Dover, 1954), p. 3.

27. Sigmund Freud, "A Disturbance of Memory on the Acropolis," *Standard Edition,* 22:242. He connects pessimism, as we might expect, with unanalyzed father-son rivalry. "It seems as though the essence of success was to have got further than one's father, and as though to excel one's father was still something forbidden" (p. 247).

tion, so that it exists at the same level of fictionality as the progress narrative. Once we agree that pessimism has no ultimate claim on truth, we are free, in theory, of a millennial mystification. How far we can carry this idea depends on the way we define ourselves as readers of the world and the self. It is possible to become angry at the decline tradition, if not at any individual practitioner: to wonder at the egotism that wishes to inflict its private sorrows and sorry expectations and hopeless interpretations on the rest of us. Bellow, revising his sense of his mission as a writer just after he had inflicted *Dangling Man* and *The Victim* on a culture coming out of World War II, decided that there was mental imposition involved. Helped by writing in *Augie March* about the way a child develops, he started envisioning his *readers* too as vulnerable individuals. He has Augie think, "My next idea was how nothing was more dreadful than to be forced by another to feel his persuasion as to how horrible it is to exist, how deathly to hope, and taste the same despair. How of all the impositions this was the worst imposition." [28]

III. Glamour and Shock, Grief and Solace

Demystification should make us better readers of both kinds of fiction: at the least, we can see clearly that each has its rhetoric of persuasion. *Each thinks it possible to persuade us:* neither takes us to be fixed, impervious beings. The decline narrative exerts various kinds of allure: its swagger that it is telling the "hard" truth to only brave ears is a mode of flattery. But many modern midlife decline narratives have been telling dangerous and sentimental soft "truths" instead. Decline was invested with a sort of glamour by the Fitzgerald of *Tender is the Night* and the Hemingway of *The Sun Also Rises* and the Waugh of *Brideshead Revisited* and in Malcolm Lowry's *Under the Volcano,* if only by being attached to expensive, wasteful, careless people—people with luxurious settings, once-large opportunities, and worldly appetites. When that old monied glamour became passé, decline drew on bohemian stylishness or existential lack of affect: Beckett's minimalism (the bicycle, the sucking stones, the pencil stub), or Camus's (Meursault's torpid crime). In our own era, decline often has mere middle-class appurtenances: it is set in well-upholstered households, businesses, hotels. Failure and loss lurk in wait in front of the TV screen, inside Detroit

28. Saul Bellow, *The Adventures of Augie March* (New York: Viking, 1953), p. 417.

cars, in Vermont country homes, on day trips, at Swiss resorts. Now the innocuous *mise-en-scène* (as in horror movies) enables readers to be shocked by the hardships of repeated loss or the sudden catastrophe or humiliation of loss. Joan Didion returns to putting outcasts in exotic settings, holding margaritas as the Götterdämmerung darkens. There has been a style in every turn of taste to give life-course pessimism an attractive updated package.

The sociological decor (like Beckett's Nowhere, Europe) is supposed to bring decline home to all of us: it isn't reserved for alcoholics, tramps, ex-consuls, prostitutes, jet-setters, women in general, or the classes below our own. What many decline narratives covertly promise readers is that their own lives may provide them with an unexpected emotional charge, rather than the sameness that they experience inwardly and realize as a true defeat. Beyond the static, the known, the boring, may be some violent and luxurious exculpatory excess of loss and fall. A doom. Any ordinary neurotic may share the glamour of decline.

For depressives who read them, such decline narratives are bad counselors. I believe they offer a spurious substitute for change, an authorization to evade the tremendous (but slow and incremental and possibly painful) effort that making positive change in oneself entails. The soft truth that decline narratives offer is that decline is a seductive alternative to improvement. And the truly vulnerable readers (at any age, but particularly those conscious of their aging) are those who feel an intimate sense of failure already and who are wondering, "Is this permanent? Is it too late to change?" For them "to be forced by another to feel . . . how horrible it is to hope" is far worse than an imposition. There is something deeply questionable about fiction that identifies with the stronger forces inimical to the individual. However sympathetic the writer's attitude (test cases could be *Anna Karenina,* or Kate Chopin's *The Awakening,* or Christina Stead's *The Man Who Loved Children),* we can't forget that the plot has been engineered to bring about defeat, that the characters' psyche has had to be constructed to internalize defeat. An older psychoanalytic view held that fiction *needs* to represent punishment, so that fear can "bind" readers' impulses: "were it otherwise, fiction would indeed increase inner tension, both by arousing feelings of guilt and by making the impulses it released more clamorous and more difficult to control." [29]

29. Simon O. Lesser, *Fiction and the Unconscious* (Boston: Beacon, 1957), p. 174. In traditional psychoanalysis, "the impulses" are conceived as being hostile and forbidden; if any wish, however innocuous, is realized, the impulses flood out. All wishes, therefore, have to be suppressed.

The midlife progress novel doesn't bind impulses in this way. If anything, it releases them. If there is truth to this reading theory, then adult Bildungsromane, embracing desires of many kinds and showing them rewarded, could be very frightening to some readers.

Nor can the genre compete at decline's level of frisson, temptation, and disjuncture. Its values are too different. For one, it depends on representing the self-in-time as a relatively smooth and meaningful continuum rather than a series of disjunctive pieces. Shocking the reader can't coexist with its adult view of experience. How likely is it that an experienced person will be shocked by reversal (or, for that matter, by ecstasy)? It actually assumes wider experience in the past of its characters than the decline narrative does. And more resilience as a result.

This range and resilience is represented by the characters' reactions to the shock of loss—fiction's typical "unscheduled event." However important the event may be to the protagonists, the main feature of their reaction is their ability to recover. Recovery may take years, depending on the shock, but the whole emotional course is shown.

The midlife progress narrative helps its protagonists recover even from the worst event most adult readers can imagine. As novels about the parenting generation have proliferated, children are beginning to die in fiction with alarming frequency: usually in accidents, but sometimes murdered; and sometimes, worse yet, killed by one of their own parents. The murder of Macon Leary's son in *The Accidental Tourist* is probably the worst event that happens in any contemporary midlife progress narrative. It could be contrasted with the deaths of children in *The World According to Garp,* in Heller's *Something Happened,* in Rosellen Brown's *Autobiography of My Mother,* in Maureen Howard's *Expensive People,* even in Lynne Sharon Schwartz's *Disturbances in the Field.* (Perhaps there ought to be a moratorium on killing a child in the last quarter of a novel—a fortiori, on the last page.) Tyler places the murder in the past of the novel, a year before. This avoids a scene of immediate horrified response. What Tyler is doing instead is helping us interpret the loss. Grief, rather than shock, is the feeling this novel wants to recognize as humanly central. It allies itself with elegy, representing a stage in the ongoing process of mourning that comes after the praise of the departed but closer to the pain than say, Leopold Bloom is, in Joyce's treatment of the midlife aftereffects of the loss of a child.

Grief is not the matter of a horrified instant, but the ruling content of a long space of time. Shock in decline fiction generates abruptness, silence, absence—at most a scene; grief in progress narratives can generate an entire novel. The decline narrative often treats the loss of the child as only the last of a series of losses that a character suffers, the clincher proving how deeply malevolent fortune is. Or it is the shock given to a protagonist who has had an easy life—a shock that's supposed to prove that trusting life is a mug's game. Either presentation of loss hammers in a curious angry way at the reader who happens to be an optimist: "*See* how wrong you were not to worry." Both are offering their narrative form as a verbal fetish (in the superstitious way I mentioned initially) as if mistrusting the world could prevent the deaths of one's children. Related to this is the way such novels can't get away from an egotism of knowledge: "How right I was to worry!" or, "How could my judgment have been so wrong!"

If decline narratives warn complacent parents direly, Tyler's story is written as if to sufferers of loss, kindly. Everything that happens to Macon, from the dispute in the rain with his wife to his last thought of his son on the penultimate page, derives in some way from his sense of loss. It certainly doesn't scant the difficulty of the recovery process: its many stages, its reluctance to relinquish mourning. When Macon reduces and comically mechanizes his life, washing his clothes underfoot when he takes his shower, it empathizes with him rather than ironizing the moment. Macon escapes self-pity, Bob Slocum's primary sentiment in *Something Happened*. When Macon creates a consoling image at the end of the book that his son is growing up by himself elsewhere, the story doesn't in any way deprecate the image or mock it as a fantasy. By giving his son, in fantasy, an independent, parallel life, Macon gives himself permission to have such a life: it marks one end within the continuum of grieving. (Progress narratives admit a category of what we might call *valuable* illusions.) By inventing a character whose solitary habits, lack of willpower, and toneless adverse judgment of life (not to mention his odd orphaned childhood) might have made him a permanent victim of grief, a decline figure, Tyler confers a degree of dignified resilience on a midlife person who is less than average on scales of luck and inner resources. While denying us the intense luxury of believing we can suffer "forever," *The Accidental Tourist* asks us to do justice to our capacity for love and sorrow and change.

In general, I would argue that the allegedly "optimistic" midlife Bildungsroman tells us enough about the evils of life. Its melioristic vision allows a wide space for the troubles that its endings show as mostly over: in D. A. Miller's hyperbolic and paradoxical way of describing fiction, its middles amply include what its endings "hate." But in fact, even in *Herzog,* a book that plainly labels suffering as evil and hateful and solipsistic, the persistence of his suffering is not merely a way of exfoliating plot or postponing conclusion (as narratologists rightly if somewhat redundantly say), but a way of making change seem slow, internally generated, and thus convincing. Who needs to be convinced? The decline reader blowing on a scintilla of hope, or the meliorist in deep trouble and doubt. The writer too, living somewhere on the spectrum.

Naive and trivial midlife Bildungsromane do exist, of course; I would describe them generically as novels in which change comes about in a "magical" way: meaning, now, not the ending of *A la recherche du temps perdu,* but fictions in which little or no attempt is made to imagine and convince the implied decline reader. They don't satisfy the meliorist either, because they don't write large enough the challenges of the self or the world. *They* are the counterpart, in fact, of the decline narrative, which typically fails to imagine and convince a meliorist reader impatient with its self-pity, plot excesses, sentimentalization of suffering, and disbelief in luck or character or will or imagination.

The midlife Bildungsroman at its best, by emphasizing not what "happens" to us from outside but the way we interpret events and respond from within, could be called an antipositivist genre, as well as a psychological one. Philosophically, it encodes a Stoic message. It asserts in a secular context what *The Golden Sayings of Epictetus* assert: that "God has . . . given us these faculties by means of which we may bear everything that comes to pass without being crushed or depressed thereby." [30] To repeat Henderson's reflective judgment: "I like to think I am always prepared for even the very worst [life] has to show me." The Stoic/Bildungsromancier goes on as if to say, sympathetically, to the decline reader, "Though possessing all these things . . . you do not use them . . . but sit moaning and groaning." The genre enables us to imagine ourselves, as adults plunked down in narrative, not becoming victims, but making ourselves beneficiaries of the drift of time.

IV. A Funny Shoe

The older the decline reader is, in our culture, and the older the protagonists of progress narratives, the harder all these Bildung lessons are for them to accept. The midlife progress narrative must

30. Quoted by Lynne Sharon Schwartz, *Disturbances in the Field* (New York: Harper and Row, 1983), p. 2.

therefore *inevitably* be the genre that will trigger the pessimism/optimism debate. The progress narrative of youth (whether a sexual initiation story or the old marriage or Wanderjahr plot) does not offend the conventions of "truth" I have been calling pessimistic. Nobody attacks *them* because they end with gladness or progress or expectation. Young people are allowed happiness—it's permissible to start out that way. Indeed, the conventions of midlife decline narrative (it's the main reason I have named it this way) often require that there be a previous high point in adolescence or young adulthood to contrast with the later years.[31] Literary pessimism discriminates, in short, against the aging. The brunt falls on those in their middle years. The comic outcome— gratified desire—cannot be permitted past a certain age.

The nature of midlife desire as the Bildungsroman figures it has to present a problem to our culture. On the whole, midlife desire in progress fiction is not generic and "universal," like the desire youth Bildungsromane are traditionally based on, to leave home, to be married or to become in one of very few other ways a culturally sanctioned adult. No, midlife desire risks idiosyncracy. Charlie Citrine, Harry Angstrom, Kate Armstrong, Justine Peck: How many among us want to read to the dead or move into a tacky suburban house, or can measure our happiness in being able to give a party and buy a potted plant, or expect to find fulfillment in being a fortune-teller in a traveling circus with one's husband as the mechanic? However symbolic these outcomes (of mental freedom, surprised contentment with the real, the importance of the social fabric, discovery of identity; or all of the above), they don't look normal. These outcomes don't affront conventional notions of desire, but they exist at a slant from it—a healthy independent slant.

Midlife progress fiction thereby runs a number of risks as a representation of reality. Its problem (as Bernard Paris phrases it, developing an idea of Northrop Frye's) is that "the wish fulfillment aspect of comedy seems to work best when the protagonist's 'character has that neutrality which enables him to represent' desire."[32] It follows that the more highly developed protagonists are, the more individualized their desires—in short, the *older* they are, as fiction is constructing them—the more they may strain some people's ability to empathize with them. Offended readers don't say straight out that their desires happen not to match those of these positive characters; they say "their fates [are not]

---

31. See Margaret Morganroth Gullette, "The Exile of Adulthood: Pedophilia in the Midlife Novel," *Novel* 17, no. 3 (Spring 1984), pp. 215–32.

32. Bernard Paris, *Character and Conflict in Jane Austen's Novels: A Psychological Approach* (Detroit: Wayne State University Press, 1978), p. 16.

commensurate with the laws of probability."[33] The so-called laws of probability, however, are problematical, culturally constructed, biased by the prestige of pessimism.

The broader though related risk that progress narratives run is that they don't mind if some midlife desires look "trivial" or even (though more rarely) ephemeral: Macon's girlfriend has sloppy diction and peculiar clothes and no great gift except that of making him feel brave and kind; Kate Armstrong will clearly want something else next after giving her party. Not just romantic pessimists but most of us have to outgrow the idea that desire—*our* desire—may not be single, ideal, or permanent. Santayana had an explanation for this mistake: "He [the romantic pessimist] thinks that what is desired is not this or that—food, children, victory, knowledge, or some other specific goal of a human instinct—but an abstract and perpetual happiness behind all these alternating interests. Of course an abstract and perpetual happiness is impossible . . . [for the fundamental reason] that we have no abstract and perpetual instinct to satisfy."[34]

For me, it's an achievement of the midlife Bildungsroman that it counters so many preconceptions. It casts doubt on the idea of ruling desire—that is, of the lifelong predominance of childhood or adolescent or young-adult desire. And it makes room for the variety of midlife wishes without labeling them as odd: it accepts the necessary individuation that comes with advancing along the life course without interpreting this situation generically as fantastic or comical or subversive or illusory, via one of the ironic distancing modes. The endings do not repudiate new longings if they differ from the longings of the beginnings and middles; they acknowledge their new priority, and satisfy them. The whole fictional endeavor validates and, from one point of view, magnifies these longings. Separate, secret, possibly inadmissible cravings are treated as if they were normal, harmless, right, and capable of fulfillment. Early on in *Humboldt's Gift,* a novel whose narrator will wind up dropping sex and money as goals and turn to reading Rudolph Steiner for a while instead, Bellow has a minor character pronounce sententiously, "A funny foot needs a funny shoe." Minus any derision, this could be a motto for the whole genre. Go on, they encourage the reader, chances are you'll find your funny shoe.

All good writers extend fiction farther into the private sphere—that's their *news,* after all. They don't have to apologize for a given that fiction

33. Ibid., p. 19.
34. George Santayana, *Egotism and German Philosophy* (London: J. M. Dent, 1916), pp. 110–11.

shares, in any case, with lyric poetry, drama, journals, autobiography—all invaders of privacy. But because the midlife Bildungsroman deals not with fear but with desire, and not with youthful desire but with midlife desire, and not with "noble" desire but with particular desire; and because it says that contentment can crown this unconventional desire, it gets labeled narcissistic. The charge is ludicrous when it comes from advocates of literary pessimism, since no character is as self-enclosed and jumpy as a deeply damaged twentieth-century decline figure who constantly presses himself against the thorns of life. Heller's Bob Slocum epitomizes this tendency when he states what *he* wants: "There are times I wish everyone I know would die and release me from these tender tensions I experience in my generous solicitude for them." [35]

The charge of narcissism needs some further rebuttal, however, when it comes from outside both kinds of midlife narratives. "Both are self-involved," this point of view would argue; I phrase it in my own words because it was one of my early responses; "one concerned with midlife fears, the other with midlife desires. Claiming to be alternatives, aren't they counterparts?" If they are counterparts, they are certainly not equal. The crucial difference in this context has to do with aging.

To maintain one's sense of being-*for*-oneself as one ages is a preliminary, genuine human assignment of some magnitude. To *construct* this sense if one has never had it before seems to me heroic, and to *reconstruct* it after having experienced adulthood as a set of trials, perhaps even more worthy of admiration. The midlife decline narrative clearly shows the dreadfulness of being-against-oneself or, in some cases, *turning against oneself as one ages*. Aging, in its conventions, appears as another punishment—for not being able to grow emotionally, or for going on biologically, which brings with it that inevitable success over one's parents, surviving them. Believing this about aging is of course a self-inflicted punishment.

The respectability and overriding importance of this adult assignment should be obvious, but it isn't always. One of our good critics complained when *Humboldt's Gift* came out, "But Citrine is primarily attracted to Steiner's ideas about transcendence and immortality of the self—a highly egotistic cause." He went on to deny "significant changes for the better taking place within him. . . . only a stronger concern with survival of the self. . . . In the final burial scene . . . I find no hint at parody, nothing to cloud the implication that a kind of redemption is

35. Joseph Heller, *Something Happened* (New York: Ballantine, 1975), p. 321.

beginning."[36] If this critic were telling a similar story about his own personal redemption to his friends, I wonder how highly he would value having them ridicule his concern with the survival of his self. At any rate, the theoretical defense of such projects in life has been left mainly to meliorist psychologists, and in their most assertive statements we still catch a hint of the defensiveness forced on them by their (our) cultural situation. Karen Horney, in validating our adult assignment, continues to accept the dichotomy of self/others, rather than asserting that our primary choice is between a positive view of our self and something worse. "The best representatives of psychoanalysis, on the other hand, would emphasize not only the responsibility toward others but that toward oneself as well. Therefore they would not neglect to stress the inalienable right of the individual to the pursuit of happiness, including his [sic] right to take seriously his development toward inner freedom and autonomy."[37] A slightly less wary attitude is visible in the Kohutians. "Through self-psychology, it has become possible to obtain a new understanding of healthy pride, healthy self-assertiveness, healthy admiration for the idealized self object, the capacity for enthusiasm, and certain aspects of the 'creative-productive-active' self."[38] Nothing more exhilarating could happen to a person, personally, than to come into a better relationship to the self, build the idea of progress into one's life, and implicitly accept aging (even via suffering) as an advance, as Keats does in his language of soul-building. If many of us could do this, the results for society—for relationships with others, projects in the social world—would also probably be quite positive (to say no more than that). Philip Rieff has said dryly (again, with those ubiquitous opponents in mind), "To call corrupt a culture purchased at a lower cost to our nerves, and at larger magnitudes of self-fulfillment, would show a lamentable lack of imagination."[39]

The midlife Bildungsroman weakens the belief that being-for-oneself means indifference to others. Readers looking for instances of mutuality, caretaking, love, and commitment will certainly find them here. But it would be naive to look for good only within the characters. In assess-

36. Roger Shattuck, "A Higher Selfishness?" *New York Review of Books* 22, no. 14 (September 18, 1975): 24–25.

37. Karen Horney, *Self-Analysis* (New York: Norton, 1942), pp. 29–30.

38. Paul Ornstein, "Self Psychology and the Concept of Health," in *Advances in Self Psychology*, ed. Arnold Goldberg (New York: International Universities Press, 1980), p. 157.

39. Philip Rieff, *The Triumph of the Therapeutic: Uses of Faith After Freud* (New York: Harper and Row, 1966), p. 12.

ing the interpersonal benefits of this genre, I have been implying all along that its relationship to its protagonists and to its readers is in itself a good.

The genre of midlife Bildungsroman challenges us, although not in expectable ways. It doesn't ask us to steel our will or to control our "evil" impulses or strain not to be dangerous to ourselves. Invading midlife privacy—the innermost self in a more or less evolved state— midlife progress writers, unlike decline writers, don't flinch. They dare to like what they see. Their look is a blessing on the evolution they allow us. Are we able to be blessed?

V. Lifelines

Anne Sexton told a story about reading *Henderson the Rain King,* "carrying [it] around in my suitcase everywhere I traveled"; rereading it; finally, she wrote to Bellow to say that Henderson was "a monster of despair, that I understood his position because Henderson was the one who had ruined life . . . made a mess out of everything." Bellow wrote back with intuitive sensitivity, not contradicting her, but taking a real risk in sending her what she was to call a "message about my whole life." He circled for her a passage that she kept over her desk, pasted in the front of her new manuscript, and remembered years later.

With one long breath caught and held in his chest, he fought his sadness over his solitary life. Don't cry you idiot, live or die, but don't poison everything.[40]

The risk Bellow took, for her, analogous to that therapists take when they choose a way to intervene, was to clarify the choice so decisively. *Live or Die* (the title she chose for her next book of poems). She realized "that I didn't want to poison the world, that I didn't want to be the killer; I wanted to be the one who gave birth, who encouraged things to grow and to flower, not the poisoner." She didn't say whether she ever read *Herzog,* that manual of instructions for delivering oneself from suffering, but she had kept *Henderson* by her for the right reasons although

40. Barbara Kevles, "Interview with Anne Sexton," in *Writers at Work, The* Paris Review *Interviews,* 4th ser., ed. George Plimpton (New York: Viking, 1976), pp. 410–11. Bellow might have been recalling Deuteronomy 30:19, "I have set before you life and death, blessing and cursing; therefore choose life."

she couldn't state what they were. What an accolade for Bellow, and for the inspiration behind progress narratives, this anecdote represents. Our Bildungsromanciers could all say, in the words of Walter Benjamin, "Only for the sake of the hopeless ones have we been given hope."[41]

We stumble over the threshold of adulthood in all our degrees of hope and doubt—most not suicidal, but all needing lifelines at some time or other. What will help any of us to live?

If we are lucky, our parents have told us, or before it's too late will yet tell us, stories about their own survival and growth. Models of the always unknowable future, on which to base patterns of expectation. If we are not lucky, they will have left us a bitter legacy, hard to shake—of dreams soured, forces unspent, a precious life judged as a span of waste. Many parents don't speak; they don't have a good story, or they don't know how to tell it. These are secret things, after all: a private success narrative may be just as unsayable as a narrative of failure; perhaps more so. Yet parents *hint* constantly at their evaluations of the life course: by, for example, dwelling affectionately and in detail on certain epochs of their life (their childhood, the years of our childhood, the first years of their marriage, the present), or by damning them mutely. Or by projecting our future, in terms of our age (and gender and alleged character). Which gender tells which story? We may go on for years thinking that our mother's story is the story of all women aging, or our father's that of all men—and that we are doomed by our gender to have the same midlife. What happens when a mother and a father tell two opposing stories of aging?

The hints they give affect us profoundly; we are the most avid listeners. Even if all they provide is a lifetime of hints, we often recompose them into a story, something with a broad clear outline: a decline or a progress narrative. We invent a midlife story about each of our parents (undeterred by classic admonitions to wait until they die to figure out what the story is). But at its best, this story is still skeletal, when what we need are intimate, vivid, complete narratives—manuals of instruction in fictional form.

Where shall we turn for these? The paucity of progress literature in the age of the novel is rather frightening. Philosophy once answered some of these needs, particularly when it overlapped with religious autobiography or pseudoautobiography. Earlier ages might have been satis-

41. Walter Benjamin, *Illuminations,* trans. Harry Zohn (New York: Shocken, 1969), p. 17. Hannah Arendt quotes this line, from Benjamin's essay on Kafka, in her introduction to this edition.

fied by Augustine's *Life,* or *La Divina Commedia,* or Bunyan's *Pilgrim's Progress*—all tales encompassing a midlife *prise de conscience,* followed by detailed instructions for advancement. Wonderful as they are in other ways, they fail precisely for us now as developmental guides, if only because the old ideal of a single spiritual goal for all has started to wither in the expansion of our own modern, secular idea of adult goals as necessarily individualistic (however much class- or gender-based) and, most of all, progressive, multiple and shifting.

Fragments of cure stories—one main model of growth—used to occur in the autobiographies of philosophers, writers, and reformers. Many people who have not discovered the twentieth-century midlife Bildungsroman have relied on the nineteenth-century cure story for its meliorist vision. In the years before "crisis" was a noun automatically preceded by the adjective "midlife," John Stuart Mill set down the successive phases of an identity crisis he suffered and recovered from in his early twenties. He tells it as a reading cure. He read the passage in Marmontel's *Mémoires* where a boy learns that his father has died and announces that he will take his place. In the terms used in Chapter Two, Mill was enabled to envision his father's death and his own survival and personal power. Marmontel's scene exactly expressed Mill's hidden wish to become a valued, autonomous person.[42] William James in his late twenties managed a cure by reading philosophy: the French philosopher Renouvier let him believe he could continue to grow in his own free way. Charlotte Perkins Gilman chose the cure by illness and then escape at the age of twenty-seven: "From the moment the wheels began to turn, the train to move, I felt better."[43] Hers was the route Elizabeth Barrett had modeled in 1845 at the age of thirty-nine—relearning how to eat with appetite, to walk, to speak in a firm voice, to go outdoors, to trust a man (a cure that so charmed Virginia Woolf, among many others, that in her fifties she wrote this version of it in a mock-heroic novella called *Flush*). Where Barrett escaped a father and a culture, Gilman fled a husband and (like all of them) an ill-fitting early self-definition. Escaping from her blind, dependent mother, Harriet Martineau also took sick, and then self-managed a mesmeric cure. "At past forty years of age,

42. For the full Marmontel passage, and a lucid, sympathetic, but not "Oedipal" reading of Mill's crisis, see A. W. Levi, "The 'Mental Crisis' of John Stuart Mill," *The Psychoanalytic Review* 32, no. 1 (January 1945): 86–101. It is not a traditional Oedipal reading because it locates the source of the son's (ambivalent) hostility in the obsessive harshness of the father's educational regime.

43. *The Living of Charlotte Perkins Gilman* (New York: Arno Press, 1972), p. 92.

I began to relish life, without drawback."[44] All of these women and men stepped off in boldly new adult directions. They identified their futures as eras of independence from constricting others and internalized constraints—mostly parents or ideological "fathers." Using our terminology, we would call most of their stories dangerous-age narratives, noticing, as we did earlier, how belatedly many of these "crises" occurred in the lives of these adult children. And how prominently (prostratingly) illness had to figure in the first stage, for both women and men, as a protective label, instigator and cover for growth. In short, they were all telling strenuous progress stories about *becoming themselves* in adulthood—to borrow from the subtitle of Nietzsche's own fragment of midlife autobiography, *Ecce Homo,* or *How One Becomes What One Is.*

The twentieth-century midlife Bildungsroman has expanded these fragments into full-length narrative; the genre that demonstrates growth has specialized itself, created a fuller discourse. Except in rare cases like *Herzog* or *The Accidental Tourist,* it doesn't construe growth in the now-popular terms of "crisis"—illness, regression, incapacity—but, as we have seen, in terms of slow, incremental, process. In treating growth as a normal aspect of life, it may entice into hopefulness ordinary, unselfdramatizing mortals—people whose miseries feel chronic. By fleshing out this proposition for use, in the words of Walter Benjamin again, it has more *counsel* to give.[45]

The new genre I am lauding honors the entire movement of growth it represents, from beginning to end. Although particular novels support many different models of growth, in general this genre's narrative strategies teach us how to reread and upgrade aspects of our lives, and possibly revise our own stories. Its length and style of narration validate patience, and its plots, calm; its events-and-outcomes validate blunders and accidents and opposition and even inaction; its secondary characters validate the contingent; its absence of irony constitutes a liking for

44. Harriet Martineau, *Autobiography* (Boston: James R. Osgood, 1877), 1:483. The passage continues, "and for ten years I have been vividly conscious of its delights, as undisturbed by cares as my anxious nature, and my long training to trouble could permit me ever to be." One should see also her proselytizing *Letters on Mesmerism,* published immediately upon her cure in 1845. They suggest that all she needed by that time was someone else's belief that she could be cured, which (given that she had had five years of invalidism and was addicted to opiates) her medical doctor could no longer provide, but her mesmerist could.

45. Benjamin thinks that the shorter and less analytic the story, the more counsel it has to give. See "The Storyteller" in *Illuminations.* I think the longer and less analytic the narrative, *ceteris paribus,* the more counsel it has to give.

a certain type of ordinary unselfconsciousness; its structure validates our learned instinct to wish ourselves well. And finally, it gives us a new ideology of aging. This is not all these novels do, of course—if they were strictly manuals of instruction they would teach nothing.

The genre does not argue that everyone should try to cultivate a higher self: it's not moralistic to that degree. (On the contrary, it assumes that we are good enough to be happy—another risky assumption.) By showing how characters grow in the ever-lengthening stretch of the middle years, it shapes a hope rather than a sense of duty. It can steady us in our relations with the future by intimating that we might become meaningful to ourselves in some more satisfactory way. Its main fault—and that can be remedied mainly by alterations in our self-deprecatory, ageist culture—is that it's not bold and brave enough, not free enough from superstition and fear of envy; it doesn't permit itself a large enough vision of what we might become. And overcome. Eventually, however, barring catastrophe, midlife Bildungsromanciers may be able to do more than make small claims about aging's good gifts. If we are to have complex, unapologetic fictions depicting heroic lives in our time, this is the genre for them. If ever we have novels that can absorb all the kinds of suffering that we know, and that can still plot survival, this is the expandable genre out of which they will arise. The projections they make now may be the mere shadow of more desirable things to come.

Index

Compositor: G&S Typesetters
Text: 10/13 Galliard
Display: Galliard
Printer: Halliday Lithograph
Binder: Halliday Lithograph